A BIOGRAPHY
OF THOMAS P.

O'NEILL

Speaker of the House

PAUL CLANCY
SHIRLEY ELDER

MACMILLAN PUBLISHING CO., INC.

NEW YORK

MACMILLAN PUBLISHING CO., INC.
866 THIRD AVENUE, NEW YORK, N.Y. 10022
COLLIER MACMILLAN CANADA, LTD.

Library of Congress Cataloging in Publication Data
Clancy, Paul R   1939–
Tip, a biography of Thomas P. O'Neill, Speaker of
the House.
Includes index.
1. O'Neill, Tip. 2. United States—Politics and
government—1945–   3. United States. Congress.
House—Biography. 4. Legislators—United States—
Biography. I. Elder, Shirley, 1931–   joint
author. II. Title.
E748.O49C55   328.73'092'4 [B]   80–13317
ISBN 0–02–525700–5

10 9 8 7 6 5 4 3 2 1

DESIGNED BY JACK MESEROLE

PRINTED IN THE UNITED STATES OF AMERICA

TIP

CONTENTS

TIP

1

AT THE OLD
BALLGAME

TIP O'NEILL went out with the boys to a ballgame on a cool October evening. The game was the last of seven in the 1979 World Series between the Pittsburgh Pirates and the Baltimore Orioles. The "boys" were several members of Congress, including Massachusetts crony Eddie Boland and Chicagoan Danny Rostenkowski; a couple of Washington insiders and television bigwigs; Bowie Kuhn, the commissioner of baseball; and Jimmy Carter, President of the United States. Needless to say, they had pretty good seats.

Although O'Neill and his friends sat in the specially built box that jutted out almost to the playing field on the third base side at Baltimore's Memorial Stadium, it was not so different from the days, a half century before, when he and another set of friends jostled the crowds for the cheap seats at the Red Sox games. It was still the same, being caught up in the roar and the press of the crowd, being part of the excitement and the drama in the clash of two great teams and, most of all, engaging like-minded men in baseball talk, suckering them with bets, and favoring them with hunches.

It was the sort of occasion that O'Neill wrapped himself around, keeping track of every play on the official scoresheet while at the same time keeping his companions informed about the fine points of the game and amused by his stories. It wasn't much different from his performance in Congress, where he can appear to be simultaneously absorbed in the process and totally oblivious to it. The game at times seemed incidental to the banter that took place in the front row of the box seats.

Neither the pizza that O'Neill consumed in heroic quantities, nor the beer that was accidentally spilled on him by an usher, nor the baseball that was viciously fouled by one of Pittsburgh's left-handed sluggers, striking the seat between him and Carter, came close to interrupting O'Neill's singular performance.

Carter had rarely before seen O'Neill in his own element. Most of their meetings had been in the more controlled setting of White House congressional breakfasts, and it is not clear what Carter thought of this

Rabelaisian character seated beside him. Carter is not one who mixes comfortably with ballplayers, cardplayers, or politicians, and his contempt for Congress has not been elaborately disguised. Yet there he was, a born-again Georgia Baptist, taking in a ballgame with a street-wise, glad-handing Boston Irish politician.

On the entire North American continent there may not be a greater fan of the game of baseball than Thomas P. O'Neill, Jr., Speaker of the United States House of Representatives. The fact that he is also one of the most powerful political figures in America has nothing to do with it. O'Neill loves sports contests almost as much as he loves political contests. Maybe even more. He can tell you more about Joe Cronin or Jimmy Foxx or Carl Yastrzemski, all fabled Red Sox players, than he can about equally fabled Boston politicians at whose feet he sat as a youngster. He is probably more at home with a Yastrzemski—whose 3,000th hit he had recently celebrated as if it were his own—than he is with a Carter.

That night it wouldn't have been unlike O'Neill to tell the story about the day, in the fall of 1978, when, upon his return from Rome where he had an audience with the newly installed Polish pope, he was greeted by Yastrzemski. It was shortly after the Yankee–Red Sox playoff series when the Red Sox almost made a comeback in the last inning. What did the pope say? Yastrzemski demanded to know. "He kissed me on the left cheek and he kissed me on the right cheek, and he said, 'What the hell happened to Yastrzemski in the ninth inning with two out and two on?'"

That last game of the 1979 World Series was a gloomy one for the Orioles. With a world championship so near their grasp, their bats, like Boston's, suddenly fell silent and their nerve deserted them. It was a gloomy season for Jimmy Carter, too. He had recently sunk to new depths in the polls and it was obvious that Edward M. Kennedy wanted his job.

O'Neill was in agony over this unholy condition. To him the Democratic Party was church, state, and family. He was brought up to believe that you never, no matter what the provocation, attempt to strike down one of your own, most especially not a sitting president. He had grown up believing that loyalty was one of the most sacred principles, not just in politics, but in life. And although his respect for Carter had been slow in developing, his fidelity toward him could never be questioned. Kennedy, on the other hand, was like family, O'Neill often said. They were not politically close, although O'Neill had a paternal love for the younger man.

O'Neill's distaste for this turn of events was exquisite. He needed an out, and that night, in the fifth inning of the World Series game in Baltimore, Carter gave it to him.

Instead of reaching for another peanut, Carter reached into his pocket and produced a note from Democratic National Committee Chairman John C. White. The note reminded Carter to put O'Neill on the spot and ask him then, more than ten months ahead of the event, to preside as chairman of the 1980 Democratic National Convention. Enormously relieved, O'Neill accepted. It meant that for the next several months, for however long the family feud lasted, he could look all of his inquisitors in the eye and say, with half-smile, half-scowl, "Hey, I'm neutral."

Had it not been for the fans looking on in the stadium, he might have embraced Carter.

O'Neill was an impressive-looking figure at the ballgame. Topped by his distinctive thatch of white hair and clad in a topcoat that did not hide his massive frame, he could be seen with the unaided eye from the farthest outfield stands. Carter, on the other hand, blended in with the crowd.

It is the same for O'Neill in his own arena, the floor of the U.S. House of Representatives. It is an impressive sight to see him, with massive rumpled frame and Bantry Bay face, enter the House chamber. Every congressman, every page, every clerk is aware of his presence. He moves about as though he were the bishop of Boston, slipping quietly into a seat and holding what he calls "confession," whispering, listening, nodding to the penitents who alternately take seats beside him. Watching the performance, you get the feeling it is the reenactment of a scene from another era.

In some ways, this bigger-than-life character is a throwback to another time in politics when big city ward bosses dispensed favors in exchange for inviolable pledges of support. He arose from the primordial ooze of politics, the Irish wards of Boston, and was suckled at its ample bosom, patronage. He learned his lessons early, campaigning door to door for Al Smith and FDR, and mixing in the company of card sharks, bartenders, and boozy, backslapping politicians.

O'Neill received his political training in the brass-knuckles school of state legislative politics, first as a member of a trampled and abused minority, then as leader of an insurrectionist and finally dominant majority. In time-honored fashion, the oppressed eventually became the oppressor. O'Neill's transition to the go-along world of Congress was not as smooth as his relaxed, one-of-the-boys manner suggested. He had a timetable for returning to Boston and running for governor, but the breaks did not occur on schedule. To some it would appear that the luck of the Irish had often touched his career—and perhaps it did—but on the other hand, he was always ready, always prepared for the next step.

O'Neill's ascension to the speakership of the U.S. House coincided with the rise of a very different sort of politician, Jimmy Carter. It must have been a rude awakening for Carter to arrive in Washington when Congress was at the peak of its post-Nixon assertiveness, to find a backroom deal-maker running the show. Carter's pureness of heart would not stand for such lapses in character. Yet he soon came to realize that O'Neill could be his strongest ally in the government and soon saw the wisdom of putting or keeping O'Neill cronies on the federal payroll. Carter's people eventually had to acknowledge that O'Neill, the old warhorse, was capable despite his faults—or perhaps because of them—of running one of the biggest engines of government, the House of Representatives, with considerable skill.

Part of the reason for O'Neill's success is his understanding of human weakness. In a system built on mutual dependence, those with no insight into the nature of frailty never get very far. O'Neill, who has supped at many a lobbyist's table and traded many a favor, knows a great deal about human weakness. Because of that he may be the perfect man for the job. As he likes to say, you put the people together, job by job, favor by favor, and you get a program, a bill, a policy. Fail in this basic rule of politics and there will be only a hollow ache in an ethically pure heart.

At first O'Neill was deeply offended by Carter's aloof attitude toward Congress. But O'Neill's willingness to forgive and forget hovered just beneath the surface of his disapproval. When Carter returned from a peacemaking trip to the Middle East in March 1979 he was almost smothered by this huge, bulky man as he stepped off the plane at Andrews Air Force Base. O'Neill took the president straight to his breast in an open display of pride and affection, an unusual sight in reserved, cautious Washington. This directness, this personal self-confidence, is only one dimension of a complex and utterly unique political character.

O'Neill came to Washington as the last of a breed. He nimbly crossed back and forth between the old and the new: tough, gentle; demanding, kind; unawed by presidents and statesmen, fiercely defensive of the institution in which he served. What his colleagues and the public see is what they get: a sentimental, God-loving, old-fashioned gentleman and patriot, a devout Democrat and thorough-going extrovert who impulsively hugs the ladies and slaps the gents on the back with a throaty Boston how-are-ya. There is, as one James Joyce politician said of another, no hunker-sliding about him. He can clobber you with directness.

O'Neill is known as a man who never goes back on his word, and if there is a serious weakness that intrudes on his public life, it is that he never abandons his friends. In the midst of the ethics-scandal mood that whipsawed the House in the 1970s, this seeming character defect landed him in one of the most unhappy periods of his life.

Professionally, he is a master of the intricate rules and folkways of the House, not a law writer. He knows what he wants—help for the needy, jobs for the unemployed, health care for the ill—but he can't be bothered with details of legislation.

Intellectuals, some of them, may cringe at his style and lack of finesse. His is the image of an overweight whiskey-drinking, cigar-smoking, poker-playing pol. The fact is that in this increasingly complex democratic congressional system of ours, O'Neill, flaws and all, makes things happen; he gets things done. He has something else: a politician's instinct for numbers.

When his term as Speaker settles into history, O'Neill may be viewed as one of the strongest speakers of the house. He is fully aware that a weak and hesitant holder of that office leaves the House open to encroachment by an assertive president or Senate—he saw it happen under Nixon—and he is determined not to let it happen again.

It was not an unreasonable hope. The Founding Fathers had intended that Congress be an equal partner with the presidency and the Supreme Court. Republican Speaker Thomas B. Reed of Maine had even refused to go to the White House to discuss legislative policy with the president. He said it would denigrate Congress. And Democratic Speaker Sam Rayburn of Texas was always careful to correct any misunderstandings of his status. "I haven't served *under* anybody," he would say. "I have served *with* eight presidents." Not all Speakers talk that tough. Like the presidency itself, the post of Speaker has few clearly outlined duties beyond presiding over the House and signing bills. Each Speaker has shaped the job by his own personality. Some have been strong, some weak, some narrowly partisan, some scrupulously fair, some lively, some dull.

One of a Speaker's more awesome responsibilities is one that has so far never been exercised: to step into the presidency if both president and vice-president die or resign before replacements can be selected. Initially, the line of succession ran through the president pro tem of the Senate before reaching the Speaker. In 1886, Congress decided that the line should run from the vice-president to the secretary of state and down through the cabinet in order of rank. It wasn't until 1947 that the order of succession was shuffled again and the Speaker and Senate president placed (in that order) ahead of the cabinet. Twenty years later, while a decidedly creaky-looking seventy-five-year-old John W. McCormack of Massachusetts was Speaker, the nation ratified the Twenty-Fifth Amendment to the Constitution setting up a new system for filling a vacancy in the vice-presidency, inserting another person ahead of the Speaker in case of a vacancy. None of the amendment's sponsors could have guessed that the new procedures would be used twice—and successfully—in the next seven years.

The prospect of being next in line to the president might be welcomed by many Speakers, but it clearly frightened Carl B. Albert, the man it happened to. For Albert was Speaker of the House when Vice-President Spiro T. Agnew resigned in 1973 and when President Richard M. Nixon followed him into private life ten months later.

In both cases, Secret Service agents immediately were dispatched to watch over Albert, and a White House telephone was installed in his apartment. The whole thing made him jittery. He didn't like being guarded, and he seemed genuinely relieved when new vice-presidents, first Gerald R. Ford for Agnew and then Nelson Rockefeller for Ford, were named, confirmed by majority votes of both House and Senate, and sworn in.

The Constitution doesn't specify that the Speaker of the House be a member of Congress, but he always has been. And it says nothing of sex nor age. Nevertheless, Speakers have always been men, and they're getting older all the time. From 1860 to 1899, no man over fifty was elected Speaker. Since then, no man under fifty has been elected. Rayburn was fifty-eight when finally elected Speaker after twenty-four years in the House. McCormack was seventy when he took over. Albert was sixty-two, and O'Neill sixty-four.

The seniority system can be credited—or blamed—for this advance in age. Congressmen must wait their turn. Older members get first crack at leadership posts, both on committees and within the House as a whole. By now it has become a tradition that floor leaders move up to the post of Speaker. There wasn't even a roll-call vote when Majority Leader O'Neill was nominated for Speaker by fellow Democrats. He got the job by acclamation and without opposition.

Only time will show whether O'Neill can turn this popularity into a strong Speakership to rank with the few giants of the past. There have been many more lackluster performances than great ones during these two-hundred years. From the list of forty-six Speakers who preceded O'Neill, historians generally have deemed only four as strong: Henry Clay, Thomas B. Reed, Joe Cannon, and Sam Rayburn.

Clay, an anti-Federalist and later National Republican from Kentucky, was elected Speaker the day he entered the House at the age of thirty-four, on November 4, 1811. Tall and graceful, he was a young man of charm and wit. Before Clay, Speakers had acted as impartial presiding officers; Clay, however, guided, and led, the House where he wanted it to go. He forced limits on debate. He made all committee assignments with an eye to the bills he wanted approved. And with his strong personality, he made the House the dominant branch of government.

Republican Thomas B. Reed came along seventy-eight years later. He was a rude contrast to the elegant Mr. Clay and the first Speaker to win the title "Czar." A huge man physically, Reed was bitterly sarcastic and ruthlessly partisan. The political cartoonists of the day had a grand time portraying the rotund gentleman from Maine in regal robes with ermine collar, his arms raised to pound a gavel or crack a whip. His biting wit furnished ideal captions: "The minority be damned," for example, or, in reference to two colleagues, "They never open their mouths without subtracting from the sum of human knowledge." To Democrats, after he reorganized and took control of the Rules Committee, he said: "Gentlemen, we have decided to perpetrate the following outrage." And when mulling over the possibility of Republicans nominating him for president: "They could do worse, and they probably will." (They did. It was the year William McKinley won.)

Reed's most lasting contribution to the forward progress of congressional government was to end the opposition tactic of disappearing quorums. He did it as he did most things, roughly and arbitrarily. But it stuck.

It sounds easy today: Reed simply counted all members in the chamber to determine whether the quorum—necessary to do business—was on hand. Until then, congressmen seeking to block action would refuse to answer their names. In the absence of a quorum, the House had to shut down. One day, Reed started counting, even when the members failed to answer the roll call.

"I deny your right, Mr. Speaker," one man shouted, "to count me as present." And Reed responded: "The chair is making a statement of fact that the gentleman from Kentucky is present. Does he deny it?"

The Democrats exploded in anger, but Reed was firm. At one point he even ordered the doors locked to keep the quorum from actually disappearing. They stayed and were counted. In future years, the opposition party had to find other ways to stall.

Reed's assertion of power obviously set the stage for "Uncle Joe" Cannon, but his heavy-handed rule collided with a growing progressive movement in the country, and in 1910, seven years after Cannon was first elected Speaker, the House revolted and stripped him of much of his power.

Cannon, a very conservative Illinois Democrat, was a scrappy little fellow but out of touch with the changing times and unable to control a restless House. He was something of a paradox. Though autocratic and tyrannical, he was personally popular, a jovial chap, cracking jokes even at his own expense. But in laughter there was some truth. "I am," he once said, "one of the great army of mediocrity which constitutes the majority."

Sam Rayburn was first elected to Congress two years after the revolt against Cannon, but he waited twenty-seven years to become Speaker. In the end, the Texas Democrat and friend of presidents served as Speaker longer than any other, from January 13, 1940, to September 21, 1961, with two two-year periods on the sidelines when the Republicans were in control.

Rayburn served in a time of great men and a great war, the era dominated by Roosevelt, Stalin, and Churchill. He outlasted them all and, along the way, became something of a legend among his colleagues in the House. In Rayburn's Congress, younger members were seen but seldom heard. Except for a chosen few, Rayburn hardly noticed them. His advice was a crisp: "To get along, go along." Tip O'Neill, who was one of those younger members who went along with the rules of the game, came to know every member of the House by name. He doubted that Rayburn knew twenty. Upstarts were in a minority.

Rayburn ran the House from the relatively small base of a first-floor meeting room in the Capitol which was known for years as the "Board of Education." There, behind closed doors, Rayburn would meet with a select few to talk politics over his favorite bourbon and branch water, and to chart the legislative course for the House. Senate Democratic Leader Lyndon B. Johnson, a fellow Texan, often dropped by, and Vice-President Harry S. Truman was there when the news came of President Roosevelt's death.

As a young congressman, O'Neill was invited into this inner circle from time to time as a friend and protégé of John McCormack of Massachusetts, the House majority leader. McCormack didn't drink and O'Neill didn't like Rayburn's bourbon, so the two would sip soft drinks. O'Neill seldom was invited to offer legislative advice, however; he was usually asked to share stories of Massachusetts politics. "Tell me about Curley," Rayburn would ask, or "How about this young guy, Kennedy?"

Times change. Today, Tip O'Neill can't run the House the way Rayburn did. Much of the time, O'Neill's "board of education" has been the House Chamber itself. And he consults with everyone. The House is getting younger and the younger members are more aggressive, more impatient. John McCormack couldn't cope with it. Neither could Carl Albert. Both quit in defeat.

But Tip O'Neill, the old Irish pol, came along at a time when history was ready for him. He bridged the gap between old politics and new. With that bearhug approach to his fellow man, O'Neill gathers young and old into his embrace. He likes everyone or nearly everyone, except maybe some members of the press and the Republican gadfly who runs against him every two years. But he doesn't care whether you're young or old, bright or stupid; if you're with him, you're OK; if you're not with him for some good reason, such as being a Republican, that's OK, too. He is not going to play "czar." He wants to be liked, to throw his arms around even the least of his friends. "As I've said in my office over the years," he says, "it's nice to be important, but it's even more important to be nice."

Inevitably, Tip O'Neill's political life has been interwoven with the comings and goings of the almost legendary Kennedys. But O'Neill was there first. He was a rising power in the Massachusetts state legislature and Ted Kennedy was a boy of fourteen working in his oldest brother's first campaign, when the two of them first met. It was St. Patrick's Day, March 17, 1946. Kennedy does not remember a specific meeting, but says, "I've always felt that I've known Tip all my life." When this reminiscence is added to O'Neill's expressed father-son feelings toward Kennedy, a strong familial relationship emerges. Even though the two have never been close politically, the personal attachment is made of binding stuff.

Cordial as their first meeting may have been, however, it is important to note that O'Neill did not approve of the first Kennedy venture. John F. Kennedy had not paid his dues to the party by starting on the lower political rungs. He ran immediately for Congress and thus angered members of his political establishment, including O'Neill. In fact, he ran against one of O'Neill's closest legislative pals.

Ted Kennedy showed every bit as much political opportunism when he decided in 1962 to go after his brother's recently vacated seat in the U.S. Senate. In doing so, he put O'Neill, the party loyalist, in an exceedingly difficult position.

Kennedy telephoned O'Neill and said he would like to see him in O'Neill's office; his brother Jack suggested that he call. They had a big political favor to ask of O'Neill. Ted wanted to run for the Senate, but he had one problem, a big one: Edward McCormack, nephew of O'Neill's mentor in the House, newly chosen Speaker of the House, John McCormack. Eddie was the party favorite and was already lining up delegates for the nomination. O'Neill himself had considered running for the Senate but had deferred to McCormack's wishes. This was not the way the Kennedys operated. They figured that with a certain amount of cooperation from old man McCormack they could roll over the lesser-known candidate.

Ted Kennedy told O'Neill that he wanted to conduct a poll among Massachusetts Democrats. It would be paid for by both candidates. "If I beat him by five percent, he gets out and runs for governor," Kennedy told O'Neill. "If he beats me, I get out of the fight entirely."

Distasteful though it must have been to O'Neill, he took the proposal to the senior McCormack. McCormack agreed to take it up with his nephew, but later reported back that his nephew thought it was a bad idea; he already had delegates committed to him, and there was no point in entering a popularity contest with a Kennedy.

Kennedy, O'Neill relates, had the poll conducted anyway, and it showed, naturally, that only he could carry the state for the Democrats. Again, Kennedy went to O'Neill, and O'Neill went to John McCormack and, as O'Neill puts it, "tried to negotiate it out." McCormack called all the party delegates and asked that they remain neutral and support no one.

Kennedy won the nomination, but he did not win O'Neill's respect.

It was November 7, a full year away from the 1980 election, and things were deceptively quiet in Washington. O'Neill had returned from Boston the night before, having stayed home to vote in local elections. Congressmen were still straggling into town after the long weekend.

It was the day Tip O'Neill did not want to see arrive. Ever since Kennedy had signaled his candidacy for the presidency by saying his family no longer objected to his running, O'Neill's days had been filled with nothing but Kennedy talk and Kennedy questions. He couldn't get it out of his mind, broaching the subject with the press when the press neglected to bring it up. But he was really convinced, and his instincts told him he was right, that Kennedy would not really do it.

He had told the press one week in September that he thought Kennedy could easily win the nomination for president if he sought it. The second part of the statement—that he didn't think Kennedy would run—was ignored. The result was a tornado of political speculation arising from the assumption that since the Speaker was a "close friend of the Kennedy family," he had inside information about Kennedy's intentions. O'Neill also had a reputation as a canny old Irish politician who got his information straight from the Druids.

Since O'Neill was not a close friend of the family and had not been consulted by Kennedy about the decision, he was aghast at the furor for which he was at least partly responsible. He quickly issued another statement, saying that Carter, "a very determined person," would be a candidate "to the bitter end."

It was a signal to Kennedy, a warning that an open challenge to Carter would be long and divisive, bad for the country and bad for the party. This O'Neill believed, and he told administration officials that Kennedy was positioning himself for a late entry into the race in the event that Carter got battered in the early primaries and was forced to drop out. If Kennedy believed this would happen, he was wrong, O'Neill felt. As if to underscore his position and his hope, O'Neill said, "I still have to take it on good faith that he is not a candidate for the presidency."

Kennedy, by this time, had gone too far to turn back—though O'Neill didn't think so. Kennedy was putting out his own signals and O'Neill wasn't reading them. Or perhaps he just didn't want to. He privately told colleagues that he might even have to support Carter against Kennedy, a prospect which, to a Boston Irish Catholic, was worse than abstinence. Leo Diehl, O'Neill's closest aide, was making bets with his friends: Kennedy would not run.

O'Neill comes from a background that is vastly different from the Kennedys'. He does not visit them on Cape Cod, even though his summer place is not far from theirs; he doesn't go sailing with them or dining with them at the yacht club. The Kennedys do not play cards or drink beer with Tip O'Neill. So when he spoke to the press about his hunches, they were just that—and not very good ones.

A few days after making his last hunch public, Kennedy called O'Neill and said he wanted to set him straight. O'Neill talked to Kennedy for over an hour "like a father would talk to a son." O'Neill talked tough. He told Kennedy the campaign would be a mistake—that it is disloyal and disruptive for a fellow Democrat to challenge the president.

Kennedy did not take O'Neill's advice, but in fact convinced him that he was close to making an irrevocable decision to run. Ruefully, O'Neill went back to his reporter friends and gave them another headline: There was a good chance Kennedy would get into the race.

"Naturally I'm torn by it," he told reporters one morning. "I've been friends for thirty-five years with Kennedy and I have great admiration for the president. I wouldn't be human if I wasn't." So it went, day after agonizing day. To further compound the problem, O'Neill's son Tommy, the Lieutenant Governor of Massachusetts, went to work as Kennedy's New England coordinator. If Kennedy could not get one O'Neill, he'd get another.

So it was a tremendous relief to O'Neill when Carter effectively neutralized him by offering him the chairmanship of the Democratic convention. It made it possible for him to spend a day like November

7—when Kennedy made his campaign announcement at Faneuil Hall in Boston—carrying out his duties as Speaker and not feeling he had to be at Kennedy's side or even watching for the news.

Accompanied by other members of the House leadership, O'Neill motored down to the White House for the regular breakfast meeting that morning with President Carter.

Carter at this point was a beleaguered man, down in the polls and under attack within his own party, and deeply embroiled in the biggest foreign policy crisis of his presidency—that involving Iran. Fanatical followers of Iran's revolutionary leader, Ayatollah Khomeini, had seized the American Embassy in Teheran and taken as hostages sixty-two embassy employees. It was a time of unbelievable tension. And yet, to O'Neill, Carter seemed calm and self-assured as he briefed the congressmen on the situation and urged them not to make any inflammatory statements.

There had been a gradual change in O'Neill's estimation of Carter. Theirs had been a distinctly cool relationship from the onset as Carter, his outsider juices still flowing from his successful campaign for the White House, had come to town flogging Congress and its mean little traditions, snubbing O'Neill and its other leaders, and displaying little aptitude for traditional political leadership.

And yet O'Neill experienced a growing admiration for Carter's tenacity and basic honesty. He had worked with Carter, not always closely, but loyally, for three years, and his admiration for the man who held the reigns of ultimate power had grown. To O'Neill that morning, Carter appeared extremely confident and unshaken by recent events, including political events.

O'Neill returned to the seat of his own power, the Capitol, shortly before noon, took time to make phone calls to Democrats around the country who had either won or lost in the preceding day's state and local elections, then went to lunch with Carter's chosen campaign manager, Robert Strauss. It wasn't meant to be a political meeting, althought the subject certainly came up, along with discussion about the Middle East and trade negotiations. O'Neill says he told Strauss, "Two months ago, it looked as though Carter was out of the ballgame. Now it's going to be a real cliff-hanger."

Later that afternoon, somewhat natty in gray suit and white shirt with wide gray stripes, O'Neill, during an afternoon snack, picked at boiled chicken and munched on heavily salted celery. He would have been just as comfortable in a storefront office in East Cambridge as in the ornate, spacious quarters in the Capitol. An aide, Gary Hymel, came in to discuss the schedule for the rest of the week. Should they take up the Federal Trade

Commission authorization bill the next day and put off action on Carter's hospital-cost containment bill? Yeah, put it off, O'Neill said. Things didn't look good for that bill. His wife Millie—he calls her "Mum"—called to talk about evening plans.

Kennedy, at the same time, was off on a whirlwind tour of cities announcing his candidacy, and spent a few moments on a flight back to Washington talking about O'Neill, "the last of the great Speakers." He forgot momentarily about the distractions of the campaign and spoke with feeling and perception.

"I think Tip O'Neill has a fine and very unique set of attributes," Kennedy said. "First of all, he has a basic kind of honesty and integrity, a directness; he's frank with people, he's a man of his word, he likes people, and he likes members of the House. He has a great quality that contributes to his success as a political leader—which I always thought both he and my brother had—and that is that he can really look at an issue from the other person's perspective and understand where they're really coming from. And he knows when to ask a person for help and support and when not to.

"I think he has a great sense of the Congress itself. There is a rhythm and motion to the Congress that few leaders understand how to move and shape and direct. Some people are overwhelmed by it. I think he's got that sense. There is a chemistry to that body [the House] and I think he's got nerve endings that can understand that."

O'Neill's nerve endings had been somewhat frayed in the preceding weeks. But now, with his newfound neutrality, he was able to look ahead with some detachment and consider his own role in the coming months. When the time came for division and strife, he would offer himself as healer.

O'Neill believed that the contest would be over long before the convention. A clear winner, he said, would emerge by March. If that clear winner was not Kennedy, O'Neill felt, Kennedy would be out of the running by convention time. "If Kennedy wins it, he's got to win it before he goes to the convention. Otherwise," he said, "delegates to the convention will be unable to resist the 'awesome power' of a president who, in exchange for support, can promise everything from water projects and apppointments to dinners at the White House."

If there is a bitter, open fight to the finish, O'Neill believes, it could be damaging to the party and to the country. "I hope this convention doesn't make a lot of wounds. If it does, I hope to be in a position to bring the party together. I've always had the ability to bring people together."

2

THE ETHNIC SALAD
BOWL

THE FIRST major-league baseball game Thomas O'Neill saw was a thing of flawless beauty. It was July 1, 1920, at Fenway Park where the once-glorious Red Sox were playing the Senators, the most pathetic team in all baseball save for the heroic efforts of Walter Johnson. There he was on the mound that day, the Big Train, mowing down the beloved home team with his ferocious fast ball. Inning after inning. Striking them out, popping them up. One, two, three.

And there was the wide-eyed kid, seven years old, watching the pitchers intently, Johnson for the Senators and Harry Harper for the Sox—Harper doing a pretty good job of it himself. Almost nobody was getting on base. In the seventh inning, the Sox managed to get one man as far as first on an error, and that was all. The game turned out to be the only no-run, no-hit game the great Walter Johnson every pitched.

The youngster was impressed, of course, but not so much by the pitcher's performance as by the statistics: the number of pitches Johnson threw in each inning; the number of times—six in a row—he got Red Sox batters to pop up on the first pitch. In the midst of the unnerving tension of a no-hitter, young Tom was carefully making notations on a score sheet. Figuring: a good pitcher—he heard it somewhere—won't throw more than 115 pitches in a ball game—maybe 120; after that you know he's weakening; six pop-ups in a row; must be some kind of record.

Not many kids who haven't already decided to make a career of bookmaking would look at a big-league baseball game and see numbers. But young O'Neill was a natural figurer, a statistician. Whether it was ballgames, boxing matches, or card games, he reveled in numbers and odds: batting averages, runs batted in, earned-run averages; the percentages in raising, calling, and bluffing. Thus cursed in boyhood, can the man ever have vision? Maybe not, but he might have the makings of a splendid politician.

Political notions would normally be far from the mind of a seven-year-old sports fanatic, but an Irish kid growing up in North Cambridge, Massachu-setts, in the shadow of Boston's Irish political machine, supping nightly at the table of an old-school ward boss, and learning early to trust his own instincts, would be no stranger to the black art.

Sports and politics. On the same day Walter Johnson was jamming fast balls across the plate, delegates to the Democratic National Convention were arguing over recognition of the new nation that was then being born of tragedy and triumph, the Irish Free State. In the O'Neill neighborhood, where the ancient language of the Celts was still taught and spoken, it was difficult not to feel intensely involved.

From the very beginning.

On a cold, blustery day in December, 1912, a tall, gaunt Irishman, Thomas P. O'Neill, Sr., thirty-eight years old, walked outside the gates of Harvard College, carrying a picket sign.

The early 1900s were a time of great expansion for the Yankee intellectual colossus sitting astride the teeming ethnic quarters of Cambridge like a red-brick Emerald City. Harvard College lay within sight of the pits where the Irish and French-Canadians dug the clay that made the bricks that helped the college expand. But if Harvard was aware of the growing sentiment among the laborers for collective bargaining, it had not shown it in its hiring of nonunion bricklayers. To the sons of immigrants like Tom O'Neill, who had slowly worked their way up in the bricklaying trade, union membership was like membership in the church.

O'Neill, like many of his fellow picketers, was the American-born son of refugees from the great Irish potato famine. Hard work, meager living, and harsh reality were their accepted lot. The first thing his father had done, upon arriving in Boston from Mallow, County Cork, in 1845, was to buy a plot for himself and his family to be buried in. The fact of death was an every-day reality for those who stayed in Ireland; for those who left home, it was a kind of dying: they would never be back. It was frequently remarked that the winds billowing the sails of the ships that brought them to Boston were the same ones that swept over the distant graves of their loved ones.

Grandfather O'Neill didn't die as quickly as he must have imagined. He took a job with the New England Brick Company in North Cambridge and, eleven years later, went back to Mallow with enough money to marry. With his wife he returned to Boston in 1867, where he settled down to stay, and in 1874, in the section of North Cambridge known as Old Dublin, the first Thomas O'Neill was born.

Tom O'Neill, Sr. grew to be tall and thin, possessing the easy grace of an athlete. He, too, worked for the brick company but soon fought his way out of the clay pits, vowing never to let his own sons work there. He learned bricklaying, began his own neighborhood contracting business, and, like his brother Bill, went into politics. He was elected in 1900 to the Cambridge City Council, a position of enormous power and influence in the one area that meant anything to an immigrant community: jobs.

The Irish were particularly adaptable to American politics, as if some genetic memory out of their Celtic past were being reawakened. The Irish were by nature talkers, poets, story tellers, companionable mixers. And they had in common a history of oppression by the English, for whom the Yankee Americans were an easy substitute. With Lord Blarney as patron saint, they had long learned to use the spoken word as soft deception, discarding literal honesty as a tiresome—if not dangerous—burden. Their wit, savage and mocking, and their flexibility in dealing with people, made them especially effective in the church-oriented, saloon-centered kind of politics that flourished in Boston.

Politics was the only way to get anywhere. As the waves of immigrant Irish flooded their city, the Brahmin establishment dug in its heels, effectively barring the Irish from banking, insurance, and other traditional Yankee power bastions. The only avenue left to what William Shannon calls "conspicuous success" was politics. The only goal of politics was jobs, especially safe, protected civil-service jobs: policemen, firemen, school-teachers, sanitation workers, city clerks. Any jobs controlled by patronage, of course, were dispensed by Irish politicians who were elected by the hoards of civil servants and other beneficiaries of the system. It was a perfect circle.

The older Tom O'Neill didn't have to join ranks with his fellow workers and walk the picket lines around Harvard College. He had already made his way in a tough town. But he did it out of a sense of loyalty. Cohesion. You stuck with your kind and they stuck with you. Belonging to the union was as important as being a Democrat. And being Irish and being a Democrat was a single concept.

A strong instinct for solidarity was something the O'Neills and most other Irish families brought over to America with them after generations of awesome punishment at the hands of their English masters. In America, they took quickly to the party whose representatives had met them as they staggered off the ships, an ache in their hearts and a sickness in their guts, offering help in getting jobs, lodgings, and quick naturalization. The immigrants responded gratefully by voting en masse for party regulars, by welding themselves into parts of the big-city political machine, by wielding great power at the polls.

Harvard's hiring of nonunion bricklayers was an unspeakable crime in the eyes of the men who walked the picket line outside the university's gates. So adamant, in fact, was Tom O'Neill that on December 9, 1912, he spent the hours that his wife was giving birth to their third child, Thomas Jr., marching in protest. It was what he had to do. It could not have been a more symbolic beginning for Thomas P. O'Neill, Jr.

Young Thomas never got a chance to know his mother. Soon after his birth she became gravely ill. The family did everything possible during the summer of 1913 to make things easy for her. They took a cabin in Greenfield, New Hampshire, in the mountains, but her health continued to decline. What hours she had during the day were spent sitting on the porch, holding her son Thomas in her lap while the other children, Bill and Mary, ran around in bare feet and played in the barn.

Only nine months after the birth of her second son, Rose Tolan died of tuberculosis. A number of aunts wanted to take one or more of the children, but it was her dying wish that the family stay together. In her absence the family became very close. Their father did some of the mothering, but much of it was supplied by a warm and possessive French-Canadian housekeeper, Rose Le Blanc. Of Thomas she said, "He's my baby," and in many respects that was true. She gave Thomas all the love he needed, and he responded in kind. It was not until Rose left the family six years later that his father remarried.

The death of his mother while he was still an infant could have had a devastating effect on Thomas, but it did not. The child adapted quickly to his new surroundings, found love where he could, especially in the persons of his housekeeper, a number of devoted Catholic nuns, and his father. Even as a child, he reached out, finding enjoyment in the company of others. It might have been natural for him to feel anxiety when left alone; if so, he subdued this feeling by constantly surrounding himself with talking, joking, laughing people.

The O'Neills lived on the second floor of a two-family home in North Cambridge. They lived a Spartan but comfortable life. Although their father was a strict disciplinarian, he was an understanding man; he didn't come down too hard on his children for bending the rules a little. But there was definitely an aura of authority about him.

Thomas O'Neill, Sr. was father and mother to his son for nearly eight years and, naturally, the children resented it when he remarried. His new wife was a proud woman who dressed Thomas beautifully and tried unsuccessfully to make him wear a straw hat. "It was not the happiest of homes afterwards," said O'Neill.

The Irish, as Chesterton said, are men that God created mad—

> For all their wars are merry
> And all their songs are sad.

By the same token, they are capable of laughing at wakes and crying at baptisms. But this legacy of sadness was not something that Thomas O'Neill, Sr. would dwell on. Nor would he pass it on to his son.

The life of an Irish Catholic boy growing up in Boston was frequently one of utter frustration and unhappiness. The accursed fatalism that haunted his landless, downtrodden ancestors came face to face with the reality of insurmountable barriers of the new order and left many Irish boys with shattered dreams and a profound pessimism. Many found escape in booze, and comfort, such as it was, in knowing that there was nowhere they could go. They wound up, like the brooding, dark characters of another O'Neill's Bedrock Bar, sitting around with the old gang, forgetting love, getting drunk, and swapping lies.

Pessimism was not a trait that the older Tom O'Neill shared with his countrymen, however. If there was disappointment in his life he never showed it to his children. He sought neither comfort nor oblivion in the bottle and was, in fact, a total abstainer, head of the local temperance movement. Such was the wreckage he saw in the lives of others that he found refuge in uprightness and security in living by the book. He became a grand knight of the Knights of Columbus and founded the K of C baseball team in North Cambridge. From his father, the young Tom must have inherited many of the characteristics that were to serve him in life: optimism, an easy tolerance of human frailty, and a regard for the rules of the game. Tom, Sr. was an activist, not a brooder, yet always sensitive to the lot of the less able or less fortunate.

In 1914 the O'Neill children were told to say a special prayer: their father was taking the civil service exam for the City of Cambridge. O'Neill was highest scorer out of a sizeable group of competitors and was rewarded with one of the most sought-after, if prosaic, jobs in the City of Cambridge: sewer commissioner. It made the O'Neills enormously proud. It established the father as a prominent and—with over a thousand jobs under him—a powerful member of the community. He also held sway over hundreds more who did private contracting for the city.

O'Neill was a man of precise habits. At exactly ten of eight every morning the Sewer Department's timekeeper would pull up at the O'Neill front door with horse and carriage and, as O'Neill joined him up front, place a fur blanket over their knees, then off they would trot. After some months of this, his Fairfield Street neighbors dubbed him Lord Fairfield.

The family eventually moved to a square triple-decker house on Orchard Street a few blocks away, and more firmly established itself as middle-class, lace-curtain Irish. In contrast to East Cambridge, which is much closer to downtown Boston and is dotted with factories and tenements, North Cambridge, lying just north of Harvard Square, was then a mecca for prospering Irish families. All it had had in the early days was a cattle market. Then the brick companies came in. But now it was mostly residential, a place where people who had saved enough from their factory or city jobs could get away from the noise and dirt and smells of industry and settle into lifetime homes. North Cambridge's population was as stable as granite. If any strangers lived there they did not remain strangers for long. Children, after they grew up and got married, stayed. The police knew everyone; the clergy knew everyone; the kids knew everyone. It was a place where neighbors came to fix meals when relatives died. It was a good place to live, to grow up, to stay. It could be a great source of strength: you did business with your own kind. You also sent your own kind to public office.

Personal relationships were the cornerstone of life in North Cambridge. It was not so much that outsiders were not to be trusted but that there were enough insiders to make things comfortable. It helped to know people. Knowing people, you didn't have to worry about going through procedures or bureaucracies. Informality was the rule. To practice politics with any amount of skill you had to develop instincts about human behavior and know how to follow them. In politics you accepted the idea that government was not created for great and noble things—although they were not, of course, ruled out—but to make life a little easier for people by helping them. You helped everyone you could, not just your friends. But you definitely helped your friends. Above all, as the senior O'Neill would tell his son again and again, politics is local.

Tom, Jr. naturally had a strong attachment to his father, but at the same time he developed a noticeably independent streak. At the beach in summer he became gravely frightened when his father tried to force him to swim by pulling him out into the surf. But when his father went back home after the weekend, Thomas ventured out by himself and mastered his fear of the water. Bill, seven years older, and Mary, six years older, had learned to swim right away, making it doubly difficult for the youngest.

Apparently, Thomas, Jr. often skillfully managed to avoid chores around the house. When it was his turn to take the ashes from the coal stove down to the cellar to be sifted and tossed out, he was known to occasionally jump over the coal bucket at the top of the stairs. When scolded he would invariably change the subject: "Hey, do you know who I met today?" Just as he effectively deflected people's criticism, he charmed them out of their anger.

One day, four-year-old Thomas had sneaked up the back stairs to the maid's room and crawled out onto the third-story roof in the pouring rain. After his sister had coaxed him away from the roof ledge and scolded him for endangering his life and frightening her to death, he stood at the window, smiling, with both hands gripping the sills, and said calmly, "Come out and watch the way the rain goes down."

Growing up Irish in North Cambridge was an intense experience. In Dublin, Irish patriots were fighting the English from the very rooftops. The aftershock of the 1916 Easter Rising was sharply felt throughout the neighborhood. On Easter Sunday, men went up and down the street, collecting for the cause. Every house displayed the sticker that said, "I gave to the IRA." Although he was too young at that time to understand the intensity of feeling in the neighborhood, the cause for which the Irish rebels fought became an indelible part of his life.

A few months after the great Senators–Red Sox game, an event of strikingly symbolic importance brought the Irish rebellion home for O'Neill. On October 25, 1920, Terence MacSwiney, Lord Mayor of Cork, died in London's Brixton Jail after a twenty-four-day hunger strike supplemented only by water and a daily eucharistic wafer. MacSwiney's nieces lived on Yorktown Street near the O'Neills. The boy was attending Gaelic school when he heard the news. It was a time of extravagant mourning for the Irish.

With so many first-generation Irish in North Cambridge, Gaelic was spoken everywhere. In their Connemara accents, people would greet each other with a gutteral "Cé Chaoi a bhfuil Tú," roughly pronounced (Kay-ke-wiltu), a kind of top-of-the-morning expression. Less common was the greeting "Dia Dhuit"—God be with you—and the reply, "Dia Is Muire Dhuit"—God and Mary be with you. A man did not smoke a pipe but a dúidin. The name O'Neill means "champion" in Gaelic.

As independence of a kind approached for Ireland, life in the Irish ghettos of Boston seemed more and more like life in exile. Every heart quickened to the excitement of revolution and ached with sentiment as popular Irish tenors like John McCormack crooned their themes: humble peasant cottages, warm talk and warm times by the auld turf fire, sweet lassies in the garden where the praties grew, marching off to fight for the queen in a God-forsaken war, sailing to America to make one's fortune—but always returning rich and warmly greeted.

Elements of the Irish-American experience—the story of famine, the passage to America, the yearning for home, the rebellion—were part of O'Neill's upbringing. The story of the lad, whether real or imagined, who published revolutionary ideas, who took a poke at a soldier of the crown, who went underground and finally escaped, making his way to the swarming south side of Boston, was an epic figure about whom countless books would be written. One such book, *Fair Blows the Wind*, a novel, was later to be written by O'Neill's brother-in-law, William H. Mulcahy. The book's hero finds himself among the dank waterfront slums of America, where "ancient warehouses and dilapidated mansions had been converted into human hives. The sight of ragged children playing in the littered streets brought a pang to his heart, and he thought how all this squalor so belied the promise and the dream of this bright new world."

Young Thomas O'Neill's maternal grandmother had come over from Donegal and the song that tugged at the heartstrings more than any otherhad this lilting refrain:

> Shake hands with your uncle Dan, my boy,
> Shake hands with your cousin Kate,
>
> Arrah! That's the girl you used to swing
> Down on the garden gate;
>
> Shake hands with all the neighbors
> And kiss the colleens all,
>
> You're as welcome as the flowers in May
> In dear old Donegal.

Instead of playing cops and robbers or cowboys and Indians, the kids in O'Neill's neighborhood played the Irish against the English. Living where they did, in the midst of so much American history, they identified with an earlier struggle against British enemies.

. . . I lived on the corner of Orchard and Russell Street. There was a retreat on April 18, 1775, on both sides of Massachusetts Avenue before the Yankees cut across the orchard. There was a fellow killed on one side of the avenue and then down on Miller Avenue, and I could just envision as a kid the skirmish taking place between the patriots and the soldiers of the king.

O'Neill and his chums could stand on top of Bunker Hill in neighboring Charlestown and sight down their "muskets" at the advancing redcoats, waiting to see the whites of the hated English eyes. Not far from there rested the awesome hulk of the U.S.S. *Constitution* and across the river in Boston was all the rest: Old North Church, Paul Revere's house, King's Chapel, Old South Meeting House, and the site of the Boston Massacre.

Exciting though this history may have been to a young mind, the sheer weight of it must also have been painfully felt by the relatively new arrivals on the Boston scene, whose people had little in the way of monuments and transplanted heroes to compare with these Yankee giants. Add to this the attitudes of the entrenched powers and the openly expressed contempt for the "Paddies," and you've got the makings of a massive inferiority complex. Nevertheless, in some cases, where narrow doors could be seen as standing open, it resulted in a burning desire to succeed. And where else could one better succeed than in politics?

At the least, growing up in North Cambridge with the name Thomas O'Neill was no liability. Tall, dapper, articulate, the elder O'Neill had for some time been a significant political force in the city. There was no organized civil service when the senior O'Neill was on the city council. When city departments or public utilities such as the telephone or gaslight companies had job openings, they called the council and asked their representatives on the council to supply names.

O'Neill formed a club that was basically a means of providing service to his people. Instead of going to the priest with personal problems, people went to "Governor" O'Neill. If a family was breaking up, if a father had been drinking too much, if a young lad had been giving his family problems— people went to the O'Neill house and took it up with the "Governor." No one had given him that title or that authority. He was a leader because people considered him a leader. It was all very informal. "Power," his son grew fond of saying, "is when people think you have power."

Everyone, it seemed, migrated to the O'Neill home for favors. He produced. Most important, he helped people keep bread on the table.

One of the duties O'Neill attended to religiously was making sure that senior citizens were driven or escorted wherever they needed to go, whether it was a parish reunion or a Saturday night whist party. The service was provided without question by the O'Neill club. It was a duty. The political benefits were a natural by-product, and while no one expected the ward boss to be on call at all times of the day and night, the one who was not soon lost his power.

Unlike other parts of Boston, there were no saloons or speakeasies in

North Cambridge. The political life of the community was centered in Catholic organizations such as the Knights of Columbus. In addition to supporting a championship baseball team, which O'Neill's father founded, the Knights held minstrel shows for ten days and nights and a Knights of Columbus ball every year. Because nearly everyone in town belonged, the K of C was a significant power base.

No one was surprised in those days to see local politicians going to the O'Neill house. There was little future without his support. One of these politicians, Cambridge Mayor Edward Quinn, respected, affable, a fine orator, was looked upon with awe in the Irish neighborhoods. Wanting some of that respectability, that magic, Thomas O'Neill, Jr. determined quite young that someday he'd like to be mayor, too.

Wanting to go into politics in Boston was wanting to play in a fast league. A number of giant political figures, some of whom would parade in and out of his own career in later years, dominated the scene. Patrick J. Kennedy had gone from saloon keeper on Boston's East Side to ward boss. His son Joe was soon to find the business climate of the city not to his liking and transferred to New York. His father-in-law, John F. ("Honey Fitz") Fitzgerald, Boston's first Irish mayor, ruled the North End. Martin Lomasney held sway in the West End from a roll-top desk at the Hendricks Club. And just coming to power in the South End was James Michael Curley, a figure whose political skills and capacity for mischief were only hinted at in Edwin O'Connor's *The Last Hurrah*.

Curley's defeat of Honey Fitz in the bitter 1913 mayoralty race ended the power of the ward bosses. Curley mistrusted them all—"Build up a ward boss and someday he'll destroy you"—and ran the entire Democratic political machine, favors and all, out of his own pocket.

Jim Curley. The name was synonymous with Boston politics and inspired sentiments of fear, awe, love, and hatred among the populace, each according to station. Yankee Republicans were positive that he was the greatest scoundrel, if not thief, that had ever held office. The Irish were equally sure he was a saint. Either way, those whose paths he crossed politically came away with impressions they would never forget.

Curley was a better campaigner than officeholder and stronger when out than in, primarily because he created such tumult when he ran. And he was always running. He served as mayor during 1914–18, 1922–26, 1930–34, swimming in and out with his own political tide. He made it as far as governor in 1934, but beginning in 1936 suffered a series of disastrous defeats. He ran again and again for the Senate, for governor and mayor, never quite accepting that his last race was his last hurrah.

Curley was an inspired street-corner speaker who played upon the deep resentments and frustrations suffered by the Irish. His stories about his childhood were mostly blather, but the crowds loved it. He claimed to have been born in a Roxbury tenement, to have studied by candlelight, to have gotten his first job at eleven to help his poor sick mother, and at last to have come home clutching his first day's pay on Christmas Eve only to learn that she had died. Curley would keep up this sort of thing for hours, as long as the crowds wanted to hear him. Then they would cheer him lustily and carry him around on their shoulders.

Street-corner rallies in Cambridge were major events in the pre-video days, a form of entertainment second only to the picture shows in popularity. The young O'Neill certainly attended his share, enjoying the high comedy and drama.

Curley was as much a master of the low blow as of the high-sounding phrase. His Catholic constituents were sure to be scandalized when word somehow happened to leak out that a Curley opponent was divorced or had been seen eating steak at the Copley Plaza on a Friday. Such eye-gouging, ear-biting tactics were tolerated and even applauded at a time when politics-as-theater was the only show in town.

A favorite target for Irish resentment sat grandly and aloofly in the midst of working class Cambridge—Harvard University. The politicians flayed away at its ivy-covered walls. Audiences loved it, even though they knew full well that the next day the politicians would be going around to the back door of the college getting custodial jobs, kitchen jobs, caretaker jobs for many of them and even helping some of the more ambitious of their sons and daughters gain admission. For that reason they didn't make too fine a point of it.

Curley promised—and, much to the dismay of the Yankee bluebloods, often delivered—jobs, schools, playgrounds, and parks. It was this kind of performance that a would-be politician like Thomas O'Neill sought to emulate. A man could make a whole career out of paying meticulous attention to details. Without regard for the cost—the money could always be borrowed—huge construction projects employing thousands of grateful Bostonians were begun. Not only did Curley bring about a dramatic change in the physical appearance of the city, he also brought about a quadrupling of the tax rate that the rich Yankees would pay.

Such was the atmosphere in which Thomas O'Neill was raised. The bread on the table was there because of politics. The people who came to the O'Neill house came because of politics. The talk was about politics—at least when it wasn't about baseball. Entertainment—street-corner rallies—was politics. Politics shaped the boy's dreams and imparted a taste for power; it supplied the urge, which so many power-starved Irishmen had, to bend others to their will.

This was the politics of ethnicity in an ethnic salad bowl in the shadow of a most Irish city. This was the politics of contrast, where grimy, smelly factories and boozy slums touched shoulders with Harvard and MIT and at least a dozen other colleges, where the money power of the Yankee aristocracy and the political power of the working-class Irish clashed seven days a week and twice on Sunday.

Above all, this was the politics of the neighborhood. Politicians came out of the streets and alleys, and those who made it—the good ones—knew everything about everyone: the families, their ailments, their weaknesses.

Government was a means of delivering help to people in the neighborhoods—food, clothing, shelter. Said ward boss Lomasney, "The politician who thinks he can get away from the people who made him usually gets what is coming to him: a swift kick in his political pants." O'Neill grew up knowing this as well as he knew his catechism.

3

BARRY'S CORNER

MAYBE it was because the first floor of the house on Rindge Avenue in North Cambridge had served as a store, then barbershop and pool hall, and, finally, clubhouse. Maybe it was because the four wooden steps leading to the front of the two-and-a-half-story clapboard building seemed an open invitation for young men to arrange themselves there in varying postures of lassitude and nonchalance. At any rate, the Barry home was, and had been for as long as anyone could remember, the hang-out for every kid who ever spit on a baseball or got in trouble for staying out late.

Unofficially it was known as Barry's Corner. In later years a mention of the place, when the setting was right and the lubrication proper, would bring tears to the eyes of men who seemed to have spent their entire boyhoods there. In reality, the passage of time on the corner may have been only a few years, but remembrance of those days, poignant and sharp, would last a lifetime.

On a Saturday night in the dead of winter, the parlor stove glowing red—from tar blocks that had been the street before they tore it up—the clubhouse, the Stumble Inn, is packed. The adjacent poolroom, run by Big Red ("the Moose") O'Connell, rings with cracking balls and shouts, but in the clubhouse, where a crowd has gathered around the card table, a respectful silence reigns. Tom O'Neill, one of the best card players in the neighborhood, keeps his cards close and his deep blue, doleful eyes on every draw. The game turns to stud poker and he delivers a running commentary on the merits of each card as it hits the table. Like most good players, he folds every moderate hand, bets the limit on every good one, and, once every so often, sets the others up for a colossal bluff. He has been more than once on the receiving end himself, but, observes a friend, "If you bluffed him once, you'd never do it again."

There is also gin rummy, a game that, more than any of the others, calls for keen powers of observation and inference.

26

When you're playing gin rummy you know it's a game of luck—98 percent luck and 2 percent skill. And what is that 2 percent skill? That 2 percent skill is the art of concentration. Fifty-two cards in a deck, four suits, thirteen cards in a suit, 340 spots in a deck. What does all that mean? If ten cards have been played, forty-two are left; ten in your hand, ten in mine—that's twenty-two left in there. The runs are this, the runs are that. How many nines have been played and how many eights have been played and how many diamonds have been played and how many spots have been played? Concentration. When you acquire that you become proficient. You may lick me tonight if you're just the normal player, but if I can catch you on a slow boat to China I can get even with you, because luck evens out along the line, and that 2 percent skill comes into being.

Some fellas like women, some fellas like booze, other fellas like cards. Cards keep you out of trouble.

In his book about Boston politics, *Ward Eight*, Joseph Dinneen writes of the dream of an ambitious young Irish kid of that era: "To get to work was his burning ambition. Then he could join the gang on the corner and live." The membership requirement for street-corner gangs in North Cambridge was not so much employment as it was age and a certain demonstrated loyalty. But the consequence was the same: living, at last.

There was a choice of hangouts—the front of Lynch's Drug Store or Barry's Corner. The Barry's Corner tradition went back at least two generations; the grandparents of Jack and Jed Barry, Tom's friends, had moved into the house when they were married. Tom's father, Thomas, Sr., "hung" with his pals there, organized them into clubs and teams and went on from there to politics. Identifying closely with his father, the boy fell easily into the pattern. He went to school with the boys on the corner, played sports with them, went to the beach with them; they were the ones who piled into his car, or Lenny Lamkin's, on Friday night and went to dances; they were the ones he played cards with endlessly into the night; more and more they were the ones who joined him in political adventures.

Being with the boys on the corner and being in politics were one and the same. Tom O'Neill didn't like being alone; he craved affection and admiration.

Tom O'Neill and his pals from the Barry's Corner were products of St. John's parochial school, an extension of the church, that sits just off Massachusetts Avenue in North Cambridge. The boys were taught by wrist-whacking Dominican nuns who applied their specialty with fearsome regularity. You learned your lesson, particularly the day's catechism, or you held out your hand: two whacks. There was never any question about their authority for doing this, just as there was little question about what was being taught. Education was not obtained, it was received.

Boys and girls were kept apart during school hours, going to classes in separate buildings. Strict discipline was the norm and few students tested its perimeters. Even the suspicion of shenanigans could be grounds for action.

Francis X. ("Red") Fitzgerald, one of O'Neill's school chums, considered the discipline rather arbitrary. Because sports were discouraged at St. John's, the kids resorted to playing hockey on the walkways during lunch hour or morning break with rulers and bottle caps, three on a side. One of the sisters didn't like it. "She saw Tom every day and she saw me with him every day and she thought there might be something wrong here. She called us into her office and said, 'I don't want to see you boys walking together, talking together, even sitting near each other.'" O'Neill and Fitzgerald made up for it after school, down at the corner.

Sports were crucial in the life of a boy in North Cambridge. At least 95 percent of the talk on the corner was sports—baseball, basketball, hockey. And it was not just the majors. The twilight team, organized by O'Neill's father, was an outlet for such local talents as Gaspipe Sullivan and Jay O'Connor. They were heroes and they could make fabulous money—$70 to $100 a week—playing Sunday afternoons at Russell Field in North Cambridge.

Charging admission for sports on Sundays was against the law. So they did it anyway and called it a band concert. The promoters held the concert an hour before game time and everybody paid fifty cents to get in. The game followed, and if you hadn't paid to hear the band you didn't see the game—unless you watched from the top of the outfield fence, as many of the kids did. It was a good example of how rules were made for the record, then broken, and not very subtly, with the full knowledge of everyone in town.

"Cheeze" McCrehan, who doubled as a stringbean when he wasn't pitching for the North Cambridge team, didn't have much speed, but used to boast that he "blinded them with science." His curve had a lovely drop. Every Saturday, as he left his house across the street from the Barry hangout, he'd tip his cap and the corner guys would applaud and cheer. Then, when he made an elaborate bow, they would give him their customary raspberry and he, in mock disgust, would fling his cap to the ground. It was a reenactment of the theatrics—throwing the cap in the dust and jawing with the umpire—that delighted Sunday's audiences.

The talk on the corner could not have been all baseball. Tom O'Neill and his friends were high school kids coming into maturity, after all, and even though most of them had been rigidly segregated from girls and sexually repressed by parents and church, they were young men and they must have talked and acted like young men. Granted there was respect—they all said that—and wise cracks and whistles were seldom made in the presence of women, a code, a standard of conduct that O'Neill, who was clearly emerging as a leader of the group, strongly encouraged.

But the interest and the tension sex aroused were there. Skip McCaffrey recalled the times his big sister would come down to the corner to get him. "She'd stand right in front of us—we were sitting on the steps—and she'd say, 'Is my brother there?' I myself would answer no. She'd say thank you and run home. She wouldn't even look, she was so tense."

The boys talked about baseball. They talked about girls. And they sat. They sat on weekday nights and weekends. They sat, in fact, so long that David Barry, the owner, would sometimes decide the front steps were his and not the property of a gang of loud-talking, late-night bums. At that point he'd toss a pan of water on them from the second-floor window, and that would bring an end to it.

Whenever two or more Irishmen get together, it is said, they form a club. Whenever the boys on Barry's corner got together, O'Neill organized them. He and Jack Barry put together a ragtag basketball team with O'Neill as captain. A tall, solidly built lad, O'Neill played a tough, physical game. He received little formal training in sports—the school discouraged it—but he and Red O'Connell, the Moose, made a fearsome pair on the court. The Moose was big, strong, and fast.

"I was a hundred and forty pounds and pretty quick," said Tommy Mullen, an O'Neill pal who later went to work for him. "I had all the moves going for me. I'd fake to his left and go to his right, but he was a big guy and he made you pay for it."

It wasn't only in sports that O'Neill led. O'Neill was just as likely to call the shots for an evening's or weekend's entertainment. Said Mullen, "Our crowd just waited for Tom to come; where are we going tonight?"

Later, when he was out of school and working nights at the brickyard, O'Neill did what favors he could for his friends. They were indebted to him for doing away with the nickel phone call. He did this by rigging the outdoor pay phone at the brickyard where he worked with a simple device—a nail in the contact.

Most nights of the week, with or without O'Neill's suggestion, everybody went down to Lynch's drugstore on Massachusetts Avenue to check out the "bulletin board." This contained a recapitulation of the day's sports scores, both local and national. A fellow pedaled around each evening at 9:00 with a printed list of the day's scores, and hundreds would be drawn to the drugstore window to feast on them.

Occasionally the boys hooked school and went to town to see the burlesque show at the Old Howard where there was, as the advertisement went, "always something doing, one to eleven." Most of the big headliners played the Old Howard, a huge converted church on Scollay Square. The boys sat on benches in the smoky second balcony.

O'Neill was captain of many of the teams and a leader of the Barry gang, but often he preferred to make things happen without being out front.

In Barry's clubhouse, while I never looked for an elective office, I was the fellow that a man if he wanted to be elected leader of the club and he had my support he kind of got elected.

One of the basics of politics my father taught me was this: if you're a joiner, fine, but never go to a meeting. I never went to a meeting of the Elks; I never went to a meeting of the Knights of Columbus; I never went to a meeting of the Holy Name. Because they'd become very factional. Don't get yourself involved in factions. Stay away from the meetings. But when the time comes, if you think it's running well, fine, support those that are in. If you don't think it's running well, be a part of the change. And I was.

O'Neill's organizational abilities transcended his prowess as a student. He was indifferent to school and his grades were average or possibly below average, although he was credited by some as having an exceptional memory. He had a strong voice and a commanding presence, good qualities for class plays and school organizations—but he was never a class politician; he had better things to do. At the time, it appears, he wanted nothing more than to direct the energies of his friends in informal ways. He had no burning ambitions, only vague career goals. He told his sister once that he thought he would be a Latin teacher, but she knew better. "I thought he'd be a salesman; he could talk you into anything."

What O'Neill lacked in acting ability he filled in with showmanship and bluster. He could fracture a line and carry it off with timing. Years later he would laugh hugely about muffing his only line in a class play, a line he had rehearsed day after day. "I was the butler, and when the star asked: 'Is my chariot ready?' I was to say: 'It is.' On opening night, the lead said: 'Is my chariot ready?' and I answered: 'Is it?'"

Like most other kids of the time who read anything—and there's no sign that he read a great deal—he immersed himself in the ponderous, stilted, moralizing of Horatio Alger. The code of the books—do or die, sink or swim, now or never—appealed to his imagination. He knew how the stories would end before they began—an ability he liked to apply to events in the real world. There was always some poor wretch of a boy who helped a would-be business tycoon who in turn heaped riches on the deserving youth. Alger's rags-to-riches heroes never really sweated for their fortunes but had them thrust upon them as the result of a chance encounter. Often they had been deprived of a mother's love at an early age; in fact, women don't really enter the stories. Life's goals are material success and position, attained by knowing the right people. O'Neill was not exactly Tattered Tom, but he could identify. He would "be somebody."

Another hero model was supplied by the various authors of the Tom Swift novels, whose pint-sized inventor gets out of one scrape after another by quick thinking and icy calm in the face of danger. "Once Tom Swift had made up his mind to do a thing," said the narrator of *Tom Swift and His Undersea Search*, 1920, "he did it—even though it was against his better judgment. His word, passed, was his bond." Everyone who grew up in an Irish neighborhood around Boston knew that already.

A more lifelike role model for Tom O'Neill—his friends now all called him that—was an old-fashioned, gentle parish priest. Father Kelly, accompanied by his woolly faced dog, often came down to Barry's Corner on a Saturday morning. He must have figured the lads could find better things to do than hang around the corner, because he always showed up with a baseball and a bat. There he would stand talking with the step-sitting boys, all the while tossing the ball. Somehow they always wound up at the park. There Kelly hit a few, passed the bat to someone else, and disappeared, leaving the corner guys to shag baseballs all day long—better than lounging on the corner. That kind of gentle, deft maneuvering of people might have been pretty impressive to a young man with a growing interest in the subtle arts of leadership.

Kelly was succeeded by a priest who delivered sermons about the beauty of the common folk while asking the city fathers to forbid sports on Sunday. Msgr. Hugh Blunt—"blunt by name and blunt by nature," as he said in his first sermon—was not O'Neill's idea of what a good leader should be. Blunt tried to improve the minds of his parishioners, starting up literary clubs and debating societies, but he didn't speak their language. And at times he seemed miles away: ". . . in my heart is something calling, ever calling to the Gael," says the line of one of several books of his collected poems.

O'Neill always hated pomposity. And although he would never show disrespect for authority, he had nothing but contempt for a spiritual leader who preached about hellfire and closed down high school sports.

O'Neill admired leaders, as he did athletes, who were tough-talking physical men. One of the other priests who passed O'Neill's way was Father Jack Cahane, Boston College football player and once New England amateur heavyweight boxing champion. "He was an amazing, amazing man," O'Neill remembers. "I can remember his belting a couple of kids because they took the Lord's name in vain. He kind of instilled a discipline in the area that you respected."

In the fall, O'Neill and his friends chose football as the most effective way of doing bodily harm to themselves. They played in a crude semipro league—wearing helmets, jerseys, pads, and all the rest—where, in exchange for banged heads, they might make $25 for an afternoon's exertion. The day they played the more deeply staffed Wellesley Town Team, they sent Lenny Kelly, Mickey O'Neill, and their captain, Tom O'Neill, to the Wellesley Hospital and had to call the game in the third period because they could no longer field eleven players. But that was a picnic compared to the games held on the stone and tar home field where just about everyone got hurt.

Playing the game—any game—was O'Neill's passion. Being in a test of wills and strength and brains—it was all that mattered. If he wasn't playing, he was watching.

O'Neill and his friends could walk down to just past Central Square in East Cambridge, turn right on Brookline Street, cross the bridge over the Charles, and be right at Braves Field and not far from Fenway Park. For five cents they could join the knothole gang in the outfield bleachers at the Braves games, which they did for almost every home game in the spring and summer. The fifty cents it cost to see the Red Sox was usually prohibitive, but—and maybe for that reason—all Boston kids were hopeless Red Sox fans. It didn't make any sense because by the 1920s the team had become a formidable loser, smack in the cellar year after year. Boston, the cradle of liberty, had become the graveyard of baseball. But the starry-eyed fans didn't seem to mind.

For O'Neill, the magic was rooting for a team that was in the same league as the phenomenal New York Yankees. Men like Babe Ruth, Lou Gehrig, Tony Lazzeri, and "Jumpin' " Joe Dugan assumed for O'Neill godlike proportions. They, more than any other public figures, were the ones he yearned to emulate and be near.

I can remember as though it was yesterday going over and seeing Harry Hooper playing, and my father says to me, "There's the greatest fielder that ever lived," and Harry Hooper dropped one that was right in his mitt.

I can remember in 1922 when North Cambridge played Gardner for the New England championship. The North Cambridge Knights of Columbus team was the lifeblood of the community. Ed Cicotte pitched for Gardner. Do you remember who he was? He was the guy out of the Chicago Black Sox scandal of 1919. He beat North Cambridge, I think, three out of seven games they played. It was a little World Series.

I was intrigued by Satchel Paige. He came up here with the Kansas City Black All-Stars and I followed him for four nights. Saw him play in Lynn one night, Worcester the next night, Lowell the next night, Taunton the next night—and boy, he was some pitcher. We were born and raised baseball buffs.

I remember readin' about the Kansas City Black All-Stars playing the National League. Dizzy Dean versus Paige. About the end of the twelfth inning—it was nothing to nothing—and Satchel went over to Dean and said, "We ought to call this thing off because my guys ain't gonna get any runs offa your guys and your guys ain't gonna get any runs offa me."

It is fitting that O'Neill took his own nickname from baseball—actually it was handed down to him by an uncle who had supposedly got it from a baseball player. The name was borrowed not from a long-ball hitter or notorious base thief, but from Edward "Tip" O'Neill of the St. Louis Browns, an artist of a different kind. His specialty was fouling off everything that came near the strike zone until, inevitably, he walked. He had the highest batting average in history, because at that time walks were counted as hits. He was probably the one for whom the third strike on a foul bunt rule was designed. The man knew how to get on first base. No flashy stuff, just basics.

It was the same with card games, the other major attraction for young O'Neill: it was the basics that mattered. He never got into big, no-limit games. But with nickel-dime games, poker or gin, he could play with the best. And it was as satisfying as waiting for bases on balls: you made them play to you, call you; you waited for your chance.

O'Neill would go anywhere for a card game. Usually they were held at the clubhouse at Barry's Corner or at the home of one of the club members, often his own. They drank unspiked tonic or, later, 3.2 beer, while they played. They played mostly Sunday afternoons after church. When a card game got started on a Saturday night, Jed Barry said, it lasted "pretty near all night."

Hanging out on Barry's Corner was a fairly harmless activity, although not everyone in the neighborhood thought it a proper thing for young men to be doing. What with rumors of cigarette smoking going on—O'Neill's father once caught him smoking and made him promise to abstain till he was eighteen—there was no telling what else they got into. Some of the lads would go down to the drugstore to buy four ounces of alcohol, then mix it with ginger ale and have a fine time of it. O'Neill was either too afraid of his father's wrath or just not interested in rotgut booze—he never acquired a taste for bourbon or even Irish whiskey; he tolerated Canadian Club, vodka and gin, but what he liked most was beer. At any rate, associating with the corner boys did not exactly enhance one's reputation in polite company.

The police in those days maintained a low profile. A close-knit community is a self-policing one; even minor infractions were quickly reported back to parents. The police, if they were not themselves fathers of "club members," knew most of them by name. If there was a problem they spoke to the parents and that was the end of it.

Red Fitzgerald found that being known by the police had its disadvantages. "When they built the Dewey-Almay Chemical Company they put a great big water tower up there. Pat Long, Danny Kelly, and myself climbed up on top of it. The policeman came along and he says, 'Come on down or I'll shoot ya.' Naturally, we came down. He says, 'I know you, Pat Long, and I know you, Kelly.' And then he says to me, 'What's your name?' And I said, 'Francis Cunningham.' He says, 'You're a G-D liar.' They all knew who you were. So even if you were inclined to be a little bit of a fresh kid, everybody knew it and they'd call up and tell your mother."

The North Cambridge police had the assistance of a notable local character known to everybody as Geezer. He was watching from his window with a shotgun cradled in his lap on the night the showdown between the Irish and the French-Canadians was supposed to take place. The conflict had been building for weeks and people had made elaborate weapons in preparation. The French-Canadians had moved in to replace the Irish in the clay pits, and relations between the two groups were generally good. Some even went to St. John's and hung out on the same corner. But at least one territory fight seemed inevitable. "Everybody was saying, 'Tonight, tonight,'" said Skip McCaffrey. "Sherman Street was the dividing line. We were down at the square. We came along with brickbats and chains and every other thing we could carry. We were marching down and they were marching up. When we got to Sherman Square, right by Geezer's house, out shot five cops; they [the police] just put up their hands and we all turned and faded away. And Geezer comes out to the window with his shotgun and,

Bang! Bang!" It is not clear what part O'Neill played in this fracas. One would picture him as negotiator rather than combatant.

There was a tramp in the neighborhood whom police were always running off. "One day," said McCaffrey, "we were walking down the avenue and we saw him following this policeman. Tom or someone said, 'Hey, there's your pal up there; he's gonna grab ya.' But he said, 'I'm following him today so he won't find me.'"

There was such loyalty, there was such a group. You admired the guys who were the great athletes. You admired the guy who could dance, who could play cards, who could sing. I admired Jed Barry—he was such a knowledgeable guy. Joe Healy, absolutely brilliantly talented. We used to kid Joe; Joe used to go to the library when it wasn't raining. You had a certain respect for all of them, even the poor guy who was the town drunk. You loved them all, what the hell.

By the late twenties, the friendships formed on the street corner began to evolve into political associations. When he was only fifteen, O'Neill helped get out the vote for "one of the boys from our part of town," State Representative Charles Cavanaugh. O'Neill's first real taste of political organizing came in 1928 when he and Red Fitzgerald threw themselves into what was for the Irish an utterly fantastic and impossible dream: the campaign of Al Smith for the presidency. The two went from house to house on Orchard Street, knocking on the doors of the Murphys, the McSweeneys, and all the others, making sure a car was waiting to take them to the voting place. According to O'Neill, they got every registered voter in the precinct to the polls except for four who were out of town. It was the leading precinct in the city—a remarkable feat for a couple of neighborhood kids.

Being involved in politics in a town where street-corner rallies often outdrew the motion picture house was being involved in theater. The actors were gut fighters and orators who shouted from trucks from one end of Cambridge to another. Lynch's drugstore was a favorite rally site and thousands would gather to hear a big-name star like Jim Curley. Torchlight parades wound through the streets and the crowds followed. O'Neill, only temporarily a spectator, studied the technique as he followed from place to place.

The speakers were not above making personal attacks upon each other, a practice that often resulted in fistfights among their respective supporters. Who you were for was a touchy subject in patronage-laden politics; it often determined whether or not you went to work. In their enthusiasm for one candidate or another, people took to hissing, catcalling, and sometimes throwing things. Or they cheered so lustily that the opposing candidate could not be heard. To hear Skip McCaffrey tell it, "You go down to East Cambridge and you hope you wouldn't be recognized as coming from North Cambridge, and you might start catcalling and sometimes the candidates would plant people around to cheer or hiss. And they'd be paid for booing and sometimes throwing missiles and otherwise raising hell."

The Depression did not hit the middle class as hard as it did the poor and the wealthy. O'Neill's father had a steady, secure job with the city that paid $35 a week. His son was aware of a steady stream of supplicants to his home. He was aware of the giving that took place, often anonymously and in the middle of the night. The family never threw anything away. The full impact of the Depression on the Barry's Corner crowd would not be felt for several years, when its members began looking for jobs themselves. "You'd graduate from college with pretty big ideas, only to have them fold up," said Jed Barry. Red Fitzgerald didn't find a job until 1934. Until then, like most others, he loafed.

For a would-be politician like O'Neill, jobs—not only for himself, but for his friends—would become the only thing that mattered. But for the time being, the most desperate issue facing the Barry's Corner crowd was finding enough cash for a tank of gas on a Friday night.

O'Neill and his friends began reaching maturity at a time when a new era, that of the big dance bands, was dawning. Glen Gray, Guy Lombardo, Red Nichols, and, later, Tommy Dorsey began making the scene at the Commodore Hotel in Lowell, a booming factory town just north of Boston. Their polished, driving rhythms could be heard and felt on Friday nights for the price of a dollar and enough spare change to gas up Lenny Lamkin's Pontiac or Tom O'Neill's Ford. The idea that they could be, in an hour or less, gliding around the ballroom floor with a girl in their arms and showing off their dancing skills, was so delicious that they rarely missed the chance.

They didn't take dates. Girls went stag and sat along the wall of the ballroom, waiting to be asked to dance. The dollar bought sixteen dances—four for a quarter—and they gave a check to a fellow on the floor as they entered with a partner on their arms. This "check dancing" system applied also at Shadowland in Cambridge and another place on Nahant on the shore. No one found anything awkward or strange about it.

Nostalgia can run pretty high for someone who was young during the era of the big bands. But for O'Neill the times he looked back on with the most acute fondness were those spent at Nantasket Beach in the summer.

After finishing St. John's, O'Neill entered Boston College in 1933 with

limited expectations. He held odd jobs in the summer. One of them was
driving a truck. But what he really looked forward to was spending weekends
at the beach.

"The Nasty Nine" was not a sandlot baseball team. It was a group of guys
from the corner, including O'Neill, who got together every summer and
rented a cottage on Nantasket Beach. It was a fashionable place, an Asbury
Park, an Ocean City, a playground for people who could occasionally afford
to forget. Reaching out spiderlike into Massachusetts Bay, Nantasket was
accessible by sidewheeling paddleboat from downtown Boston.

Jed Barry was chief cook and treasurer. The Nasty Nine paid a total of
$300, approximately, for the entire summer; since quite a few more than
nine eventually took part, the individual kick-in was less than $10 a month.
Most of the guys worked during the week and drove or took the ferry down
on weekends. Others who were officially loafing stayed all week, subsisting
on the leftovers from the enormous meal that Barry fixed on Sundays for
about twenty people.

They were probably pretty well behaved as young men go. But with a
dozen or so energetic young men participating, it became necessary to rent a
different cottage every year.

Mildred Miller from neighboring Somerville, German-born daughter of
a trainman on the Boston elevated, and a number of other young women
made Nantasket their weekend destinations, too. Millie, a grade behind
Tom at St. John's, was a quick-minded, spirited girl, dark-haired and
attractive. She took a dim view of some of the crowd's rowdy ways, but she
was quickly becoming Tom O'Neill's best girl. For fifty cents each the
women rented rooms in a private home across the street from the cottage.

Being young, full of spirit, and close to friends: these were the happiest
days of O'Neill's life.

Jack Barry was by then a sportswriter for the *Boston Globe*, a position
that entitled him to great esteem among his fellow sports fanatics. Part of his
job entailed the privilege of computing, for a little extra money in each
paycheck, the batting averages of every player in the big leagues. With
perhaps sixteen teams of twenty players each, this chore might seem pretty
deadly, but Barry had a system. Every Sunday night, without fail, the gang
gathered around the kitchen table in the cottage and, player after player
after player, they divided his number of hits into his number of times at bat.
To a lad who was a born statistician, this was having a great time.

We'd sit around and say, y'know, Jimmy Foxx: 112 hits, 267 times at bat.
Somebody would do it and somebody on the other side would check it out down to

the decimal point. So you knew everybody's averages in all the leagues. It was part of our life.

There were plenty of other things to do: singing, dancing, beach bumming. There was an amusement park and, as it was just before the end of Prohibition, speakeasies. Said Jed Barry, "Danny O'Brien's was the main one we went to—right off the beach, near where the cottages were."

O'Neill had not been seized by an overpowering desire to go to college. His sister, Mary, was a teacher who went on to become the first woman principal in the Cambridge public school system. His brother, Bill, had gone to Holy Cross and then on to Harvard Law School, and would soon pursue a successful career as a lawyer and judge. Both were difficult acts to follow for Tom, who was not so achievement-oriented. His work in school had always been just fair. He made up for his lack of scholarship by his easy, open gregariousness. Although he lacked the drive to succeed, success came easily enough in his chosen work.

After St. John's High School, O'Neill began driving a truck for one of the brick companies. It was great at first. He was earning three dollars a day and hanging around with his chums at night, risking some of his earnings at the poker table and going to those Friday night dances. But by the first of November, the numbing cold began to gnaw at him. "Geez, it was lousy," he said later.

When his parish priest encouraged him to get on with his education, he enrolled at Boston College Prep School to make up for lost time and missed language credits. He took special Latin classes six days a week and learned something about discipline in the process. Once, because he and three others hadn't done an assignment on time, Jocko Clary, their teacher, made them go to school every day during the Christmas holidays. "Jesus," said O'Neill, "he was the toughest disciplinarian I ever saw." It was a trait O'Neill clearly admired.

Boston College was not the place to go if you expected to compete for a piece of the action in Boston's financial world. Most of the money in the city was old money, tightly held by conservative Yankees. At the height of the Depression, when O'Neill was in school, there was no incentive to invest in risky ventures. The banks and insurance companies controlled the city's wealth and the doors of these institutions were by and large closed to any one who had not graduated from Harvard. Still, the Irish maintained a pride in "BC" that was matched only by their hatred of Harvard. They sent their sons to the school that had only recently been erected by the Jesuit fathers

on the hills of Chestnut Hill overlooking Newton. Unable to compete with
Harvard grads when they left Boston College, many of these Irish sons went
to the closely related fields of politics and the ministry.

O'Neill entered Boston College in 1933 and took part in the "famous"
Fordham trip of that year, one of the most memorable events of his college
career. To hear Tim Ready tell it, the group that went down for the game
with Fordham lived up to, and perhaps exceeded, the expected behavior of
college freshmen on their first unchaperoned weekend in New York City.

They left Friday after class, five of them jammed—three in front and two
in the rumble seat—into Tom O'Neill's Ford convertible. The boys in the
back were pretty cold; they had to drive slowly to avoid problems with the
ticket-happy Connecticut state police. Fordham, naturally, trounced BC
and, as Ready put it, "we had to do *something*. We were staying in a hotel in
Times Square. Some of the boys were kind of rambunctious and started
throwing water bags out of the hotel windows. The manager called the house
detective, who threatened to call the police if they didn't stop." Apparently
they did, for no serious repercussions ensued.

Ready, one of the best athletes and most popular members of the class of
'36, was later, with O'Neill's help, to become a subcontracting specialist for
the Small Business Administration. O'Neill took care of many friends that
way.

O'Neill was a "day-hopper" at college. He traveled every day from
Cambridge to Newton on the recently expanded subway system. In this way
he never lost touch with the life of the city or the people in the
neighborhood; it is unlikely that he ever could have disappeared into the
secluded world of the on-campus student.

Higher education came to O'Neill straight out of the Renaissance,
carefully handed down by the priests of the Society of Jesus who believed
that moral development, not knowledge, was the end of education.
"Morality must be the atmosphere the student breathes," the priests said in
a course description for 1933–34. "It must suffuse with the light all that he
reads, illuminating what is noble and exposing what is base, giving to the
true and false their relative light and shade."

The curriculum, weighted toward Greek and Latin, mathematics and
philosophy, was supposed to give the student a kind of "mental elasticity"
that would allow him to cope with life. The only way to "purify the heart,
and guide and strengthen the will" was a continual grounding in the
"evidences" of the Catholic faith.

O'Neill was not much of a student. As Tim Ready put it, "Studentwise,
he was like all of us: he graduated." Reading Horace in Latin and Homer in

Greek was tough going, but O'Neill figured his mind was getting a workout. He considered going into law like his brother who was an officer in the School's Law Academy. But by this time politics—although you certainly couldn't make a living of it—was thoroughly embedded in his character and foremost in his mind. His sister said she believed he would cast his first vote for himself.

He had already gotten plenty of political experience working for others. Jed Barry's 1932 campaign for the Cambridge School Committee had been enough to whet his appetite. Barry was having a hard time finding a job so he ran for office. Said Barry, "I had a Packard touring car with a loudspeaker in it. It would run around the city streets and Tom—he was supposed to be in school—would be sitting in the car and talking over the mike, until he'd notice his father's car. He'd stop talking and duck down on the floor. He wasn't supposed to be in politics on account of his father's position." Civil Service and politics didn't mix, even then. Barry didn't get elected. But thanks partly to the politics that dominated the selection of teachers in the city, "I got a job teaching out of it."

By the time O'Neill had entered his senior year at BC he was twenty-two years old and ready, himself, for a lifetime in politics. He took his first shot at his father's old stomping ground, the Cambridge City Council. The cycle had been completed and the senior O'Neill was neither surprised nor displeased. "The apple doesn't fall far from the tree," he said when his son broke the news to him.

Politics for O'Neill was an extension of the camaraderie of the card games he had joined in the Barry clubhouse. The admiration his comrades felt for him was soon transplanted into footpower as they hustled up and down the streets of the city, getting out the vote for their friend.

O'Neill found the new game to his liking. The best part was the recognition that went with being an O'Neill. "Are you the Governor's son?" they'd ask. Many had known his father since before young Tom arrived on the scene, had gone to him with their problems. The Governor had delivered. Certainly they owed him favors; voting for his son was the least they could do.

But Cambridge is a big, sprawling city of which North Cambridge is only a small part. Whereas North Cambridge was predominately Irish and French-Canadian, East Cambridge was a potpourri of Portuguese, Poles, Armenians, Italians, Irish, and blacks. With eight canadidates on the ballot for four seats, the vote went in as many directions as there were ethnic groups.

Although the story may be apocryphal, repetition has given an early

O'Neill story a life of its own. On election day, Mrs. Elizabeth O'Brien, an elocution teacher who lived across the street from O'Neill, is supposed to have told him, "Tom, I'm going to vote for you even though you didn't ask me." "Mrs. O'Brien," replied a surprised O'Neill, "I've lived across the street from you for eighteen years. I shovel your walk in the winter. I cut your grass in the summer. I didn't think I had to ask you for your vote."

"Tom," the lady replied. "I want you to know something: people like to be asked."

One other rather important person in North Cambridge whose help O'Neill failed to seek was his father. Possibly the oversight was due to confidence or stemmed from the universal need of sons to show their fathers they can do it on their own. Unfortunately, the failure to include his father probably cost him the election, because O'Neill got only thirteen hundred votes in North Cambridge where he should have gotten eighteen hundred. His vote total was 276 shy of earning him one of the four City Council seats. He came in fifth—impressive enough for a twenty-two-year-old college student on his first time out, but, nevertheless, not a victory. He had established himself as a comer, and next time he wouldn't spread himself out so much. He had learned something important—all politics is local; begin with the neighborhood.

June 10, 1936. . . . Alf Landon clinched the Republican nomination for president. Herbert Hoover complained that gigantic expenditures would soon sink the nation in debt, while Franklin Roosevelt spurred his fellow Americans to march forward and meet the needs of the common man.

. . . Massachusetts Governor James Michael Curley stressed the "continuity of employment of the worker" with adequate compensation for his labor. At the same time a Suffolk Superior Court heard testimony that most of Boston's bond business during Curley's last term as mayor had gone to a dummy investment house.

. . . Jimmy Foxx lashed a wicked drive up against the high left-field wall at Fenway Park, an easy homer if he had lifted the ball only a trifle. But Goose Goslin artfully played the caroom off the wall and held Double X to a single. The Red Sox, in their third year under the ownership of Tom Yawkey, were beginning to show the effects of money and total reorganization. They beat the Tigers that day 4–3.

. . . And in a ceremony that was as Irish as it was Catholic, 411 seniors at Boston College received their degrees from William Cardinal O'Connell and then knelt and kissed his ring.

O'Connell, who reigned as cardinal from 1911 to 1944, was an impressive and powerful figure. Two years before the graduation a bill setting up a state lottery had sailed through the Massachusetts legislature. That very night O'Connell came out against the bill and, on reconsideration the following day, the bill was slaughtered.

The cardinal was conservative in outlook and acted suspiciously like a Republican to Democrats like O'Neill. Because of his frequent trips to property he owned in the Bahamas, he had acquired a very untheological nickname, "Gangplank Bill." He also countenaced the activities of Boston's silly Watch and Ward Society [the censorship board]; Eugene O'Neill's new play, *Strange Interlude,* was banned in Boston and forced to open instead in a suburban movie house.

Tom O'Neill, his political instincts by then already finely honed, familiar with the difficulties being encountered in his own and other neighborhoods, must have found O'Connell's message to the Boston College graduates laughable.

"Success, the real value of success, comes in doing God's will in this life. That is why so many shallow-minded people are so afraid of this thing called a Depression. Where are their minds, their knowledge of history? These things will disappear if they don't lack faith in God."

"There is no real Depression," he said, "it is a depression of faith."

O'Neill's evaluation of O'Connell was probably understated because of his respect for authority and the church: "He wasn't that close to the people."

The senior class at BC voted for Fred Allen as their favorite humorist. Others were: Charles Dickens, novelist; W. C. Fields, humorist; Charles Laughton, movie actor; Myrna Loy, movie actress; Guy Lombardo, orchestra leader; Bing Crosby, singer; "Goody, Goody," song. Tip O'Neill—they were calling him that by then—was voted "class caveman" and "class politician."

"He stands 6 feet, 1 inch [actually he is 6′ 2″], weighs 215 pounds, and is every inch the famous 'Tip O'Neill.'" said the 1936 yearbook. "Last year he plunged into Cambridge politics and astounded the veteran Cambridge politicians by the run he made as a candidate for Alderman. He was barely defeated. As that campaign was his first he is confident of success in the next."

"He intends to go to Engineering School and to keep active in politics until he is Mayor of Cambridge."

But that was an old dream and new ones were beginning to take shape.

4

THE STATEHOUSE

IT WAS obvious from looking at the city council election returns—and O'Neill and his friends pored over them as though they were baseball statistics—that his strength was in his own community, where his friends were, where the O'Neill family power base was still very much intact. The other city wards had voted, as they always had, along ethnic and family lines, and there was no reason to expect they might change. By narrowing his focus and putting all of his energy into a race for the North Cambridge seat in the state legislature, O'Neill figured he could win in a walk. And this time he wouldn't forget to ask everyone, even his friends and family for support.

Once more, his friends from college and the neighborhood worked for him, trudging up and down the streets of the district in the heat of the summer of 1936, wearing their only suit coats. They worked hard. He was one of their own. And they knew he would not forget them. He won easily.

O'Neill took his seat in the State House of Representatives in January, 1937. He was twenty-four years old and full of himself; he was both college-educated and street-wise, a rare combination; he was caught up in the excitement of politics in a highly political time and place; he was energetic and ambitious, already talking, among close friends at least, about greater things—perhaps the governorship someday; he was Irish to the core, full of blarney and banter, possessing certain insights into human character and a deeply ingrained sense of loyalty.

His personality was ideally suited to the life of a state legislator, where decisions are made on an informal, what-have-you-done-for-me basis. Keeping the folks at home happy, with jobs and favors and access, is far more important in this small potatoes world than securing a grasp on weighty issues. Knowing how to maneuver is a skill more highly prized than being able to make brilliant speeches.

When O'Neill went into the state House the ratio of Democrats to Republicans was a lopsided 62 to 178. Christian Herter, the Republican Speaker, was not overgenerous about committee assignments. With the majority running roughshod over them, there was little the members of the Democratic minority could do except, working their contacts right, provide jobs for constituents.

America and Boston were still in the grip of the Depression; the main thing was to try to be helpful. At least there was a Democrat, Charles Hurley, in the governor's office and Democrats headed most job-producing state departments.

There were a few legislative bright spots. Although not an issues man, O'Neill was capable of taking courageous stands when his sense of right and wrong was deeply offended. During his first term he was one of a handful of Democrats to vote against a state teacher's loyalty oath bill. The American Legion thought this downright un-American of the young legislator. When O'Neill ran for reelection in 1938, the Legion placed full-page ads against him in the newspapers and sent Legionnaires to the polls in full uniform to campaign for his opponent. O'Neill's response was to send his own Legionnaire supporters to the polls. His friendships ran deep. He had no problems with that election.

But, by and large, the gut-level issue was patronage. Each representative had a certain number of slots he could fill. Mostly they were temporary positions: sixty-to-ninety-day summer typists, emergency road-repair work crews, and the like. The jobs weren't much, but during the Depression any help at all was appreciated and remembered. And O'Neill had a way of remembering not just his Irish buddies but worthy job seekers of all ethnic varieties. That would come in handy someday.

He never forgot a bit of basic wisdom given to him by that master of favors, Jim Curley. "The true, quick, sure way of success in politics is to remember this: You will have literally hundreds of people over the course of the years ask you for favors. Some of them may be great, some of them may be small. Some of them may be important, some of them may be ridiculous. Some of them may be easy, some of them may be hard. But remember the person who asks you for a favor—to him it is the most important thing in the world. Treat them all alike. You will be able to take care of more of the small ones than you will the large ones, but you will make as many friends doing the small ones as you will doing the large ones."

The Democrats, at the mercy of an enormous Republican majority, got no office space and had to content themselves with a tiny room just off the House floor to answer mail and make up their patronage lists. Eddie Boland, a legislator from Springfield who would later join O'Neill in Washington, had an indispensable skill: he could type. O'Neill and Jimmy Burke, another

Washington-bound colleague from near Boston, spent many hours huddled over Boland, shouting instructions as he typed up the lists.

The most successful legislator was he who made the best use of this system. Burke, O'Neill once joked, would have his list typed double-spaced and then, after getting it signed by the appropriate department head, return to the typewriter and fill in more names between the lines.

There was also patronage from sources other than the state to be used. Like his father before him, O'Neill got a large quantity of "snow buttons" from the City of Cambridge, the Boston Elevated Railway, and the Massachusetts Bay Transit Authority. The buttons entitled the men wearing them to work on snow-removal crews for $4 a day. On nights when it snowed, people would begin gathering at O'Neill's house at three or four in the morning.

In spite of this, the quality of snow shoveling in the city was scandalously poor. It inspired poet David McCord to write

> In Boston, when it snows at night,
> They clean it up by candle light.
>
> In Cambridge, quite the other way.
> It snows and there they leave it lay.

Cambridge Mayor John W. Lyons, whom O'Neill supported, added to the folklore—if not his reputation—when he made the comment that "the Almighty sends the snow . . . He will in time remove it."

Big favors, little favors, medium-size favors. People did not forget them. And, like the Curley-Skeffington figure in *The Last Hurrah*, neither did O'Neill. He, or the people who helped in his campaigns, kept a list. Those who owed him favors were eventually called and asked to help get out the vote on election day.

The key to the system was the checker at the polls, who was equipped with a list of registered voters.

As each person came in you checked their names off. You already had the list the night before: you had 'em red marked; you had 'em blue marked. A blue mark meant you could be assured a person was going to vote; you didn't have to worry about 'em. A red mark was a person that was with you, but you weren't sure he was going to vote for you. And so came five o'clock at night you'd check your red marks and you'd say, here's the people who have not voted. And so you sent your automobiles out to get them, and you made your telephone calls. And you made sure you were going to get them.

In the fall elections when there was an occasional Republican to contend with, the question was one of numbers.

You didn't have to go on the basis of asking them to vote for you; you worked on a percentage. My district was so highly Democratic you knew that 92 percent were going to vote the ticket. You didn't have to ask 'em to vote for Tip O'Neill or Paul Dever or anybody else. Once they came, they voted the ticket.

Jim Ferguson, one of O'Neill's early campaign workers, said city firemen would, as their contribution to the campaign, drop off their cars with a full tank of gas to be used for chauffeuring voters.

O'Neill considered himself a pretty good soapbox orator. He liked to impress crowds with his youth and the vigor of his ideas. The bigger the crowd the better. He had a politician's sense of crowds. He got some of that by watching Jim Curley. And he had some of the crowds handed to him by Jim Curley. If Curley was expected at the corner of North Harvey and Massachusetts Avenue on Saturday night, eight o'clock, there would automatically be six to eight thousand people there, some of them from as far away as Manchester, New Hampshire. Curley would make the swing, Concord Avenue at Huron, Cushing and Cushing Place, Cary and Massachusetts Avenue. The crowds followed him and so did Tip O'Neill, jumping up to speak to them before they drifted away.

Running. It was less a game of chance than of skill. O'Neill was not always infallible when it came to how the votes would go. He tended to be pessimistic but, as he told his son years later, he believed whatever happened happened for the best. One time he almost lost.

His district was a three-member district he shared with two other seasoned politicians, Jerry Sullivan and Tommy Gibson. When the legislature cut the district from three to two members, it appeared that O'Neill was the one whose blood would be shed. And, in fact, he came in third in the three-way race and would have been through if Gibson had not been offered, and accepted, an appointment as city assessor.

At a meeting of O'Neill supporters the following year, Joe Healy got up and urged them to make a strong showing or "everyone is going to say that Tip is the luckiest guy in the world" who, like the hero of a Greek play, is saved from an impossible situation by a god who comes down out of the blue, a *deus ex machina*, and is whisked to safety.

Badly outnumbered in the legislature, the Democrats could do little but sit in the back row of the chamber, Murderers' Row, and cause trouble by objecting to everything the Republican majority tried to do. A premium was put on the member who could get up and shout the loudest. O'Neill referred admiringly to Jimmy Burke as "a real bomb-thrower."

But mostly, being in the legislature was rocking quietly along and getting to know people, being helpful to his fellow legislators, and being thoroughly one of them. Jim Shannon, a young, modern-day congressman from Lowell who wrote his senior thesis on O'Neill's rise to power, said the Democratic minority was "renowned for its ability to smile in the face of adversity. While the Democratic platform was being voted down by the Republican majority, a keg of beer or a poker game could always be found for the faithful Democratic members to forget their sorrows. O'Neill was one of the main participants in these 'after-hours caucuses.'" Shannon wrote that kegs of beer and poker games could always be found in the basement of the statehouse and it was possible "to place a bet without leaving the House floor."

Charles J. ("Chick") Artesani of Brighton, who later became one of O'Neill's floor leaders, said the card games went on incessantly in the boiler room or in empty rooms on the fifth floor of the capitol. "Some guys played all night long," Artesani said, "some even all weekend." O'Neill was a compulsive card player, he said. "When we were sitting around the Gas Light Club, drinking, he said, 'I'm pooped; I'm going home.' Instead, he left us there and went and played cards."

Silvio Conte, then a Republican state senator from Pittsfield, was chairman of a joint committee on insurance on which O'Neill served. Conte, now a congressman, remembers that he and O'Neill were part of a group of legislators who went to New York every Washington's Birthday for a big meeting of insurance commissioners. They took the train both ways, playing cards en route. They would rent a large suite at the Lexington Hotel, order a big barrel of ice and fill it with beer, strip down to their shorts, and play poker sixteen to eighteen hours at a stretch. They never went to any meetings of the convention.

O'Neill and his friends did not lose their addiction to baseball games either. Every chance they got, when they weren't in session, they'd be hanging out at Braves Field or Fenway Park. And every bit as much as they loved the game itself they loved hobnobbing with the greats. Like the legislature, but more so, it was boozy, macho, man-to-man.

I can remember one night back about nineteen hundred and thirty-nine, Labor Day. I was in the company of Jimmy Foxx; Eddie Boland was there. We were down at Falmouth in this home. Eddie Boland said to Foxx, or Foxx said, I dunno, it came up:

"Who's the greatest clutch hitter in baseball?" We all said, "Joe Cronin! He's the greatest clutch hitter in baseball!" Foxx said, "Jesus, all you Irish are alike. The greatest clutch hitter in baseball is Jimmy Foxx!"

O'Neill quickly established himself as one of the boys in the legislature, a key ingredient of his growing effectiveness. His open, gregarious nature, his "happy faculty," as he put it, for getting along with people of all kinds and parties, began to translate into an ability to make things happen. Although still in his twenties, he came to be regarded as unofficial minority leader. Groups interested in getting hospitals built, seeking special legislation for schools, or interested in mental health programs, tended to gravitate to the big guy with the jokes, the big laugh, and the "happy faculty."

He didn't do so well with his own legislative efforts. In his second term he tried to get bills through to clean up, with the help of WPA funds, the Charles River and the Alewife Brook, a body of water that was once so clear Cambridge residents could spear basketsful of herring from it on an April afternoon. The legislature wouldn't hear of it.

O'Neill didn't expect, at least not then, to be able to make a living in politics. After college, he went briefly to Boston College law school—no doubt influenced by his brother—but found that it wasn't for him. The study of law was, no doubt, too tedious for someone as extroverted and as uncomfortable with rigid, formal undertakings as O'Neill.

Besides, with his contacts it was obvious he could easily land an undemanding job with the city. Which is exactly what he and his good pal Leo did. He met Leo Diehl, who lived near North Cambridge, that first year in the legislature and the two young politicians became lifetime friends. Diehl, droll, loyal, circumspect, a short, barrel-chested guy crippled by polio, was the perfect Mutt to O'Neill's Jeff.

The legislature adjourned on May 29 that year, 1937, and Tip and Leo got "sunlight" jobs behind the cage in the city treasurer's office. They worked eight-hour days collecting taxes in Cambridge's City Hall. O'Neill was cashier, pulling down $35 a week.

The job afforded him enough security to propose at last to his old sweetheart, Mildred Miller. They were married in June 1941. As they left the church, his father issued an order to her. "It's about time you stopped calling him Tip." She did. To his old, close friends he would always be "Tom." But he was "Tip" to all others, and that is how he liked it.

Tip's idea of a great way to spend a honeymoon was to go to New York and, the first night on the town, go to Yankee Stadium and watch Joe Louis fight Billy Conn. Louis knocked Conn out, but not until the thirteenth round. The following night, Tom and Millie O'Neill danced to the strains of Guy Lombardo's orchestra, then motored to Atlantic City, where they stayed at the elegant Claridge Hotel: five dollars a day—breakfast included.

Millie O'Neill did not suspect that she was marrying a lifetime politician. "I was very foolish not to realize it," she would say years later with a hearty laugh. "When you're young you expect change. I didn't think the only change would be that he'd go from one job in politics to another."

O'Neill could probably have stayed in City Hall indefinitely. As Diehl said, "You get in the routine and it's tough to get out. You're making thirty to thirty-five dollars a week; it wasn't easy to come by." O'Neill could have gone all the way to city clerk or something and been lost to history.

But disaster—or maybe good fortune—struck.

There had always been fierce rivalries in Cambridge politics, and election campaigns could split apart families that had been close for generations. O'Neill supported John W. Lyons ("The Almighty sends the snow") for mayor over John D. Lynch and thereby got on the wrong side of the political fence for a time. After Lyons was indicted on charges related to fee-splitting, the voters of Cambridge had had enough.

In November 1940, a new and puzzling plan for local representation was adopted in Cambridge that had the effect of giving the Harvard-Protestant establishment more power than that to which they would normally be entitled. Few people understood "Plan E," and even fewer could explain it. O'Neill and his colleagues, however, thought it atrocious, a blow to democratic (Irish-controlled) government.

The plan went into effect in January 1942, a month after the bombing of Pearl Harbor. The new city manager, Colonel John B. Atkinson, was determined to perform his job without regard for political influence. Tip and Leo were among the first to be weeded out by the Colonel. It was a snowy day in January. As Diehl quickly understood, to Atkinson he and O'Neill were simply politicians taking advantage of their connections.

O'Neill was incensed. "You know, Jack," he said to Atkinson, "you're firing me and I don't understand it. You got more goddamned bums on the payroll. What are you firing me for? Because you get a headline in the paper?"

"No," Atkinson said—(this is O'Neill's version of the conversation)—"I'm firing you because you're in the state legislature where you're getting forty bucks a week and you're getting forty-five bucks a week here and I think it's a waste a'yer talent."

O'Neill didn't think so at the time but he later realized it was the greatest thing that could have happened to him. He might easily have stayed in the cage at City Hall and played it safe. Naturally he was concerned about himself—he was always a worrier, and his wife by then was pregnant—but he was more upset for his friend Leo, who had more limited opportunities.

O'Neill, always a big man, could appear menacing, and he must have done just that when he went in to see Arthur MacKenzie, the city treasurer who had done the firing. He only wanted to put in a word for Diehl but that's not the way MacKenzie took it. "MacKenzie thought he was going to have a big argument or a fight or even slug him," Diehl said. "He panicked and called for the police officer."

There was no need for MacKenzie to panic. O'Neill never hurt anyone. In fact, if MacKenzie had shown a little remorse later on, O'Neill might have appointed him, as he did Atkinson, to other positions. O'Neill never stayed mad very long.

Tom Eliot, formerly a member of Congress who had been recently knocked off by Jim Curley, was solicitous for the two ousted bureaucrats and quietly offered to help them. In a letter to Cambridge City Councilman Ed Crane, he said he had heard that O'Neill and Diehl had fallen on hard times. In what now has a nice ironic ring, he asked, "Any idea as to what kind of experience Tom O'Neill has had? What can he do?" A friendly gesture toward someone he hardly knew.

O'Neill didn't so much need to be able to "do" anything, as long as he could impress the right people with his special talent for getting along with others. He finally nailed down a job working the night fire watch at Bethlehem Steel's East Boston shipyard. At the same time he took out an insurance broker's license. His life was full: he was doing a little legislating, selling a little insurance, doing the overnight shift at the steel plant. He was working hard. He had lots of energy. But still, he felt something was lacking.

O'Neill had been exempt from the draft by virtue of his service in the legislature. But he wasn't exempt from uneasy feelings of guilt, since most of his friends were going off to war. This could be doubly difficult for a man with political ambitions. O'Neill volunteered for the Army and received a shattering blow. He was rejected for being a borderline diabetic: even though he did not suffer from diabetes, there was a history of it on his mother's side of the family.

O'Neill didn't stay home and mope. He began doing well for himself. Insurance was the perfect occupation for politicians because it could be a part-time job. Jim Curley sold insurance, perhaps, as James Carroll said in *Mortal Friends*, because "nobody knows what an insurance business is."

"I started to move things," O'Neill said. "In 1952 I made forty-three thousand dollars in the insurance business—the year before I went to Congress. I had a hell of an insurance business. Christ, there wasn't anybody on Massachusetts Avenue that I didn't insure."

He was doing pretty well in the legislature, too, mostly because he developed friendships on the Republican as well as the Democratic side.

Roy Smith from Holbrooke was chairman of Ways and Means. He and I were great pals. Freddie Willis was the Speaker. He and I were great pals. I used to fight them like a tiger, positively fight them like a tiger. And they respected me for it. They had the votes; once in a while we'd win one.

O'Neill was a hard guy to dislike. He played cards, sang Irish songs, told stories, and handed out, whenever he could get his hands on them, foul-smelling cigars.

Though O'Neill liked a good Cuban cigar and was something of an authority on the subject, he would, in truth, smoke anything that burned. His addiction dates back to 1940, April 19, to be exact, when he and Eddie Boland were handed cigars at the finish of the Boston Marathon. His favorite was something called the Boston Elko, made by the brother of Honey Fitz, Jim Fitzgerald. He became a classic side-of-the mouth smoker, left or right, except on the putting green. Then he held it right in the middle, lining up the stogie with the club and ball.

By the end of the war, O'Neill was beginning to make his moves in the legislature. He had been sitting back for almost ten years, not showing any signs of moving out of the narrow confines of the state legislature. He had been a back bench warmer in a place where limited expectations and petty concerns dominated, where small-time politicians could be lured away by secure jobs in dusty corners. For him it had been no more than a place for camaraderie and contacts. Now it was time for all of that to pay off. Before he could get going, however, he received a bothersome call to duty.

Monsignor Blunt, his old parish priest, was on the phone. Could O'Neill and Jerry Sullivan come see him; he had an urgent matter to discuss with them. It had to do with Cambridge city schools, an area in which O'Neill had never, ever, wanted to get involved. The Cambridge school committee was as politically sensitive as any governing body one might ever want to see. As Jed Barry explained it, "A few years before Tom got on the school committee, everybody who worked for the schools was pretty much a Yankee Wasp type. And then they finally got four people who all graduated from BC on the committee and it turned right around and you couldn't get a job unless you were a Catholic."

The aspirations of every Irish mother in Cambridge centered on her daughter getting a teaching job with the city school system. Because there were only so many positions open every year and far more applicants than jobs, every time the school committee approved the hiring of one young girl just out of two-year normal school, nine others had to be turned down. It was a terrible situation for a politician to get into.

Even the superintendent of schools, John Tobin, had gotten his job through politics—heavy politics. The son of Teamsters boss Dan Tobin, his appointment had been engineered, according to O'Neill, by no less a personage than Franklin Delano Roosevelt.

At any rate, there was, Monsignor Blunt and the Irish suspected, a Harvard plot to get rid of Tobin and replace him with a high-powered educator who would turn the city's schoolchildren into guinea pigs. Irish power on the committee, thin because of the war, had to be strengthened.

"One of you two fellas has got to run for the school committee in order to hold that seat until the war's over, and someone from North Cambridge can win it," Blunt told O'Neill and Sullivan. The two politicians swallowed hard and told Blunt that they had an awful lot of obligations and didn't see how they could do that. Couldn't he find someone else?

Blunt was not a man to say no to. "I will go to the altar," he said gravely, "and from the altar say I have asked one of you to run and you have refused."

O'Neill confesses, "Jerry Sullivan and I flipped a coin, and I lost."

O'Neill's service on the Cambridge school committee was anything but memorable. But he did manage to get into the spirit of most of the school committee's business: squabbling. In April 1946, he charged that the Cambridge Community Association, the good-government organization that tried to run the city, had solicited contributions from a school textbook firm and when turned down had threatened to retaliate by refusing to adopt their books. "Who told you?" a committee member demanded. "A friend of mine who works there [at the textbook firm]," O'Neill finally replied. Asked to make a public apology for impugning the integrity of the CCA and to disclose the name of his informant, O'Neill declined on both counts. With the help of Tobin, who was "feeding" him the information, he made a mockery of a $25,000 consultant whose report, critical of Tobin's administration, had actually come word for word from reports made for other school systems. (O'Neill admired "Knowledge Tobin" for his near-photographic memory.)

O'Neill's biggest contribution to the schools of his city was railroading through pay raises for school employees whenever he got the opportunity. And he always managed to get a few jobs for friends.

Jed Barry tells a story illustrating the coziness of the patronage system to which O'Neill adhered. A man named Red Linsky, a hash slinger at a place near the *Boston Globe*, had become friendly with Jed's brother Jack. When they were out riding with O'Neill one night while he was on the school committee, Linsky mentioned that his uncle was a school athletic coach in New Orleans, and he was interested in the same kind of deal for himself. Between them they figured out a way: Linsky got a job as an athletic coach in the Cambridge school system.

An editorial in the *Cambridge Chronicle* in December 1947 observed that the school committee never discussed educational matters but instead occupied itself with "wrangling over patronage, preferment and pay." Patronage, the newspaper said, "determines voting line-ups and is the unseen factor that controls a large part of the committee's actions. . . . It's high time for a change." It was for O'Neill, too. "I was glad to have one term and get the hell out of there."

But before he could do so, a classic bit of small-time political intrigue took place that must have left him gasping.

O'Neill had worked out a deal with John D. Lynch who, as mayor of the city, was automatically school committee chairman: he would vote for Lynch's crony if Lynch would vote for his.

The vote took place at the last session of the committee for the year and the last of O'Neill's term. On Lynch's motion, O'Neill voted for the nomination of Lynch's brother-in-law, Tom Danahey, as assistant principal of the high school. But when it came time to vote for Jed Barry, O'Neill's old friend, as assistant headmaster, Lynch made a motion to adjourn and three others, as planned, voted with him. He banged the gavel and that was the end of O'Neill's term on the committee. He had been caught flatfooted.

O'Neill, recalled *Cambridge Chronicle* editor Eliot Spalding, was "bughouse, beside himself with the kind of rage only a double-crossed politician can muster." But there was nothing he could do about it. The newspaper reported simply that the committee ended its session in utter confusion and acrimoney.

After quitting the legislature in 1941, Leo Diehl retained his close friendship with O'Neill. Unmarried at the time, he spent practically every evening at the O'Neill house and knew the children "like my own."

O'Neill wasn't spending many evenings at home those days. "Tom was always out and available to members," Diehl recalled. "He'd make it a point

to be around. He knew where the members from the western part of the
state stayed and he'd make it a point to be there. He'd stay in town. He
knew more members than any man I ever knew."

O'Neill was always working. There wasn't a night, he said, after he and
Millie were first married, that he wouldn't have a dozen people come to his
home. He kept his phone listed and liked having people call on Sundays.

Millie didn't think it all that wonderful. "That is the one thing about
politics that bothers me more than anything, the lack of privacy. We've
always had our phone listed in the book, which means you have very little
privacy when people have access to you." For his part, O'Neill didn't want
privacy. "Tom doesn't like to be alone," she said. "He likes people very
much; he likes to be with people."

O'Neill was still campaigning. For what he wasn't exactly sure. Something would come along.

In early 1946, Mike Neville, a close friend of O'Neill's in the statehouse,
dropped out as minority leader in order to run for Cambridge City Council
and eventually mayor. John Flaherty became Neville's successor but just in
time for Governor Maurice Tobin to appoint him clerk of the South Boston
Court. It looked as though it might be O'Neill's turn.

It was obvious right from the start. I had managed Joe Rowan's campaign against
Flaherty. Tobin was with Flaherty. Old Joe Rowan was an old-timer, very well liked,
probably over the hill when he ran for the job. But he was my friend. We gave
Flaherty and the governor one hell of a fight. Afterwards they were saying, 'Ya know,
Tip, if you had run instead of Joe you would have beaten 'em.'

When Tobin appointed Flaherty to the South Boston job, the rung on the
ladder directly above O'Neill was suddenly open. He ran for minority leader
in the state House against Danny Sullivan from Lowell and trounced him 58
to 17. His years of political obscurity were drawing to a close.

It was the last time O'Neill had formal opposition for a leadership
position. "Why? I don't know. I campaign three hundred and sixty-five days
of the year."

O'Neill had come into power by doing favors for others—running their
campaigns, voting for their pet bills and being available when they needed
him. Another skill for which O'Neill, the all-purpose politician, was
recognized was that of playing broker in difficult situations.

Jim Curley had run into a streak of bad luck. He lost his bid against

Paul Dever went to the old man and tried to get Jack Kennedy to run for lieutenant governor. Dever in 1938 or '40 had lost the governorship to Saltonstall by 3,000 votes. He was the strongest man in the state, always has been. He's in the service, Tobin is elected governor. He gave him his word that he would run for lieutenant governor when he got out of the service. He wants to get into the practice of law and make some money. The guy's broke. He went to Tobin. He said I gave you my word, I'd like to get out of it. He said I'd like to get back in the practice of law. Lookit, you promised me. If I can get young Kennedy to run, would you accept him? He says yes. So he went to Joe Kennedy, the old man. There was a question at that time whether Jack would run for Congress or for lieutenant governor. The decision was made in March at the Bellevue Hotel. The old man says my son Jack will be a candidate for the United States Congress. And I can remember it as though it was yesterday, he says there'll be no contributions of less than a thousand dollars and he says they'll come from personal friends of the family and everything will be done legally.

Had Neville beaten Kennedy, O'Neill's path to Congress would most likely have been inadvertently but permanently blocked. As it was, he now held Neville's old job as minority leader in the legislature and he also had the experience of running a congressional campaign in his home district.

That fall, the Red Sox won their first pennant in twenty-eight years.

O'Neill had once been mesmerized by the colorful, irrepressible Jim Curley—his street-corner oratory, his stylishness, the way he had of appealing to the common folk. Curley once took O'Neill in hand after a particularly awful speech the younger man had given and convinced him to memorize certain all-purpose poems that he could draw on in future speeches. There would be one for labor union gatherings, one for political meetings, one for the old folks:

> Around the corner I have a friend,
> In this great city that has no end;
>
> Yet days go by and weeks rush on,
> And before I know it a year is gone,
>
> And I never see my old friend's face,
> For life is a swift and terrible race. . . .

A little corny, maybe, Curley had told O'Neill, but "it gets them."
But O'Neill, like many others, grew weary of Curley and his constant

attempts to dominate city and state politics. After Curley got out of jail, he immediately attempted to control the selection of delegates to the 1948 Democratic presidential convention, naming only two state representatives, O'Neill as delegate and Jerry Crowley as alternate, among thirty-two possible slots. O'Neill and Crowley were to run at large and undeclared.

The subject came up at the Monday morning caucus of House Democrats, always fiery and explosive sessions. O'Neill started off with his usual soft approach:

Hey, listen, lot of bullshit out in the corridor about the way I'm leading the party; now say it to my face. It's easy to criticize when you're sitting out there but I'm sitting on the front seat, carrying the ball. You got anything to say, say it to my teeth.

At that point, Johnny Asiaf, "an old fighter" from Brockton, got up and said, according to O'Neill, "That Curley, that jailbird son of a bitch, who does he think he is?" He promptly moved that the minority leader go down and inform Curley that the House Democrats demanded four delegates and four alternates. The vote carried, and O'Neill went down to see "the boss."

Curley was not happy about this confrontation.

"You go back and tell 'em for me, they're goddam lucky to have you and Crowley. I'm running this show and that's all there is to it."

O'Neill's report to the caucus made them even madder. A motion was made to run a full slate of delegates and alternates against the Curley slate. "I put the motion and, geez, it passes," says the innocent O'Neill. A monumental confrontation was in the air.

One of Curley's lieutenants tried to head it off with promises of patronage for the boys and whatever else they needed. O'Neill said nothing doing. He had given his word and if he tried to go back on it he'd be dead politically. "We're in this thing all the way," he told the alarmed side.

Would O'Neill go down and see Curley? No. Would he talk to him on the phone? Sure.

Curley got on the phone with O'Neill and in his most sonorous voice tried to persuade O'Neill. Then he threatened him. According to O'Neill, the conversation went like this:

"I want you out of that fight," Curley said.

"Governor, I'm awfully sorry, there's no way I can get out of it."

"Does that mean you're staying in?"

"Yes."

"Well, all right, you fat son of a bitch, I'm going to give you the lesson of your life. I'm removing you and Crowley from my slate and I'm putting Shag

[Dr. Silas] Taylor [a black] on there and Frank Goon [Chinese], and I'll lick you with a black and a Chinaman."

A number of prominent Democrats dropped off the Curley slate of delegates but others, like John McCormack stayed.

Every day O'Neill and Jim Burke went down from the Capitol to Scollay Square where, O'Neill estimated, there would be upwards of 10,000 people. Tip would bellow, "John McCormack, you've been down in Washington long enough," and, "Curley, you've been fifty years in public life, like a Hindu prince; how long is this going to go on? Any chance for a young fellow in public life?" The Democratic party, he said, "will have no future until the bosses have had their past."

Said the *Boston Globe* of April 21:

The fight of the all-Representative slate is bound to prove highly interesting. For years political observers have conceded that men in the district fights get out the vote. This time, says O'Neill, the Democratic Representatives are working intensely all over the state.

Each Representative is planning to send at least 300 personal letters in his own district. The aid of 400 former Democratic state Representatives is being enlisted. O'Neill figures as many as 100,000 Democrats may go to the polls Tuesday and if they do, he further figures the all-Representative slate, Group 2, will win.

Curley won, although it has never been exactly clear how, since the O'Neill slate carried thirty-eight of thirty-nine cities. O'Neill had his own idea: "They waited until the early hours of the morning and stole the goddam election on us in Boston. They waited till the figures came in and they just transferred figures."

O'Neill's crowd was in an uproar, but after conferring with Paul Dever, the Democratic nominee for governor, they declined to contest the election. "He says, 'Jesus, the Democratic Party's in bad enough shape. We can't have a recount. Christ,' he says, 'it'll show corruption in the election system within our own party.'"

O'Neill had lodged a protest, but withdrew it "in the overall interest of the Democratic party." But he got in a parting shot at Curley, who, he said, "has long since read himself out of the Democratic party."

The fact that O'Neill and his friends declined to contest the election had little or no impact on history. But it had a great impact on his career because it showed party regulars like McCormack that he could be both an effective campaigner and discreet.

O'Neill remembers that McCormack called him down to his office;

McCormack said they met at a convention in Springfield. Wherever it was, the meeting was crucial to O'Neill's career and the future of Massachusetts politics. In spite of O'Neill's opposition in the fight over the delegates, McCormack liked the young man's ability. It was obvious that he could do wonders for the Massachusetts Democratic party.

There were several state House of Representatives districts, McCormack said, where Republicans were getting a free ride and quite a few where, with a little effort, they could be turned around. "You could be the next Speaker of the House and the first Democratic Speaker in Massachusetts if you organize right," McCormack said he told O'Neill.

The idea definitely appealed to O'Neill, although he told Tom Mullen that the chance of it ever happening was "a lot of bullshit."

But a week later, Mullen came back with some convincing figures. They showed that if Democrats were to win in every district carried by Maurice Tobin in 1944, the trick would work. Quickly, O'Neill and Mullen put together a list of thirty-eight seats where they thought they might have a shot. They would need some money.

O'Neill didn't stay enemies with people very long. He always managed to patch up a quarrel with a joke, a fistful of cigars, or a favor, and it was that way with Curley, who contributed $1,000 to a war chest. So did Jack Kennedy, John McCormack, Paul Dever, Maurice Tobin, and others. He raised about $26,000, and went after forty seats.

They supplied each of the candidates with the voting records of their Republican opponents, records that were swollen with damaging nay votes on "pocketbook" issues. And they supplied the candidates with a campaign package. O'Neill went around the state recruiting candidates and handing out money. It wasn't wasted. Most of it went to candidates who had a real chance of winning.

O'Neill and his group called all the shots. They sent brochures to a mailing list supplied by the candidate. They placed ads in his local newspapers and paid for them. "Nobody got ahold of our money. We gave them nothing. We didn't trust anybody."

They were aided that fall by heavy Democratic registration throughout the state, due to referendums on labor organizations and birth control— issues they were, respectively, for and against.

When the ballots were counted, the O'Neill-backed candidates had won in thirty-six of the forty races. The Massachusetts House was about to be Democratic for the first time in more than a hundred years.

It would need a new Speaker.

5

IRON DISCIPLINE

AFTER the 1948 election, there was no doubt about who was entitled to the Speakership of the Massachusetts State Legislature. Tip O'Neill had served as minority leader, he had successfully engineered the Democratic takeover of the House, and he had moved quickly to get the pledges—in writing—that he needed to lock up the election. There was no opposition among his fellow Democrats.

In December 1948, O'Neill, thirty-seven and prematurely gray, already showing evidence of his weakness for beer and sweets, moved into the Speaker's office on the third floor of the Massachusetts statehouse on Beacon Hill. He was just down the corridor from the office of the new governor, Paul Dever, his old Cambridge pal.

The statehouse was an ancient and venerable place with ancient and venerable traditions. One of these traditions had been that the Republicans shall control the legislature. O'Neill had contributed to the unheard-of shattering of honored tradition.

The Speakership was and still is an enormously powerful job, more powerful, relatively speaking, than its counterpart in the U.S. House of Representatives. And it was to become more powerful. Transferring this power to another party caused near-apoplexy among those who had controlled the office throughout history. The Speaker appointed the chairmen and members of all committees—even members of the minority party—and he could remove them at will. Thus he had absolute control over what legislation went to the floor and what didn't. He also, indirectly, influenced the awarding of jobs throughout the state, not the least important of these being judgeships. He could ram through, with total cooperation from the majority and acquiescence from the minority, any bill he chose. He could make or break a governor's legislative program.

Naturally, the Republicans, long accustomed to having this power unto themselves, desperately sought to keep it. Jolly and amiable though he was,

O'Neill was not without a healthy politician's paranoia. And he discerned, or thought he did, a Republican plot.

It is a story he says he never told publicly.

On January 5, 1949, the day he was to be elected Speaker, O'Neill and his allies picked up talk of a Republican attempt to buy votes on the question of who should be Speaker. With a slim 122-to-118 majority, the defection of only three votes could swing the election over to the Republicans.

As O'Neill said, "They were losing the Speakership for the first time in history. They were offering $5,000 for walks and $10,000 for votes."

Incredible? Maybe not. Anything was possible in Massachusetts politics in those days. And the buying of a few votes or absences on such a crucial issue would have saved the Republicans from their awful fate. For the turncoats, it could have been a tidy sum to add to their meager $2,000 legislative salaries. O'Neill's men kept digging for information.

Now we had the eight guys we figured were going to walk on us. The governor called each and every one of them in. We laid it out on them: by Jesus, we weren't going to stand for it. And don't think we weren't operating in the same manner, 'cause we were.

The Republicans weren't the only ones capable of enlisting opposition support. As a counter move, O'Neill and the governor lined up five people on the Republican side who would, if need be, switch their votes in favor of O'Neill. The enticement was every bit as compelling: "They were either going to be heads of departments or they were going to be judges."

That's how it was till the very end. And you should have seen them: We had our five guys locked up waiting for their eight, to make sure, because we were going to win it by one vote, regardless of what happened.

Then, only a few hours before the vote, another crisis was perceived: One of the Democratic legislators had to sing at a funeral mass in Lynn and might not make it for the session. The alarms went up, panic set in. But he finally made it. The Democrats sat tight.

O'Neill got 122 votes to 116 for Republican Representative Charles Gibbons of Stoneham. At last, Gibbons and Bob Murphy, O'Neill's chosen floor leader, escorted the new Speaker to the rostrum where he said, in a statement that could be read several ways, ". . . [we] extend to our Republican colleagues the same courtesy and consideration which they have extended to us over the past three years."

The bargain with the five Republicans had not been put to the test and so, of course, there was no need for special favors, but the five Representatives were thereafter given very particular consideration by both the governor and the Speaker.

On the day he was sworn in, he and Millie and the children went by trolley to the statehouse.

O'Neill took over his first Speaker's job with energy and political skill, moving to put through Governor Dever's progressive legislative program, increasing his own power within the House and strengthening the party's new-found majority in the state. The latter goal he attacked with what one reporter called "missionary zeal." He wanted to be sure the power he was putting together would last.

O'Neill developed a reputation, in his first few months on the job, for being "a strict disciplinarian and scrupulously fair" said Charles E. Currier in the *Worcester Telegram*. But off the rostrum, the story went on, he had become "a militant partisan. He spends much of his time outside the House chamber conferring and figuring on ways and means of advancing the cause of the Democratic party in Massachusetts. It is almost a second religion with him."

The story also said that O'Neill, despite a hectic schedule and the weighty matters of office, "literally is waxing fat in his new job," putting on forty pounds since the first of the year. (O'Neill's weight has been a persistent problem for him. In later years, he has joked about having lost one thousand pounds. He has tried all kinds of diets, including Weight Watchers—he was the only white male in his Washington, D.C., group— and an "Overeaters Anonymous" effort where members counsel one another when seized with an impulse to eat too much. He has tried Air Force diets, Scarsdale diets, and "drinking man's" diets, but none has worked for long.) At the end of the session of the Massachusetts legislature he tried to trim his figure on the golf course.

Tom and Millie played golf together occasionally and attended boxing matches and baseball games, but not as often as they had in the early years of their marriage. They lived on the ground floor of a rented two-family house on Norris Street in North Cambridge. She decorated the living room in silver blue, kept the place neat as a pin and made sure her busy husband got his meals on time. He called her "the speaker of my house."

There were three O'Neill children by then: Rosemary, who was then five; Tommy, four; and Susan, three. Two others were to follow, Christopher (Kip) and Michael. The children are, like their mother, strong-willed and outspoken and, like their father, engaging and politically savvy.

Tommy was to become lieutenant governor of Massachusetts and someday, maybe, governor. He remembers that his father rarely brought up the subject of politics, the in-fighting, the nuances, at the dinner table. But issues of the day were always discussed and the children, when they grew older, took part and often clashed with their father and each other.

The more time O'Neill spent away from home, the harder he worked at being a father. In later years, when he went to Congress, the fathering became aggressive. He took the kids bowling every Saturday afternoon and took Millie out every Saturday night. As Susan put it, "On weekends, he worked his ass off being a father."

The by-now overcrowded O'Neills yearned for a house of their own. When he wasn't practicing politics, Tip worked like a tiger selling insurance, and eventually they moved into a comfortable three-decker on Russell Street, just around the corner from his Orchard Street boyhood home.

When power changes hands, especially in government, it is axiomatic that heads will roll, departments will be shaken up, old hangers-on will be replaced by new hangers-on. And nowhere would this be more readily assumed than in the Speaker's office in the Massachusetts legislature where the spoils system was in such robust good health. It is therefore most interesting that when this not-so-young pol with fifteen years of patronage dispensing under his belt went to the top of the legislature, nobody was fired. O'Neill's instincts to promote his friends were overcome by his unwillingness to turn anyone out. Administratively, this may have been a weakness, but politically it was shrewd. For in politics you never know when you'll need a friend.

O'Neill brought his old neighborhood chum, Tommy Mullen, into the office as administrative assistant; he handled the legislative calendar and the favors. But O'Neill kept the woman who had been secretary to Republican speakers for over four decades, a deed that won her total loyalty. A new formality crept in. Visitors to the office, even old friends of O'Neill's, were crisply informed that he was no longer "Tip" to them, but "Mr. Speaker."

With a slim four-vote majority in the House, O'Neill could not afford any lapses in party discipline. As chummy as he had been with most of his Democratic pals, he had to quickly disabuse them of any notion they may have had that he would tolerate disloyalty.

I was the toughest disciplinarian they ever had in the Massachusetts legislature. You know, Christ, you couldn't rattle a newspaper or talk. Nobody would dare read a newspaper; nobody would dare smoke a cigarette till after six o'clock—if you gave them permission; nobody would dare put their feet up on the chair in front of them; nobody would dare speak: absolute discipline.

O'Neill pushed through a prodigious number of bills—573, all told—in his first session. During one six-and-a-half hour session over highway bond issues, he banged so hard for order that he shattered the gavel. He kept the House in session each day until its calendar was clear, and frequently ordered the chamber's doors closed to keep members in their seats. Or, as he once put it, to "keep a fella from taking a walk." On at least one occasion, a vote was taken on a close bill while Republicans were attending the funeral of one of their members.

To someone who had spent his youth memorizing baseball statistics and figuring batting averages and runs batted in, keeping track of a complicated legislative calendar was easy. "He could tell you everything," said his friend and confidante, Joe Healy, "what was involved, who the opposition was and why—all the way from a complicated bill to making some local fire chief permanent."

O'Neill was committed to getting through Paul Dever's "Little New Deal" program of social legislation for the state. One of his proudest achievements, even after a quarter century in the U.S. Congress, remains the construction of new mental health hospitals and the improvement of care for mental patients in his home state. He also boasted of great gains for labor, partioularly inoroaooo in unomployment componsation and equal job rights. He supported increased housing for veterans, with extra help for the disabled; greater benefits for the elderly; and vast new highway construction, which he once called a "boom" to motorists. At the end of his four years as Speaker, he would list all these programs as accomplishments. Dever would kid him: you son of a bitch, that was my program. O'Neill would say, yeah, but you would've never got it through without me.

O'Neill was lavishly celebrated by his supporters for his accomplishments that first session. At a testimonial dinner in May 1949, eight hundred friends chipped in and bought him a new car. Dever praised him as being "firm without being tyrannical, keenly intelligent without being pretentious." In June, at another such gathering, he was given a mahogany spinet piano—which he did not play—and more praise. Dever predicted he'd be governor some day.

O'Neill told a reporter in June 1949 that he thought he might like to go to Congress someday, although he knew he might have a long wait unless the incumbent from his district, John F. Kennedy, decided to seek higher state office.

It was not a tradition for Massachusetts Speakers to make the U.S. House their next jump. The line of progression, established by others like Leverett Saltonstall and Christian Herter, had led straight to the governor's office.

O'Neill seemed to have already had his eye elsewhere, and he must have understood something of the restlessness that Kennedy was feeling in Congress. O'Neill, always the figurer, had to have a plan, even beyond going to Congress. He didn't plan to stay there very long.

More than just bullying and keeping order from the Speaker's rostrum, O'Neill's leadership ability depended on a system of punishment and reward that he took to exquisite lengths. Primarily his system is one based on loyalty, a virtue easily measured in a statehouse. A man's voting record and his willingness to push bills through committee can be gauged rather simply in this setting and his performance duly rewarded or punished. Committee assignments, totally controlled by the Speaker, were largely made on the basis of performance. O'Neill had the power to shape the legislative leadership to fit his and the governor's program and philosophy. He might tolerate small indiscretions, but obstruction and disregard for party loyalty he would not stand for.

For example, when Dever asked O'Neill to produce a certain piece of health legislation and the chairman of the committee on health, Frank Oliveira of Fall River, failed to get the bill to the floor, O'Neill went to him: "Frank, either put the bill on next Monday or I'll put a man there that'll put it on." When Oliveira failed not only to produce the bill but even to hold a hearing on it, O'Neill simply banged the gavel and ordered him replaced by someone who would. The bill went to the floor and was passed.

The Oliveira incident turned nasty when the legislator charged O'Neill with "racial discrimination" in making committee assignments. In its morning edition of January 18, 1951, the *Boston Globe* reported Oliveira's charge together with O'Neill's response that it was "groundless and outrageous." The newspaper account is revealing. It reports that O'Neill disclosed he had taken into consideration Democratic voting records in naming members of committees and that Oliveira had voted against the party's program on nearly fifty occasions, although his district was eight-to-one Democratic. "Upon that voting record," the story quotes O'Neill, "he is not entitled to his own choice of committee assignments." O'Neill's record-keeping system was irrefutable.

A similar fate awaited any dissenting committee member. O'Neill: "If you wanted to get a bill out and they didn't vote with you, you'd remove the fellas from the committee and put somebody else on, so you'd get your votes out. Everything was party loyalty. You hadda get the governor's program to the floor."

The reverse of dismissing committee members, of course, is appointing them. Good assignments in the House meant more prestige and more patronage. Committee chairmen got half again as much pay as representatives. Friendly Republicans got friendly assignments.

The idea of a majority leader appointing members of the minority to committees is today unheard of in Congress, but the practice persists in many legislatures, including Massachusetts, where periodic attempts at change have failed. There was nothing wrong with it, O'Neill would say; it simply made cooperation easier. Republicans appointed to the Ways and Means Committee, one of the choicest assignments, knew they were not to cause trouble. They could be relied on to take occasional walks when their presence in the chamber might cause a close vote or require them to make a long speech. In exchange, when they wanted some local bill passed that was not a party matter, O'Neill could be very cooperative.

O'Neill was also cooperative in the matter of study commissions, one of the more popular fringe benefits available to the hard-working legislators. There was no pay involved, but members of the numerous commissions might get expenses-paid trips to tolerably nice cities like New Orleans and Montreal to do their studying at first hand. It was not unheard of for Republicans to be appointed to such commissions.

The reward system followed legislators beyond their service in the statehouse. Charles J ("Chick") Artesani, the Speaker's floor leader from Brighton, said O'Neill was helpful in getting permanent jobs for people even after they left the legislature. "If they were loyal friends, he went out of his way to help; if not, they were pretty much on their own."

The other devastating weapon was patronage control. Not only did the Speaker directly control the greatest number of patronage jobs, but indirectly he controlled the jobs his friends controlled.

If you had ten people working on the state and you went off on a bill, you'd be called in on a Thursday and told that your ten men were going to be laid off. Or if you had five guys working on the state or out cleaning the beaches in Dorchester, then they got assigned out to Salisbury where they had to travel forty miles or something like that. That's the way it worked. It was iron discipline.

The Speaker's office didn't do the actual axing. But it did keep performance records and sent its instructions through the liaison people in the governor's office, the public works office and the highways office.

Meanwhile, O'Neill had his own seemingly inexhaustible patronage supply. From the comments he has received in later years from people he had helped put through college by giving them summer jobs, it seemed nearly everyone in the state owed him a favor.

Because of his position as Speaker and because of his ties in the community, O'Neill also had power to influence hiring by the companies that did contract work for the state and the public utilities that were regulated by the state. He found neighborhood ties useful in making sure that friends were not unfairly treated. If a friend told him he couldn't get a bank job because he was a Catholic, O'Neill paid a visit to the bank president. Somewhere during the conversation, O'Neill advised him that, with all the parochial schools and other neighborhood groups investing their money in his bank, he'd better wise up. In one report, O'Neill is said to have told a banker, "I could walk from here to Fresh Pond Parkway telling them you're a bigoted son of a bitch. I could have a run on your bank in twenty-four hours." Within a week, three Catholics had been hired.

Because O'Neill controlled the membership of the Judiciary Committee, he also controlled the appointment of judges. Artesani, a big, solid guy who became a municipal judge in Brighton after leaving O'Neill's service, put it this way: "If he supported you for a judgeship, it was practically a guarantee you'd get on—or else no bill was passed."

When a bill went through the legislature creating a new probate judgeship for Middlesex County, two of O'Neill's old friends, Jerry Sullivan and Freddie McMenimen, wanted the job. Jerry had always been close politically to Tip, but Freddie, a former BC football player, was closer. He got the judgeship. Sullivan got one later.

O'Neill played the game as well as it had ever been played in the statehouse, with his combination of old-style whip-cracking leadership plus his talent for working the back rooms. The votes on the House floor were, whenever possible, mere formalities, ratification of agreements long since worked out behind the scenes. O'Neill never played his hand unless he had the cards and had a good idea of what his opponent was holding. At the same time he was already thinking about and planning for the next game.

The political strategy of general elections was constantly a subject for planning. One of Tommy Mullen's jobs in the Speaker's office, besides handling the dispensing of favors, was compiling voting records of Republican legislators. It was a very tedious chore, going to the office of the clerk of the House and pouring over several years' worth of records. How has so-and-so voted on labor issues, health issues, job issues? Then the representative's vulnerability on the issues would be matched against his vulnerability with voters in his home district, and an early decision made to oppose or not to oppose him in the next campaign.

Out of the never-quite-disbanded structure that O'Neill had set up to elect Democrats two years earlier, sprang a new organization, the Committee to Retain a Democratic Legislature and Congress, with O'Neill as chairman. Again, contributions were solicited and collected, this time from a broader base. Thirty-two Democratic legislators with little or no opposition were persuaded to contribute, providing the Democratic war chest with the same $20,000 to $25,000 in campaign funds.

Once more the money was parcelled out strategically, most of it going into races where a close fight was projected. Voting records were laboriously compiled and supplied to voters. Brochures and paid ads were also provided. O'Neill took it upon himself to muster and inspire the troops. He was a persuasive and formidable leader.

In the fall campaign of 1950 O'Neill, then thirty-eight, was an impressive and imposing figure, six two, 260 pounds, with a deep, booming voice and a pounding, I'm-gonna-level-with-you delivery.

At a meeting he and Dever set up at the Parker House in Boston, O'Neill told all of the assembled candidates, "The day of electing a fellow to office because he is socially attractive is over. The people are educated politically and realize that the ballot box is the bread box. The campaign was made on current issues and not on a philosophy that went back to the time of gas lamps and high button shoes."

The campaign was a tough one. The *Boston Globe* of November 23, 1950 reported the election as "the stiffest struggle for the lower branch the state has ever witnessed." When the votes were counted, the Democrats still had their slim, 122-member majority. This time, however, contenders in nine districts were calling for recounts. O'Neill, with a sort of flying squadron of fellow legislators, went from town to town—Athol, Royalston, Nahant, Revere, Sherborn, Everett, Cambridge—to observe the recounts and hold the line. The final tally was Democrats, 124, Republicans, 116. O'Neill would be Speaker for two more years.

Not long after, on February 22, 1951, at the Belmont home of Joe Healy just over the Cambridge line, Tip O'Neill heard the not surprising news that Jack Kennedy was ready to make his move. It was not surprising because O'Neill knew Kennedy was restless in the House and ready to go forward. As O'Neill told a college audience years later, Kennedy was regarded as a maverick in the Massachusetts party with many influential social friends but few political ones. He was thought to be something of a lightweight. "The Democratic leadership [in the House] almost despised him because they couldn't count on his vote or even on his showing up." O'Neill's opinion of Kennedy, formed instinctively six years earlier when the neophyte had burst upon the Cambridge political scene, had been changed by Kennedy's performance in Congress.

Kennedy had never hung out with the guys on the corner and in his early years in politics was visibly uncomfortable in a crowd of people. Tip had known his brother Joe and felt he was much more the natural politician. Joe had frequented the bars where the politicians hung out, and seemed to take to the politicians with grace and humor. When O'Neill and Jack Kennedy once appeared together at a firemen's breakfast in East Cambridge, O'Neill was surprised to see Kennedy sneak out the back door after his speech. O'Neill knew you didn't win votes that way. "He hated the part of politics of the shaking of the hands. He just hated it."

But O'Neill gradually gained respect for Kennedy and his political ability. "I never saw anybody grow like that." And Kennedy, who had once considered O'Neill little more than a political hack, eventually returned the admiration and even affection. As a senator and later as president, Kennedy retained an interest in his old district, especially in how well he ran among the different ethnic groups and neighborhoods. As O'Neill told Myra MacPherson of the *Washington Post:*

In 1952, in one precinct in our district, I came up four votes less than Kennedy when he ran for the Senate and I for Congress. Nothing would do but to find out who voted for him and not for me. We finally pinpointed it as the LeFevre family. Then, at the 1960 inauguration, here's Kennedy, the president, and he yells at me, "Hey, Tip, what was the vote in that precinct?" I told him he was still ahead by four votes. Kennedy roared and said, "Tip, that LeFevre family is still off you."

Such good-natured rivalry had not, however, entered their friendship as of early 1951. Kennedy and O'Neill remained about as opposite as two Irishmen could get, a corner guy and an Irish Brahmin, now dining together; talking about the future of Massachusetts politics at Joe Healy's dining room table. Healy was the perfect go-between—neighborhood pal of O'Neill, and Harvard graduate, like Kennedy.

During the evening, the discussion covered much ground. At one point Kennedy turned to O'Neill.

"Tip, are you interested in going to the Congress?" he asked.

"Yeah," O'Neill deadpanned.

Like the good card player he was, O'Neill probably did not betray any more emotion than that. He had thought quite a bit about Congress in the past few years, but he was also interested in being governor some day, a dangerous job for a big-hearted man. Still, he was interested in the honor and the prestige. And he was ambitious. Congress he would have to think about: he'd let Kennedy play out the hand.

Kennedy himself wasn't sure what he would try for; governor or senator, but Kennedy told O'Neill, "I'm either going to move or get out of politics." Kennedy asked O'Neill to keep it to himself, but he said, "I'm giving you the inside; you've got a year to work on it."

O'Neill figured Kennedy would go for the Senate. As Healy advised Kennedy, he had no state administrative experience and he might well get chewed to bits running for governor.

"Jack was sort of impatient in the House, with restrictions on debate and formal rules for getting stuff on the floor," said Healy. A nice man, Healy: bank president, Harvard educated, gentle. He knew both Irishmen well and he loved both of them. "Intellectually, that process [the House] did not appeal to Kennedy. On the other hand, I think it's the kind of process that appeals to Tip O'Neill."

Kennedy reasoned that, if he decided to run for the Senate, Paul Dever, the strongest statewide politician in the party, should be prevailed upon to seek reelection as governor. Dever would help the ticket in what would be a tough year for Democrats, 1952.

O'Neill was keenly interested in the unfolding scenario. Although the Speaker's job was enormously powerful, it wasn't considered a lifetime job in Massachusetts. O'Neill decided to take the chance and run for Congress. He could see where it could lead—or at least he thought so. "I had my life mapped out and planned," he said. "I was going to be six years in Congress and then run for governor in 1958 when Jack Kennedy ran for reelection."

Kennedy had put O'Neill onto what seemed then a sure thing, the sort of arrangement that appealed greatly to a politician. O'Neill honored Kennedy's confidence, but quietly began accepting speaking engagements outside his legislative district, in places like Allston, Brighton, Charlestown, moving restlessly about the district but never really revealing his intentions to run for Congress.

On April 16, 1952, O'Neill announced his candidacy, citing the record of Dever-O'Neill accomplishments of the past four years. A newspaper story the next morning commented that O'Neill "has won recognition for the manner in which he conducts the meetings of the House and for his work in drafting the state Democratic platform in 1948."

Thanks to Kennedy, O'Neill had a tremendous head start over the other candidates but soon found himself in a crowded field, anyway. Six other candidates, four from Cambridge and two from Boston, entered the race, although only one, Michael LoPresti, a state senator from East Boston, spelled real competition. With the backing of the burgeoning Italian neighborhoods in Charlestown, East Cambridge, and East Boston, LoPresti was sure to be a tough challenger in a wide-open ethnic primary election. It turned out to be one of the dirtiest fights ever in Boston politics.

Meahwhile, Paul Dever, who wanted to get out of politics and practice law, was talked into staying on the ticket by Kennedy's father. He was given the choice of running for governor or senator, with Kennedy taking whatever was left. It was expected he would seek reelection as governor.

Nevertheless, according to Healy, Kennedy had prepared two campaign statements, one for the Senate and one for governor. Dever and Kennedy met on Palm Sunday, 1952, at the Ritz and confirmed the arrangement. Fine, said Kennedy, and called to have the statement released. The next day he announced his candidacy for the Senate.

But Dever, as O'Neill said, was a reluctant candidate. "You can't win with reluctant candidates. And he campaigned lousy and they ran a rotten campaign and everything went bad." To make matters worse, Dever lost his voice before delivering the keynote speech at the Democratic National Convention. "It was a disaster," according to O'Neill. At that point, Kennedy, who had talked Dever into running, began putting distance between himself and the man who appeared to be a loser.

I remember being in Chinatown the Sunday night before the election. We had a big rally. Dever said, "Tip, how do you think it looks?" I said, "Geez, absolute disaster. Eisenhower's going to bury Stevenson." He said, "How many votes?" I said 300,000. Dever said to me, "Gee," he said, "I figure I can overcome 250,000. Whatever he wins by over 250,000 carries the state and I lose." You know, I couldn't conceive of Dever losing. He was running against Herter. I said, how about young Kennedy. He said, "He's going to be stronger than I am." You know, if my memory serves me correctly, Eisenhower carried the state by 268,000 votes, Kennedy carried the state by 72,000 over Lodge, and Dever lost the state by 12,000 votes. That's how accurate Dever had it.

If there was one thing O'Neill did not like to get involved in it was an intra-party fight, especially one between the Kennedys and the McCormacks. He had seen just such a dispute coming in 1956 over who would lead the Massachusetts delegation to the Democratic National Convention and got out of the way. It involved one William ("Onions") Burke, the Democratic state chairman, a friend of McCormack's but not of Kennedy's—and Kennedy was worried.

Suppose, he told O'Neill, in a phone call from Palm Beach, "lightning strikes" and he is nominated for vice-president. "I don't want a son of a bitch heading my delegation who'll be opposed to me." He asked O'Neill to become state chairman. "Oh, Jesus, I'm not interested," O'Neill replied. "I'm too friendly with McCormack." After a lot of back and forth, in which Paul Dever said he'd take care of McCormack but didn't; in which O'Neill got in, saw the predicament he was in and got out—Kennedy put up another candidate who beat Burke and locked up the delegation.

Then, in another "if lightning strikes" appeal, Kennedy asked O'Neill, who as congressman could choose four delegates, to name his brother Robert as one of them. O'Neill was reluctant; he had already named the slate—three friends and himself—and didn't particularly like Robert Kennedy. But he did what he was asked. He got off the slate himself to make room, and that was how the younger Kennedy, then chief counsel of the Senate Investigations Subcommittee in Washington, went to the convention in Chicago. O'Neill never even went to the 1956 convention because the day before it was to take place, his house in Cambridge burned down. It wasn't lightning.

The road for Tip O'Neill from speakership of the Massachusetts House to membership in Congress was rougher than expected. The year 1952 was a convulsive one in state politics and O'Neill found himself face to face with disaster on several occasions. The first, although he did not see it at the time, walked into his office in the person of James Michael Curley.

The man who had once been O'Neill's idol, then his adversary, was by then a pathetic figure. Although nearly seventy-seven, a defeated politician and an ex-convict, Curley had never reconciled himself to the notion of being out of public life. He had often come by to sit in O'Neill's outer office, seeking to gain what favors he could for himself and his friends from whatever crumbs were left under the table.

Now, in the spring of 1952, he wanted something specific, a pension for his more than fifty years of service to the City of Boston and the Commonwealth of Massachusetts. O'Neill had performed a similar service for former Republican Mayor Malcolm E. Nichols. Nichols had written to O'Neill saying that after years of public service he was destitute. At the time, O'Neill said, "Jesus, heaven forbid that such a thing would ever happen to me; I feel sorry for the poor old guy." It was a disgrace. He called Nichols and asked for details of his years in the legislature and elsewhere, then put through a special pension bill for him.

Now, reasonably enough perhaps, Curley said to O'Neill, "Hey, listen, you did it for Mal Nichols, why don't you do it for me?"

Curley, of course, was a different case. "They'll kill me if I do it," O'Neill protested. The old man was not to be denied and talked him into it, saying it was not so much for himself but for his wife. Curley had found O'Neill's soft spot. O'Neill finally agreed to do it, but first he had to check with everyone—"I check everything in my lifetime"—before making a move. He cleared it with the Republican leadership in both houses and with the most dangerous man in the state—on this issue, Norman MacDonald, head of the Taxpayers Association, a citizen watchdog group.

I called him and I said, "Lookit, here's a piece of legislation that's meant for Curley." But I said, "if I put Curley's name on it, I don't have a chance of passing it. Now, you know the Nichols thing went through and nobody ever objected. Have I got clearance from you?" He said, "Tip, fine, excellent. I'm glad the old guy is going to be taken care of."

So, in the wee hours of the morning on the last day of the session, July 1, 1952, an innocuous-looking amendment to the recently enacted legislative retirement law was mumbled through both houses and sent to the governor. It was signed on July 4. Said Walter Sullivan, then in the House, "We had been sitting for thirty-five to forty hours straight. It was during that time. Tip brought it to the House and suspended all the rules—the lights were shut off—and he just pushed it through." Immediately afterward, the legislature adjourned.

No name was mentioned in the bill. It simply changed the retirement law to permit persons over seventy who had once served in the legislature—Curley had in 1902–03—to qualify for a pension. No hearings had been held and few members who had not carefully examined it knew that the bill applied to Curley. But as one state official put it at the time, "It fit him like a glove." He, and later his wife, would be entitled to $1,000 a month. That is, if things could be kept quiet.

There was more trouble in store for O'Neill, for earlier in the legislative session he was being set up in a vicious legislative maneuver. In December 1951, a House member named Eddie Donlan had filed a bill seeking a legislative investigation into communism in the state. It was a ridiculous bill, but given the climate of the times, nobody dared oppose it. One of the Boston papers, the *Post,* was then serializing a book called *McCarthyism, the Fight for America,* which allegedly exposed the "traitors and potential traitors in government." The whole country was in a fever over supposed Communist infiltration in government.

Because the bill had been filed after the first Wednesday in December, it was automatically sent to the Rules Committee, chaired by the Speaker. O'Neill felt that McCarthy "was completely outta line—although you couldn't tell your own Irish people that." He had quietly pocketed the bill in early 1952 and the subject never came up until the last day of the session, July 1, 1952, when Donlan suddenly requested a hearing. O'Neill refused. Chester Dolan, president of the Senate and a friend of O'Neill's opponent, LoPresti, then immediately accused O'Neill of blocking the investigation.

"Holy Jesus, the thing was absolutely devastating," O'Neill said. It was reminiscent of the teacher oath blow-up fifteen years before. O'Neill stood firm in spite of the dangerously heated atmosphere. He refused to reconsider his decision, and he never replied to his accusers in kind. He just redoubled his already frantic efforts to get himself nominated.

One thing O'Neill certainly had going for him was loyalty. It was a quality no amount of campaign money could buy. The people who had been for him were always for him, and he never forgot to ask his friends for help. One of these friends was Chick Artesani, who had been O'Neill's floor leader. The name is Spanish, but a lot of people, especially voters in Artesani's Brighton neighborhood, assumed that anyone with a name ending in a vowel was Italian. "With 1,500 Italian votes in the district," he said with a big laugh, "I was not about to disillusion them. Even LoPresti thought I was Italian and when I went out for Tip, LoPresti got very mad at me."

There was also John O'Connell, the Moose, or Red, one of the greatest athletes, one of the greatest card players O'Neill had ever known. The two men went back together to the basketball courts and football fields near Barry's Corner. O'Connell once lost $18,000 in one memorable night of cardplaying. He owned four bars, one of them a kind of soup kitchen for all the neighborhood deadbeats. Red O'Connell made good money, although not fast enough to get rich; he liked to spend it and he didn't mind losing it.

I'm running against LoPresti and that was the biggest and toughest fight I ever had. The Bartollos, they were the fighters, they came to Red. They knew that Red was a kind of power in our town and that I'm a boyhood pal of his. And they said, Red, we'd like to have you be with LoPresti against Tip. You can help us in the neighborhood. "Number one," he says, "I grew up with him since I was four years old. Number two, I'd take off both my arms before I'd ever do that." I mean, the trait of loyalty was inbred in us. So the fella says, "Well, you know, he'll never be able to match LoPresti for money," he says. "LoPresti's going to spend a ton of money on this fight and O'Neill's never gonna be able to raise the money." Red says, "Well, I just want you fellas to know one thing: I figure I can always go to the bank and get $200,000 on my barrooms, just so you don't think Tip will run out of money. Anything he needs up to that, I'll go to the bank and get the money and give it to him. He's my pal." They turned around and walked out.

Now when I look back on that first fight and I think about the money that Red wasted and I didn't even know—I mean, my God, it was something awful. He was spending money all over the place, thinking he was doing me a favor. He was wasting it. In those days there was no reporting or anything like that. But he was my pal, and to him they had questioned his loyalty, and to question Red's loyalty to me, that just aroused him to the most. Without even my knowledge, he went out and went crazy.

Less than three weeks before the September 17 primary election, the first explosion occurred, threatening to damage O'Neill's candidacy. The *Boston Post,* then in its waning days, gained a temporary reprieve by means of a story its editors undoubtedly felt would rock the government. They were right. On August 30, the first of several screaming banner headlines appeared:

EX-MAYOR CURLEY IS HANDED $12,000 PENSION BY SOLONS

Legislature Stretches Back to Service Performed for State 50 Years Ago—Passed During Rush of Late Marathon Session on Beacon Hill and Signed by Governor— Boston Would Pay the Entire Sum

In a copyrighted story, the *Post* spelled out in great detail how the bill had been "slipped quietly through the legislature and signed by Governor Dever." In subsequent editions, the newspaper detailed how Curley had had the bill written and introduced, how it had been referred to House and Senate committees and then brought to the floor. "Somewhere in the legislative mill," the *Post* said, "the name of James M. Curley was taken off the bill so that the measure could not be readily identified as a pension measure tailored to a single individual." Just how this had occurred could not be ascertained, "as legislators who voted on it developed severe cases of amnesia."

Oddly enough, except for one mention that Speaker O'Neill had referred the bill to the committee on pensions and old-age assistance, O'Neill's role in the affair was never revealed. Instead, the stories focused on the roles of the committee chairmen. Several legislators expressed their surprise. Said one, "I never dreamed this bill was for Curley. It was pretty trickily worded."

For his part, Curley seemed to enjoy the whole affair, since it gave him a new opportunity to remind the press of his tireless efforts on behalf of the poor and downtrodden. He sounded the old familiar eloquence: "Censure is the tax a man pays in the public for being eminent." Then, quoting the Irish satirist Swift, he said, "It was an excellent act. It was a very generous act." Finally, he produced a classic Curley line. "It's hard to foretell what the future will hold," he said. "I might even run for public office again." He did, one last time, in 1955, when he tried to beat "the little city clerk," John Hynes, and failed. Before the next election came around he was in his grave, and in fact, Curley never saw the pension.

The uproar over the pension continued in the press and public. Curley had never done any particular favors for O'Neill. But for politicians, (and others of position), it isn't so much a question of payment for specific favors, but a mutual looking after, taking care of one's own. The proposed pension was the ultimate gesture, the final payment of respect to a man who had been, in his day, a magnificent politician. O'Neill's own involvement seemed unlikely to be revealed, but Governor Dever, however, sliding badly in his bid for reelection and under agonizing pressure over the affair, called O'Neill a few days before the primary election. Dever told O'Neill he had no choice but to call the legislature back into session. O'Neill was mortified. "Jesus, no way," he said. It would be admitting error when what they had done was actually an act of decency. They couldn't let the *Post*, a desperate newspaper, do that to them; they'd be murdered on election day. Dever said he was sorry, he had to do it.

As a result, Tip O'Neill's last act as Speaker of the Massachusetts House was to preside over a chamber of panicky legislators in an extraordinary session in which the politicians threw out the baby with the bath water. The House, in a rousing 213-to-12 vote, repealed the entire pension act, cancelling pension for all legislators, past and present.

O'Neill, who had publicly opposed the special session, was furious. To Norman MacDonald of the Taxpayers Association who, O'Neill was sure, had leaked the story to the *Post*, he said "You gotta be the lowest bastard I ever met in my life. We *cleared* this with you." MacDonald, according to O'Neill, shrugged and replied, "This was a natural for me." To a man like O'Neill, a special place in hell was reserved for people who failed to honor a bargain. It was the worst kind of sacrilege. Not long after, he publicly attacked MacDonald as "a $28,000-a-year hoptoad."

Privately, O'Neill was in anguish. The repeal process lasted until two o'clock election morning, forcing him to miss a big election eve rally at the Harvard Theater in North Cambridge to which more than 2,000 supporters had been invited. A friend, Joseph Harrington, father of Michael, (who later served five terms in the U.S. House), and one of the great spellbinding orators in the state, kept the crowd happy and entertained.

The pension scandal proved to be a disaster for a number of Democratic legislators. In fact, whether because of the scandal or simply because of the Republican sweep in 1952, the Democrats briefly lost their majority in the

Massachusetts House. O'Neill personally was unscathed, although the election did prove to be a heart stopper.

The big Irishman had run hard and scared. For a seasoned politician, it is surprising how often he succumbed to fears that he was losing a race. Jack Kennedy had advised him not to waste his time in the Italian-dominated East Boston wards, where he felt a non-Italian didn't stand a chance. But O'Neill told Leo Diehl, his campaign manager, "I'm still going to be over there." "He was," said Diehl, cringing. "He got murdered, shellacked."

O'Neill and Diehl placed ads in local newspapers and used some television, a live five-minute appearance the night before the primary. They used the old neighborhood gang to speak for O'Neill and hired others they could not get free.

"Leo, we got any money left? I need a couple hundred dollars. I want to put workers on," an edgy O'Neill said one day. Diehl, who was trying to save enough to pay all the bills in case they went down the drain, protested but finally gave in. O'Neill was running the show.

The masterstroke of the campaign, however, was one that left the LoPresti people scratching their heads and crying foul. O'Neill was aware that because there hadn't been a real primary fight in Cambridge for years, Democratic registration was way down. So he decided to appeal to the independents (who could vote in Massachusetts primaries), sending letters to thousands of them saying that if they wanted a Cambridge man in Congress, they should vote for O'Neill. In the letter, the independents were told that the day after the election, they could ask to have the "D" removed from beside their names and return to independent status. O'Neill: "LoPresti could never understand it. There were only 21,000 registered Democrats and 27,000 voted. How the hell did they do it? There were like 2,000 registered Democrats in Ward 11 and 4,400 voted. We got every independent; they all came out and voted."

Even though O'Neill knew the votes from East Boston and the North End were machine votes and would be in first, he imagined the worst when he saw himself trailing by 12,000 votes the night of the primary. He and Millie went to headquarters where, crestfallen, he concluded, "It's all over." Diehl told him to go home and stop worrying. It was going to be a long night.

More pressure was added during the evening when the *Boston Herald* went to press. Diehl remembers that "John Harris of the *Globe* called me and said, 'Leo, the *Herald's* on the street saying LoPresti won.' I said, 'Don't print it! He hasn't won. Cambridge isn't in. Somerville isn't in. We'll catch up.'"

The September 18 edition of the *Cambridge Chronicle* ran its headline:

TIP TOPS FIELD IN HOT RACE FOR SEAT IN CONGRESS. He had beaten LoPresti in Cambridge, 13,378 to 4,493. In the same edition, the paper reported that the Eisenhower Cambridge Committee was beginning to swing into action for "Ike and Dick."

In the face of the Eisenhower landslide, however, O'Neill won the election that November in a walk, beating out Republican Jesse Rogers by better than 60 percent.

Tip O'Neill was going to Washington. He figured it would be a short stay.

6

TUESDAY-THURSDAY
CONGRESSMAN

THE Eighty-third Congress came to town on a cold and cloudy Saturday in January 1953. It was not a happy time for Democrats. They had lost the White House in a landslide to a grandfatherly Republican, the wartime hero Dwight D. Eisenhower. Eisenhower had carried his party into control of both the House and Senate for only the second time in a generation. Speaker of the House Sam Rayburn was about to yield his gavel to Joe Martin, and Lyndon Johnson would be only "minority" leader to the Senate's new GOP boss, Ohio Senator Robert A. Taft.

O'Neill's family drove down from Boston for the swearing-in ceremony but they couldn't stay long. The older children had to get back for school. For them, a high point on the trip was a ride on the old Senate subway with the new young senator from their state, John F. Kennedy.

O'Neill wasted no time getting down to business that first day. One of the Bostonians who crowded into his two-room office in the Cannon Building for the congratulations that traditionally follow the brief opening House session was Kenneth T. Lyons, then head of the Federal Employee Veterans Association (later the National Association of Government Employees) who represented workers at the Boston Navy Shipyard. Lyons had worked with Kennedy in the past but knew O'Neill only casually because his responsibilities were limited to federal workers.

Now, as O'Neill moved from statehouse to Congress, Lyons was one of the first on the scene. "What can I do for ya," the new congressman asked with his customary heartiness. Lyons went right to the point. He said his union men at the Navy Yard needed more work or some would be laid off. O'Neill, apparently unaware that freshman congressmen are considered rather insignificant in Washington, picked up the phone and called Navy Secretary Robert. B. Anderson. Anderson was new in town too; he came to O'Neill's office immediately. And, after listening to the O'Neill-Lyons plea, he put in a few calls himself. The result: Boston received a new order from the Navy to build a small warship, an LST.

80

O'Neill was off to a great start. The quick, well-placed telephone call was to become a trademark of his congressional style. For the Navy Yard, however, that call on January 3, 1953, was only the first move in O'Neill's twenty-one-year losing effort to keep the facility alive. Eventually, the Yard was closed down finally by President Nixon on July 1, 1974, a little-noted triumph by Nixon over O'Neill, who had become, by then, a leading Congressional advocate of the impeachment of Richard Nixon. In the months and years that followed that first O'Neill initiative on behalf of the Boston Naval Yard, Nixon would resign in disgrace, O'Neill would become Speaker of the House, and the Naval Yard would become a national historical park.

The 1952 Republican sweep created a nonpolitical but related problem for newcomers like O'Neill and Eddie Boland, who had also been elected to Congress. They ran into a serious housing crunch. The two, who had served in the Massachusetts legislature together, drove to Washington from Boston together and apartment hunted together. Democratic bureaucrats, who hadn't seen a Republican president in twenty years, apparently found it hard to believe they would actually soon be out of work, and were slow to move. At the same time, great numbers of Republican office-seekers swarmed into the city.

Luckily—and typically—O'Neill had a friend who had a friend who knew a real estate agent, and somehow or another, the two freshmen congressmen wound up in an efficiency apartment in a building owned by the International Brotherhood of Electrical Workers at 1500 Massachusetts Avenue, N.W.

Boland and O'Neill had decided to share an apartment to save money. Besides, it didn't seem necessary for each to have his own apartment when neither would be around much. O'Neill planned to spend every weekend at home in Cambridge while Boland would return to Springfield for his weekends.

The efficiency, however, turned out to be a little too cozy, and after a few months, they found a one-bedroom apartment in the same building. They furnished the place like most bachelors do, with a little of this and a little of that. Boland arrived with what he considered the basic necessities, a toaster and a coffee pot. O'Neill, outfitted by his wife, did a little better. He had sheets and towels. Friends from Massachusetts, including Maurice J. Tobin (the former governor who had been President Truman's Secretary of Labor) and his wife, loaded the two up with chairs and lamps. They had to buy a couple of beds.

O'Neill and Boland were an unlikely pair, the big rumpled O'Neill,

shedding coats and papers on any available piece of furniture, the neat and
orderly Boland, picking up after him, making beds, emptying ashtrays. But it
worked. They shared apartments for twenty-four years, and maintain to this
day they never had a fight.

"Millie would come and check on us once in a while," Boland said, "to
make sure the apartment was in great shape. And my responsibility, of
course, was to make sure it was in great shape."

He was meticulous, neat as a pin. Eddie would spring-clean the place, scrub
floors, do the laundry. I'd come home at night and drop my coat over a chair and
Eddie would whisk it up and hang it in the closet. Eddie would get up at 6:30 in the
morning, shower and shave, then he'd tell me "Okay, big fellow, it's your turn."
Then he'd raise all the windows, air the beds for ten or fifteen minutes, shake the
sheets and blankets out, and then make the beds.

O'Neill made the instant coffee.

They moved twice. After seven years at 1500 Massachusetts, friends
recommended another apartment house on 17th Street, where they moved.
Here, they were robbed twice. They decided it wasn't a safe neighborhood
and moved again three years later when a one-bedroom apartment became
vacant at the Calvert Woodley, 2601 Woodley Place, N.W. They stayed
there until O'Neill became Speaker in 1977.

In any man's career, circumstance can play a significant role—even one
as unimportant-seeming as where (or how) he chooses to live.

Many interconnecting threads of accident and luck led Tip O'Neill to the
Speakership. One may have been the fact that his family never moved to
Washington. O'Neill lived, therefore, like a "bachelor," sharing an apartment with his old friend, unencumbered by any serious domestic duties.
The two men never cooked a meal, but ate out every night, palling around
with other bachelor congressmen, real and temporary. As a result, O'Neill
quickly slipped into a comfortable role as one of the boys, playing cards at
the University Club or the Army-Navy Club, a cheerful, self-confident
fellow. He was good company and an excellent low-stakes poker player. He
made lots of friends, Democrats and Republicans, conservatives and
liberals. The common bond was made up of a mixture of politics and
friendship and playing cards.

In those days, there was a regular poker game held Monday nights in the
fifth-floor office of former Rep. John Bell Williams, the archconservative
Mississippi Democrat who bolted from the party in 1964 to support the
Republican candidate for president, Barry Goldwater. At the poker table,

differences in persuasion were of no concern; O'Neill left his political liberalism at the door. It was, he said simply, "a helluva fun game."

There also was a regular Wednesday-night poker game, usually at the University Club. One of the regular players was the late Michael J. Kirwan, an Ohio Democrat. Kirwan, who was sixty-six when O'Neill came to town in 1953 and who had been in Congress since 1937, took a liking to the big Irishman. By the time Kirwan died in 1970, he had smoothed the way for O'Neill to take over from him a post uniquely important to the internal Democratic politics of the House, chairman of the Democratic Congressional Campaign Committee. In that job, O'Neill was to control the flow of a congressman's lifeblood: money. The job brought with it enviable side benefits, for in a twist on the story of the king killing the bringer of bad news, anyone running for Congress is likely to embrace the messenger who arrives with campaign contributions in his hand. O'Neill made a few more friends.

The Wednesday-night poker game produced strange alliances, O'Neill and the late Sen. Karl E. Mundt, for example. Mundt, a Republican from South Dakota, was just about as conservative as a man could get, a consistent roadblock in the path of Democratic party programs. But he and O'Neill were friends. "Amazing thing," says O'Neill, "there wasn't anything in the world Karl Mundt wouldn't do for me."

It was Mundt, in fact, who stepped in and saved an O'Neill constituent from the public embarrassment of appearing at a televised Senate Committee inquiry into labor mismanagement. Both the committee chairman, John L. McClellan of Arkansas, and the chief counsel, Robert F. Kennedy, were adamant. No special treatment for anyone; all would appear in public.

O'Neill had never cared much for Bobby Kennedy, the super-bright rich kid. He found it ironic that the man called to testify by the McClellan Committee was closer to the Kennedys than to himself. He came from the wealthy Irish end of the district and had contributed handsomely to John Kennedy's two Senate campaigns. O'Neill didn't even know him personally. But he heard his plea—that the man knew nothing of the union misdeeds and that public scrutiny would ruin his business, labeling him guilty forever. So O'Neill went to Karl Mundt. Put a man on television, he argued, and you condemn him for life. It's like being indicted. No one remembers you were found not guilty.

Mundt walked down the corridor and into McClellan's office. O'Neill waited. He could hear the two senators talking. "I've never asked you for a favor," Mundt said, "and Tip O'Neill's my friend." Finally McClellan agreed. "We'll hear him in executive session. At 6:30 tomorrow morning."

Did O'Neill do favors for Mundt? Of course. If Mundt wanted something for South Dakota, O'Neill would talk to his friends in the House to try to help it along. "He was my friend," said O'Neill. "That's the way the ballgame works."

For all the men's club camaraderie of O'Neill's life in Washington, he says he always felt guilty about not being a full-time husband and father. It was a difficult decision to leave the family in Cambridge instead of moving them to Washington. He had strong emotional and philosophical ties to his family. Reverence for family stood right up there with his church and his political party. But when O'Neill was first elected to the House, his five children ranged in age from one to nine. The oldest three were in school. O'Neill and his wife decided it would be best for them to stay in Cambridge.

Also, in those days, Congress hadn't yet become a year-round job. In 1953, congressmen went home for the year on August 3. Those who moved their families to Washington then had to decide what to do for the rest of the year. Any who stayed in Washington risked criticism for neglecting their homestate constituencies. Yet maintaining two houses was impossible for most members.

O'Neill's children in fact have quarreled with his assessment of his performance as a father. On the contrary, they all testify that he was a splendid father and probably spent more time with them the three days he was home than full-time fathers spent with their children over an entire week. O'Neill certainly tried harder. They did more things together. They bowled and played ball. Dinners were family gabfests, political seminars. There was always something going on. The family was highly competitive and plunged into every new activity vigorously.

Susan O'Neill, the middle child, looked back on those years fondly when talking to a *Cambridge Chronicle* reporter recently. "It was never just the five of us kids," she said. "It was a cast of thousands, always people in and out, all of our friends." And, of course, politics was very much a part of their lives. Only the youngest O'Neill, Michael, stayed out of public affairs. "I really don't enjoy politics at all," he said. "The two big things I have together with my father are watching football games and playing golf." But there's an oft-told family story about the oldest son, Tommy, at age ten, racing into the water at a Massachusetts beach and hollering: "Last one in is a Republican."

Although these were generally happy times for the children, they often were hard times for Mrs. O'Neill. "It's not the easiest life in the world," she said of her marriage and the responsibility of raising five children. "I honestly think you have to be a strong character to deal with it. . . . You have to be prepared for not having your husband around in any emergency. You have to know who you are and what you can do."

Millie O'Neill learned well. She became independent and tough—"a tough woman," Tommy once said, "with all kinds of love." Mrs. O'Neill was also a strict disciplinarian. The children remember their father as a "soft touch" and their mother as the strictest mother of all their friends.

It was a recurring theme in many political families. The wife must be both mother and father. She is strong and beautiful but she is still mother and father. She's the one who's there when a child breaks a leg or needs help with homework. It's not an easy life, and even when the husband-father is home, he's likely to be out politicking somewhere.

There'd be times when I'd say to myself, Geez, I'm going to get out of this, or Millie and I'd have an argument or something. I was never home when a catastrophe happened. When Kip fell out of a tree and broke his ankle, I was down here. When Rosemary was in an automobile accident, I was in Washington. So, every time there was a crisis, I'd say, Jesus, I'm going to get out of here. What the hell, I can make more money in the insurance business. What the hell am I doing down here? And then I'd always say, hey, someday you're going to be Speaker.

After O'Neill went to Washington, he remembers that John Kennedy gave him only one piece of advice: "Tip, don't do what I did down there. Be nice to John McCormack."

It wasn't hard for O'Neill to be nice to McCormack. They had worked together in the past. They respected each other, McCormack admiring O'Neill for his skills as Speaker of the Massachusetts House, O'Neill admiring McCormack for his position as majority leader (and minority whip during the Republican eighty-third Congress) in the U.S. House. And they both were Irish, Catholic, cigar-smoking, Democratic politicians and poker players from neighboring districts in Boston. They differed only in two aspects of life-style. McCormack was a teetotaler, and his wife lived with him in Washington during his entire forty-two-year congressional career. They became famous for dining together every night of their married life.

O'Neill fell into step with McCormack easily. Their alliance was sealed at the breakfast table and enhanced on the cocktail circuit. Every morning they were in town, O'Neill, Boland, and a floating group of other McCormack followers met for breakfast in the old House dining room, a smaller and less formal version of the present restaurant. There, they swapped stories, information, and legislative plans over their coffee and sweet rolls. O'Neill soon became known as "McCormack's man," someone close to the old man who possessed some influence with the House leadership. Many new loyalties clicked into place, to be called up years later when O'Neill himself started moving up the leadership ladder.

In the evenings in those early years, McCormack regularly accepted the dozens of invitations congressmen receive to cocktail parties, receptions, fund-raisers, and the like, sponsored by lobbyists, business groups, fellow congressmen. He didn't drink, of course, but he felt a responsibility to go, as an elected leader of the House. At each affair, he arrived promptly, at 5:00 P.M., for example, and left just as promptly at 6:15 P.M., for dinner with Mrs. McCormack.

Soon he decided to take Tip O'Neill along. O'Neill's circle of acquaintances grew larger and valuable friendships were formed as he, with his political instincts sharpened, met the city's power elite, both in and out of government. At first people asked who's the big fellow with McCormack all the time? Tip O'Neill; he's very close to the Speaker. And they'd come up and shake his hand, introduce themselves, have a drink.

Eventually, O'Neill knew, or claimed he knew, the name of at least one person he could ask for help in every major government agency. This was part of the talent he called his "happy faculty." It would pay off, not only for Massachusetts, which consistently ranked high in federal government spending, but among his colleagues in the House. As younger members came to Washington, it became known that O'Neill had good contacts downtown. More friendships clicked into place.

McCormack was an unabashed O'Neill booster. He often said that Tip O'Neill knows more about Massachusetts politics than anyone else, he was Speaker of the House there, y'know. And, occasionally, because of this, O'Neill would be invited into the House inner power circle, Speaker Rayburn's "Board of Education." There, in a small meeting room on the first floor of the Capitol directly under the House chamber, Rayburn met in the late afternoons with a small group of old friends and political allies.

There was a bucket of ice and a bottle of bourbon and some water. What kind of bourbon? I don't know what the hell it was. I never drank it. Never could drink bourbon. Bourbon to me is like medicine. John McCormack would have some soft drinks there. But they would sit around and they would talk about politics. Rayburn loved to reminisce: tell me all about Curley. Tell me all about this young guy, Kennedy. He'd want to know how we ran the [Massachusetts] House, how we won control for the Democrats.

O'Neill was not a regular at "Board of Education" sessions, where membership was by invitation only. Invitations were highly prized because it was from that first-floor meeting room, behind closed doors, that Rayburn ran the House. As legislative issues developed, the committee chairman handling the subject would be invited to discuss strategy. Few rebelled. It was an era that matched a Rayburn motto: "To get along, go along." He could not possibly have envisioned the internal revolutions of the '70s that would open up the process and spread power around to more than a hundred committee and subcommittee chairmen.

In spite of his easy entrance into the Washington political-social circles, O'Neill's first days in Congress were frustrating to him. He had gone from Speaker of the Massachusetts House to a freshman in the U.S. House. And that's the way he was treated, like a freshman. He applied for the rich pork-barrel committee, Public Works, only to be given a choice of three favorite dumping spots for freshmen: the District Committee, Government Operations, or Merchant Marine and Fisheries. He took Merchant Marine.

The committee met only four times that first year and the only discussion O'Neill can recall concerned a Republican demand that all former (Democratic) staff aides be fired. O'Neill argued that they should at least be given thirty days' notice. The Republican chairman turned to him and said: "They got their notification November 6 when the House went Republican." O'Neill remembers thinking, "Yeah, that's it, that's the way the ballgame works."

Back in Cambridge, O'Neill wondered aloud whether he had made the right move. In the first place, he found himself pinched for money. The $12,500-a-year congressional salary stretched thin when it had to cover his home in Cambridge, the apartment in Washington, and his weekly commuting costs. (Beginning in 1953, congressmen were allowed a $3,000 income-tax deduction for Washington living expenses.) He had earned $32,000 the year before in his insurance business, but now that work would often have to be neglected. Gradually he found that if he wasn't on the scene regularly, the business went to others—out of sight, out of mind.

"I never saw a more dejected man," Leo Diehl recalled later. "For the first six months he complained, 'What the hell am I doing here?' It was a tough adjustment for Tom."

But he stayed, and things slowly began to improve.

First of all, the Democrats won the congressional election of 1954. The election marked a milestone of sorts for Eisenhower: it was the first time since Rutherford B. Hayes that a Republican president had to face a

Congress in which both House and Senate were controlled by the opposition party.

Then, in 1955, congressional pay went to $22,500 a year, easing the strain on O'Neill's finances. Still, the O'Neills felt they could not afford to move to Washington. Perhaps more important, they decided it was best not to uproot the children from their familiar neighborhood and school friends.

O'Neill once again put in for assignment to the Public Works Committee. Support seemed to be growing for a "defense" or interstate highway system and O'Neill, ever alert to methods for guiding federal money toward Massachusetts, wanted a piece of the action. The highway program was to become the most extensive public works project in the nation's history.

McCormack, however, had other plans for O'Neill. The new Congress, though Democratic, was generally categorized as middle-of-the-road politically—like Eisenhower. This was largely because the Democratic Party was still strong in the conservative South. More often than not, the Southern representatives formed a Dixiecrat alliance with the Republicans in Congress, voting with them on a large number of issues.

A critical outpost of conservative strength was the House Rules Committee. In 1955, the brilliant mastermind of the Southern coalition in the House, Rep. Howard W. Smith, Democrat of Virginia, became chairman of the committee, effectively gaining control of the machinery for scheduling House action on all major bills. The committee was, in short, a roadblock for all progressive legislation, Republican or Democrat, that the conservatives opposed.

There was little Speaker Rayburn and Majority Leader McCormack could do about it except to try and make sure that future appointees to the committee were party loyalists. That way, perhaps someday they could outvote the Smith group.

O'Neill was sitting at his customary breakfast table one morning when Rep. Francis E. Walter, Democrat of Pennsylvania and Communist-hunting chairman of the House Un-American Activities Committee, stopped by and said, "Congratulations." Walter was one of the House's old bulls. He had been around since 1933. It was the first time he had even seemed to notice O'Neill, let alone speak to him. O'Neill asked what was going on.

Walter told him that Rayburn was about to name O'Neill to the Rules Committee. It had been decided the night before. McCormack had assured Speaker Rayburn that O'Neill was a man who knew a lot about politics and could be trusted to be loyal to the party. O'Neill didn't believe the story and went calmly on with his breakfast.

O'Neill knew there had been some talk earlier of trying to get him on the Rules Committee. McCormack had told O'Neill and Boland that he would attempt to place one of them on Rules and one on Appropriations. McCormack prided himself on the way he watched out for the state of Massachusetts by winning choice committee assignments for the state's congressional delegation. But the final decision would of course be Rayburn's.

"You take Appropriations," O'Neill had said to Boland, at the time, and thought nothing more of the matter. The Appropriations Committee is a workhorse committee and O'Neill still was a Tuesday-Thursday man, his eyes focused on Massachusetts politics. It was important for him to maintain close ties with state party leaders because he still planned to go home and run for governor some day.

As Walter continued his way through the dining room, O'Neill shrugged the news off. He still had his application in for the Public Works Committee. Five minutes later, the House doorkeeper, William ("Fish Bait") Miller came in and told O'Neill Rayburn wanted to see him. Upstairs in his office, as O'Neill remembers it, Rayburn was blunt:

He says, John McCormack tells me you're a former Speaker of the House. I says, that's right. And you know what loyalty is. I says, that's right. He says, you know what it means to get legislation to the floor—you could be opposed to the legislation but I would expect you to get votes for me to get it on the floor. I says, that's party loyalty. He says, you're going on the Rules Committee.

Up to that time only one other congressman had been assigned to the Rules Committee in his second term: Howard W. Smith.

O'Neill went onto the Rules Committee just behind a Rayburn protégé, Representative Richard Bolling, a thoughtful and intelligent liberal Democrat from Missouri. For eighteen years, the two sat side by side in varying degrees of frustration over a succession of staunchly conservative chairmen. Finally, in 1979, Bolling himself became chairman and, with O'Neill as Speaker, formed a strong leadership partnership between the Rules Committee and the Speaker's office for the first time in several decades.

There are two basic approaches to the job of Congressman. Some go to Washington determined to have a hand in developing national policy, eager for a place in the spotlight and generally uninterested in the day-to-day trivia of what is called constituent service. Others take a different approach, men like O'Neill who rarely issue a press release, operate very much within the Congress and spend most of their time watching out for the folks back home. O'Neill's attitude toward the job was, in short, parochial, and he made no

apologies for it. "My life is politics," he would say, "and all politics is local."
(In contrast, old Joe Kennedy told his sons that local politics was "an endless
morass from which it is very difficult to extricate oneself.")

The O'Neill style was evident even before he was sworn in as
congressman. Immediately after the 1952 election, he found himself
swamped with job-seekers and other requests for favors. With a *Boston
Globe* reporter close at hand, he visited his temporary State House office
one December day and found a dozen or so of his new constituents waiting
with special problems. He was not offended, then or later. He did not feel
imposed upon. This was all part of his job representing the people, looking
out for their interests.

That's the way you operated in public life back in those days. You never got any
letters on legislation. Everything was public service. Business people came in—you
opened the door for them. What could you do? You could open doors. I was one of
the best door openers in town.

In his early years in Washington, O'Neill continued this patronage
tradition that was so much a part of Boston political life and O'Neill family
life. He simply switched from the local to the federal level. In those days, a
person couldn't even get a job in the post office without clearance from the
local congressman. "And we'd put literally hundreds of women to work
during the Christmas rush," O'Neill said. "Their pay might average out to
$87, but it made a difference between a good Christmas and a poor
Christmas." He recalled Mayor Curley's saying that hundreds of persons
would ask him for favors over the years, big ones and small ones, and his
advising O'Neill to treat them all alike.

Twenty-six years later in an office high in the steel-gray John F. Kennedy
Federal Building overlooking Boston's city hall, O'Neill said things hadn't
changed much. "We run a public service operation here," he said. "Every
time they got a problem with the federal government, they wind up in our
office." Maybe it's just the Boston area, he suggested. Public service,
personal favors, are the norm, the way the politicians operate. It's the way
the Irish moved up and took care of their friends.

In Washington in those early years, Congress watchers hardly knew
O'Neill. He seldom spoke in public and took little active part in Rules
Committee deliberations. "He just sat there like a big, fat Irishman," said
one reporter. "I wouldn't have guessed he'd be Speaker one day." It was
Bolling who caught the public's attention, the one tagged as a comer and
praised for his rules skill and his generally constructive, although acerbic
criticism of the House.

There were important differences between the two men, however. For one thing, Bolling could not abide ineptness, whereas O'Neill was more tolerant of human error. Bolling could be cruelly sarcastic with colleagues who came to the Rules Committee inadequately prepared or who muffed parliamentary signals on the House floor. O'Neill didn't even notice. "That's just not my nature, to make judgments on people," he said. "If you're the dumbest guy in Congress, that's all right with me."

The differences, in personality and in style, probably denied higher leadership positions to Bolling while aiding O'Neill in his advancement. When the chips were down, it seemed O'Neill had no enemies.

The Rules Committee turned out to be the perfect place for O'Neill. Its schedule suited his: meetings were held on Tuesday mornings, or sometimes Wednesdays. Its jurisdiction touched every committee and every member of the House. He was, therefore, not thrust into the narrow legislative confines of a member of a housing or an education subcommittee. And it put him (along with other Rules Committee members) in a special position between the rank and file and the leadership. In the course of a two-year Congress, he would be likely to come into contact with nearly every member of the House. More friendships clicked into place.

As a member of the Rules Committee, I would have the Johnny Fogartys come to me and say, "Tip, what's comin' up next week? What went through Rules? Will there be any roll calls, anything controversial? What's in the bills that would affect the economy of my area? What anticipated amendments do you see?" On Fridays, I'd have the Harold Donohues asking, "Do I have to be back Monday or Tuesday?" I'd have thirty guys call me on a Friday. I'd make up my own list so I'd have answers ready for them. I had the New York crowd callin', the Chicago crowd callin', until it became known that Tip knows what's going on. Call Tip, he'll tell you. . . . People would call because there was no whip organization to speak of in those days. I was kind of created whip.

One of the few times O'Neill stepped into the spotlight in these early years occurred on a characteristically political issue, the question of whether segregationist Dr. Dale Alford should be seated as a duly elected member of Congress from Arkansas. As a write-in candidate, he had beaten a popular and racially-moderate Democrat, Brooks Hays. O'Neill was chairman of a special House committee on elections—another gift assignment from McCormack—and, contending there was evidence of fraud at some of the Arkansas polling places, he advocated that Alford step aside until a full investigation could be conducted. But Arkansas Representative Wilbur Mills threatened to challenge the seating of three Northern Democrats who had run afoul of the law: Adam Clayton Powell of New York, William J. Green, Jr. of Pennsylvania and Thomas J. Lane of Massachusetts. Rayburn and McCormack decided that the resulting fuss would tear the party apart. So they blocked O'Neill from making the anti-Alford motion and from opening the question to debate on the floor. O'Neill accepted the rebuff philosophically. He was a get-along-go-along guy, loyal to Rayburn and McCormack. Alford served two terms in the House and there was no further talk of investigation.

In Congress, O'Neill became an inside man, a master of the internal House processes and the political nuances of the men and women who served there. On the rare occasions when he was involved with the specifics of legislation, it was usually on behalf of his own constituents. He kept up a running battle, for example, to keep the Boston Navy Shipyard alive despite repeated efforts of various presidents, Democrat and Republican, to close it down or cut it back. And he was credited with drafting compromises on such measures as the Federal Aid Highway Act, with its millions of dollars for Massachusetts, and a federal housing bill, which included money for much-needed college dormitories in his district. Often, through friends on committees, he could accomplish his goals with amendments to bills. National parks were created this way and a complicated land switch deal arranged to give Boston a new jail and a multimillion-dollar federal office building. All this was perfectly consistent with O'Neill's view of the best way to do his job.

The Rules Committee had twelve members in O'Neill's early days, eight Democrats and four Republicans. Whenever anything important came up, however, they deadlocked at 6 to 6, as Smith and his fellow conservative, William Colmer, Democrat of Mississippi, voted with the Republicans.

Although the Rules Committee's philosophical lineup reflected the House as a whole, it became the single most visible symbol of the frustrations of liberal Democrats, O'Neill included. Plots and counterplots were mapped but "Judge" Smith seldom was outsmarted.

On two or three different occasions, Ray Madden, Dick Bolling, and I would sign a petition to call a meeting [on something Smith opposed], and we'd file it with the clerk under the rules requiring a hearing in ten days. Always on the ninth day, old Smith would have a hearing. We never would get to the point of having a vote. The old-timer, y'know, would close down the shop and leave here, saying his barn burned down. And he was tough. He was able too. Jesus, he was able! We had our problems in those days.

In the Eighty-fifth Congress, 1957–58, liberal Democrats led by Eugene J. McCarthy of Minnesota and Frank Thompson of New Jersey, tried to blast loose the solid conservative grip of Republicans and Southern Democrats. They decided they needed something to rally around. So they drafted a legislative program based on the 1956 national Democratic platform and urged the support of fellow Democrats. The next year, they organized formally as the Democratic Study Group.

But O'Neill remained neutral. Although blocked by Smith, his first loyalties were to Speaker Sam Rayburn and the institutional framework in which they operated. He shared neither the liberals' anger at Rayburn nor the anger of more conservative Democrats at the DSG. O'Neill was not a legislative innovator, partly because he wasn't assigned to a legislative committee and partly because he wasn't interested. He would speak grandly of overall objectives, jobs for the unemployed or housing for the poor, and leave the details to others.

If the Rules Committee was a frustration in a Republican administration when the flow of liberal legislation was quite modest, it promised to be a nightmare for a Democratic one. After John Kennedy was elected president in 1960, one of the administration's first projects was to do something about the Rules Committee. The problem was discussed even before the election when Bolling, who was chairman of Kennedy's liaison committee to Congress, met with Robert Kennedy in Los Angeles. The Kennedys clearly believed that without a change in the Rules Committee there would be no New Frontier program.

The question was, What to do? Purge Colmer, who had bolted the party by supporting an insurgent slate of Democratic electors in Mississippi? Add new members to tip the balance away from Smith's control? Change the rules to take away committee power to pigeonhole bills? Cut a deal to let just a few Kennedy bills out?

There were plots within plots. Rayburn vetoed rules changes. Purge Colmer, he said, or expand the committee. Smith said no: "No purgin', no packin'."

Behind the scenes, a group of young liberal Kennedy friends, organized around the new Democratic Study Group, were frantically trying to line up votes for the expansion idea.

Armed Services Committee Chairman Carl Vinson of Georgia, the grand old man of Southern politics and second only to Sam Rayburn in length of service, finally stepped in. He called a Southern caucus meeting at which he warned that Rayburn had the votes to win. He advised that they support the expansion idea to save Colmer—and just possibly they might also save three other Mississippi Democrats who also bolted their party.

No one knows how many votes Vinson swayed. But when the roll was called, the House agreed by a margin of three, 217 to 214, to expand the Rules Committee by three. Two Democrats and a Republican were added. Votes would shift to 8 to 7 in favor of Kennedy programs.

O'Neill played only a minor role in the Rules fight. He supported the expansion effort but was not one of its organizers. Such battles were not his style. He was not a reformer, even though he seemed sympathetic to their aims on occasion.

In politics it's the little things that count. As in Massachusetts, O'Neill's major interests were the politics of legislation, not the substance. In all likelihood, he probably never read a bill completely through. By the time he ran for Speaker the Fogartys and the Donohues were gone, replaced by a new generation of younger, more activist Democrats. But the O'Neill reputation remained—that he was a man who could be counted on to help out a fellow Democrat. "I knew everything that was going on," O'Neill said. "Like learning the rules at a baseball game, I learned the rules of the House. They just came to me naturally."

The need to know a little something about everything had taught him valuable lessons. In order to be well informed, he needed to make wise use of his staff. Later, of course, he was aided by the basic political fact that as he rose higher in Congress more talented staff aides sought him out.

In the 1950s, congressional staffs were relatively small. O'Neill had one full-time secretary in his Washington office and one part-time (Mrs. O'Neill's sister Evelyn) plus three in Boston. All were paid from a $20,000 annual office allowance. Although congressional staffs have grown steadily and, in some cases, spectacularly since then, O'Neill was convinced early by a young Mount Holyoke College professor that he could get invaluable help from student interns, to beef up his small staff.

The professor, Dr. Virginia Schuck, who later became president of Mt. Vernon College in Washington, D.C., said O'Neill's office became one of the favorite spots for interns. Unlike some other congressmen, O'Neill treated the students as full-fledged staff, giving them substantive work and making them feel important. Too often, in other offices, student interns wound up sorting mail and making coffee.

O'Neill was generous in his praise of the student aides. They became his Rules Committee brains, studying bills scheduled before the committee and drafting brief summaries for him. As a result, he said he and Bolling probably were the only ones who knew anything about upcoming legislation. (Bolling read most bills himself.)

The key to successful use of staff is an ability to spot bright people, give them responsibility, and trust their judgment. O'Neill mastered that art with his student interns. In return, he received their affectionate loyalty. There was no grousing in an O'Neill office and very little turnover. Tommy Mullen was manager of O'Neill's Boston office from the day he went to Congress until January 1979. Dorothy Kelly, who started as a secretary at the same time, retired in 1971. Lenny Lamkin, head of a satellite office in Arlington, Massachusetts, was one of the boys from Barry's Corner. His assistant, Herbert D'Arcy, was from another gang, but remembered playing ball with the Barry's Corner crowd at Russell Field in North Cambridge. As congressional allowances and staffs grew, others who came in the 1960s were Francine Gannon and James P. Rowan in Boston, Dolores Snow and Leo Diehl in Washington. Diehl had served with O'Neill in the state legislature and remained his closest personal friend, eventually becoming his administrative assistant. O'Neill took care of his people and they took care of him.

Members of his personal staffs weren't the only ones who owed their jobs to O'Neill. When he went to Washington, he left behind a statehouse full of men and women, some of them former legislators, who had found work during the years he had served there as Speaker. These people, along with later members of the legislature, provided a continuing link between O'Neill's Washington office and Boston. They also expanded his constituency beyond his eleventh (later eighth) Congressional District. Many sought aid from his office before they went to their own congressmen.

O'Neill encouraged this contact. He wanted to retain as much influence and visibility in Massachusetts as possible because he still had plans for returning to his home in 1958 and running for governor when John Kennedy would be up for a second Senate term. Many of his friends tried to get O'Neill to speed up his timetable and run for governor in 1956. But he was unopposed for reelection to the House, there was no Kennedy at the top of the ticket, and to his surprise, he found in an informal poll that he was not well known outside his own district. He decided to stay put, and Foster Furcolo became governor.

In 1958, the year O'Neill had thought would be his chance at the governorship, Foster Furcolo decided to run again. Furcolo was unpopular with many of the state's most influential Democrats, but O'Neill decided not to run against him. Instead, with his own House seat safe, he agreed to manage Furcolo's reelection campaign. It turned out to be no easy task. Many state Democrats had been warring with Furcolo, and the governor had tried to bypass the regular party leaders. Four years earlier, when Furcolo had sought Republican Senator Leverett Saltonstall's seat in Congress, Kennedy had quietly opposed Furcolo. Now the two would have to run together.

O'Neill preached solidarity, urging the Democrats to forget their past differences. Let bygones be bygones. He organized Democratic officeholders throughout the state to get behind the entire ticket, Kennedy, Furcolo, and the House candidates. When the votes were counted, it was a big Democratic sweep. The *Boston Globe* reported that O'Neill was not surprised: a pollster had told him it would happen.

The pollster, Dr. Louis H. Bean, the economist who had stood alone among his fellow pollsters in 1948 to predict a Truman victory over Dewey, told O'Neill that in 1958 many Republicans and independents would switch and vote Democratic. The reasons may sound familiar to us today. Bean estimated 9 percent of the Republicans and a large number of independents were angry with Eisenhower over inflation, the high cost of living, a recession, the president's vacillating foreign policy, and the lack of a defense buildup. They were mad enough, he said, to vote Democratic. Bean was right and O'Neill learned to respect the pollsters' art.

O'Neill flirted with the idea of running for governor of Massachusetts several times over the years. All evidence points to the fact that he really wanted to be governor, but that he finally gave in to strong advice against it from the closest of his friends, including his wife.

Newspaper speculation that he would seek—and could win—the Democratic gubernatorial nomination in 1960 began shortly after the GOP rout O'Neill engineered in 1958. First he was described as a "dark horse" possibility, then as "unannounced but active," then as "unbeatable," and, toward the end of 1959, as almost certain to run. In December, two old Statehouse colleagues, Lawrence F. Feloney and George W. Spartichino, mailed copies of a pro-O'Neill flyer to 5,000 potential delegates to pre-primary conventions. "The Democrat for '60, Recognized by All as a Great Democratic Leader," the two proclaimed. "He Will Be a Great Governor."

But O'Neill at the last minute stepped aside. Old friends told him in blunt terms that the governor's office was a dangerous place for a man like O'Neill who couldn't say no to people; he would be vulnerable to grafters and sycophants. "I always felt that Tip O'Neill in a top executive capacity was much too kind to be an effective guy up there," said longtime confidante Joe Healy. "That part of his character troubled me. Tip is the kind of guy that if someone came in with eight kids and was in trouble, Tip would do anything to see that he was taken care of. Nothing illegal, but this human characteristic worried me at the time in terms of his ultimate survival and whether or not he might be chopped up."

Millie O'Neill said she had opposed her husband's running for governor for many of the same reasons. "I always felt it was a dead end in politics," she said. "Everyone wants a job. You lose friends. I kept saying to Tom that you lose strength as governor; you never gain any. Tom could never say no to anybody."

O'Neill's publicly stated reason for seeking a fifth term in the House instead of running for governor was that John Kennedy had asked him to take on a key assignment for the 1960 presidential campaign. His job was to try to drum up support for Kennedy among House members. The Kennedy people were concerned that they were not picking up congressional support outside the Northeastern delegations. O'Neill was to arrange a series of meetings between Kennedy and congressmen from other sections of the country who might be expected to endorse the Massachusetts senator.

There is still some confusion about O'Neill's relationship with Kennedy and his role in the presidential campaign. Despite their geographic and philosophic closeness, the two men were not really friends. Largely, it was a matter of class distinction. The Kennedys were the wealthy Irish who rode in limousines and toured the Continent. They were educated at toney Eastern prep schools and colleges, like Harvard. The O'Neills, on the other hand, were the wage-earners who kept the streetcars running and toured North Cambridge, getting their education at public high schools, on the streets, and at BC.

Shortly after O'Neill announced that he was Kennedy's man in the House, Eddie Boland revealed that he and O'Neill were to share the task of coordinating Kennedy's campaign among House members. No one was more surprised at these announcements than Dick Bolling, who had been invited by Bobby Kennedy to do exactly the same thing. Bolling said he went to the younger Kennedy to tell him he didn't mind, that O'Neill could have the job. But Kennedy insisted he needed a man like Bolling—from Missouri—out front, and issued a press release saying Bolling had the job. That was the end of the matter. O'Neill never said another word.

After the election, Bolling suggested that the White House use O'Neill as its spokesman on its upcoming legislative program because of O'Neill's closeness to McCormack, the majority leader who soon would become Speaker. But O'Neill deferred to Boland. "He didn't want to apply himself to that kind of [legislative] detail," Bolling said later. "He didn't want to be a technician." Boland was the logical contact man, anyhow; Kennedy's chief congressional liaison man, Lawrence F. O'Brien, was an old friend of Boland's from Springfield. As a member of the Rules Committee, O'Neill continued to be consulted on White House strategy, but the Kennedy people generally felt more comfortable with legislative detail men like Bolling and Boland. O'Neill never claimed to be "Kennedy's man in the House" though occasional newspaper articles described him that way during the three years of Kennedy's presidency.

In spite of their differences, O'Neill maintained an easy, friendly, professional relationship with Kennedy. In fact, he thought John Kennedy the ablest politician of the clan. He was the kind of politician an O'Neill understood best, a man who could read the country the way he read his own congressional district, analyzing vote patterns down to the smallest detail.

One of the reasons I have always looked at Kennedy—so sharp, so far ahead of his own organization . . . [is that] after the '58 election, I'm sitting in the office one day and who walked in but Jack Kennedy. And he said to me, "I understand that Tommy Mullen knows more about the congressional district than any person on earth. . . . I understand he knows Cambridge inside out." I said, "That's right." "Fine," he said, "let's get the figures." So we laid out a ward map . . . went over every precinct—where the Polish lived, where the Jewish lived. . . . And, you know, I said to myself, this guy's really a sharp individual.

But Kennedy, from a standing start, was a national politician, while O'Neill remained steadfastly provincial. It is interesting that the one time O'Neill can remember taking an active role in a Kennedy vote roundup came on the trade expansion act in 1962. The story of O'Neill's work on this bill for Kennedy is indicative of the way the House operated in the days before the revolts of the 1970s, and it reveals much about Tip O'Neill.

At the time, President Kennedy was seeking broad authority to reduce or eliminate tariffs on imports, particularly on items largely produced by the United States and Europe. His aim was to strengthen the European community and to expand international trade. In lining up support for the bill, Kennedy publicly promised American producers there would be "ample safeguards" to protect American industry from cheap foreign imports.

Candy manufacturers were concerned, however, because they were being undersold in the candy bar business and didn't want to see Kennedy allow cheaper candy into the United States from England and the Netherlands. The basic problem was peanuts, which make up a large part of most candy bars. While U.S. domestic supports kept the price of peanuts high in this country, foreigners could buy the nuts at a fraction of the cost in India and Egypt.

Candy was big business in O'Neill's district, and he wanted to be sure the industry was protected. He knew little about the rest of the trade bill, however, and was willing to accept Kennedy's word that the legislation was needed.

American candy makers were also centered in several other large cities, including Chicago, Brooklyn, and Philadelphia, each of which had a large Democratic delegation. Kennedy strategists figured they would need all those old-guard Democratic votes to pass the bill. Republicans and some Southern Democrats were organizing to oppose the bill. Unfortunately for the Kennedy people, the Democratic delegation from Chicago, Philadelphia, and Brooklyn voted the way their respective city bosses told them to. This time, all were threatening to vote against the bill because of the stiff opposition from the candy makers.

O'Neill went to Kennedy to explain the problem. The president understood the problem; after all he had represented the Eleventh District six years. No problem, he said. Tell the candy manufacturers there is an escape clause in the bill and candy will be the first product protected. Similar assurances were to be passed on to the other cities.

Somehow the word failed to reach Chicago Mayor Richard Daley. The senior man in Chicago's Democratic delegation Thomas J. O'Brien, reported to O'Neill that they would have to vote against the bill. When O'Neill went to McCormack with the news, he said, "Well, we can let Chicago off the hook, the vote won't be that close."

I says, "Supposin' New York goes and Philadelphia goes. You know you could be in trouble." And he says, "You're right. I'll call in Larry." So we get Larry O'Brien and he says, "Geez, I meant to have the president call Daley last night. I'll have him call right now." O'Brien was familiar with the fact that I was interested and the president was interested because he had represented my district and he had made an agreement. So he [Kennedy] called Daley and he said, "Lookit, we made an agreement with the candy manufacturers. Under the escape clause, they'll be the first ones in."

From Chicago, Daley promptly called Tom O'Brien in Washington and the delegation switched back into the Kennedy column. The bill passed easily after a Republican motion was defeated, 253 to 171. Only forty-four Democrats, mostly from the South, voted with the Republicans.

O'Neill counted it a good day's work. He had watched out for his constituents and he had helped bring in a winner for Kennedy. It wouldn't be as easy in future years after the old city machines disappeared. White House lobbying in the '70s would require contact with nearly every member of the House, not just with a handful of bosses.

O'Neill broke with Kennedy on only one major bill, a 1962 proposal for $2.3 billion in public-school aid. Ironically, this Catholic president's bill for school aid was defeated because of opposition from Catholics—including O'Neill. The Catholic Church hierarchy argued that school aid should go to private (and Catholic) as well as public schools. Kennedy argued that such government aid would violate the Constitution's demand for separation of church and state. The issue came to a head in the Rules Committee, which had been carefully rearranged in 1961 to tilt 8 to 7 in Kennedy's favor. On the school issue, however, two Catholics, O'Neill and James J. Delaney, Democrat of New York, voted along with the Republicans and the Southern Democrats to shift the balance the other way and block the bill from coming to the floor of the House.

Larry O'Brien was philosophical: "That was just a case of Tip representing his district and the president feeling that it [the school aid bill] was an integral part of the New Frontier program. Both Tip and Delaney had problems with our version of the bill. Nothing personal."

O'Neill broke with the Democratic majority on the Rules Committee on one other occasion, after Lyndon Johnson became president, by refusing to vote for an administration bill to ease federal regulation of rail rates on perishable commodities. O'Neill had no particular quarrel with the details of the legislation; he was simply mad at Johnson for threatening to close the Boston Navy Yard. In this instance, O'Neill's influence was felt. Johnson was worried because he knew that without O'Neill, other, more important Great Society bills, the antipoverty program, for example, would be threatened: the Navy Yard remained open a few more years.

Again it was vintage O'Neill; he was representing his constituents. He was virtually unknown outside these two spheres, his home district and the back rooms of Congress. Painfully consistent, he operated the same way in both places. Only the names of his colleagues changed. Neither the Washington papers nor more scholarly studies of Congress those days mentioned him much if at all. Congressional reporters, speculating on future leadership challenges, ignored him. Frank Thompson, who went to Congress two years after O'Neill, recalled that the only time he noticed his Massachusetts colleague was once a year when he offered a St. Patrick's Day resolution of support for Ireland.

"Congressman O'Neill?" asked a senator when his name came up at a 1963 hearing. "Is he still in Congress?"

It took an unwinnable war in Southeast Asia, a family growing into political awareness in the 1960s, and a student heckler at a political rally to propel O'Neill into a position where he gradually became the logical—and unopposed—choice for congressional leadership.

There was one more burst of speculation in Massachusetts in 1961 that O'Neill would be a candidate for governor the next year. He hadn't seemed to close the door tightly two years earlier and the Democrats were looking for a winner. Republican John A. Volpe had won in 1960, and was likely to run again. But by this time O'Neill had made up his mind. He would lend a hand to Democrats in Massachusetts (he did, in fact, get much credit for the Volpe upset by Endicott Peabody), but he would stay in Washington; he would be Speaker of the House of Representatives, or at least he would try. Rayburn had died of cancer November 16, 1961, at his home in Bonham, Texas. McCormack moved up to Speaker. Most people, including O'Neill, expected McCormack to serve only a short time and then retire, but as O'Neill said in 1979, "McCormack stayed a lot longer than I anticipated."

7

VIETNAM: MOVING UP
ON THE INSIDE

THE last edition of the *Washington Evening Star* came off the presses at about 4:30 P.M. on September 14, 1967. Within a few minutes, copies were delivered all over town. Half a dozen were dropped off at the White House; one was placed on a small cabinet just outside the Oval Office.

President Lyndon B. Johnson walked into the office at 5:00 P.M. He was just back from a fast trip to Kansas City where he had spoken to the International Association of Chiefs of Police and had visited briefly with former President Harry S. Truman in Independence.

Johnson glanced at the *Star*'s front page and noted with satisfaction that the lead story was based on the speech he had delivered at noon: "Johnson Blasts Negro Militants." He had decided it was time to speak out against men like Rap Brown and Stokely Carmichael who were urging blacks to rise up in violence to assert their rights. In his speech he had called them "poisonous propagandists."

Johnson skipped over the rest of the page. There didn't seem to be much good news. The Federal Reserve Board warned of inflation; B-52s bombed missile sites north of the demilitarized zone in Vietnam. He would get back to the paper and the stack of wire-service clips later. First he had to get a haircut. He was to meet the parents of daughter Lynda Bird's fiancé, Charles S. Robb, for the first time this evening.

Back in his office before the 9:00 P.M. dinner, an aide called the president's attention to a four-paragraph story on page six of the *Star*. It had been overlooked earlier. "O'Neill Splits with Johnson Over U.S. Vietnam Policy." Headlines are always noisier than the small type in news stories, and this one jumped out at the president. Sonofabitch. Not O'Neill, the good loyal Democrat, consistent supporter of the president? He picked up the phone: Get me Tip O'Neill.

The House had convened at noon that day. Two LBJ supporters took the floor to deliver short speeches in praise of the government's Vietnam War policy, all part of the Johnson administration's orchestrated response to critics. The statements had been prepared by various presidential aides. "It's high time the American people joined ranks in support of the wonderful efforts of our fighting men," said one. The other offered the prediction that "from now on, Communist losses will increase substantially and their ability to hold out will decrease markedly."

Eddie Boland wished LBJ a happy fifty-eighth birthday. Tip O'Neill said nothing. Less than a month earlier, he had come to the decision that the Vietnam War was unwinnable, and that the U.S. should figure a way to get out. He had sent this word out to his constituents in a newsletter but had said nothing to reporters. Today he was totally unaware that someone had given the *Star* a copy of the newsletter and that the story would run in the afternoon editions of the paper.

Opposing the war had been a fateful decision for O'Neill and a profoundly difficult one for him to make. He thought it would ruin him among his hard-working blue-collar constituents at home who dutifully sent their boys to fight in Vietnam. "The day he changed on the Vietnam War, I'll never forget it," said O'Neill's oldest son, Thomas P. O'Neill, III. "He felt he was absolutely gone politically. That was the worst time in his life." O'Neill's wife, Millie, agreed. "The reception he got at home was very rough. . . . People were furious to think that he would do such a thing while their boys were still in the service. They thought it was very unpatriotic at the time."

As it turned out, his opposition to the war did not ruin him politically. Far from it. O'Neill began to try to turn his constituents around on the war, accelerating his already heavy schedule of speaking engagements around his district, cajoling hostile audiences with the same report on the progress of his thinking that he would later personally give the President of the United States. In the process, he became the most visible war opponent among the so-called Establishment politicians, the first to break with LBJ. His actions also had an unexpected side effect: the younger congressional activists who had paid O'Neill scant attention in the past soon began to view him as a possible contender for House leadership. His new position showed them he could blend loyalty to old politics with sensitivity to new ideas. But to Lyndon Johnson, he looked like a traitor.

On September 14, the House session dragged on until 8:45 P.M. Speaker McCormack wanted to finish action on the Appalachian Regional Commission bill. In a concession to the Tuesday-Thursday group, he didn't want the House to have to meet again Friday. O'Neill was mildly interested in the bill but only as it affected a similar commission in New England. He cast his vote in favor of the amendments—and went off to join a late game of poker at the Metropolitan Club.

At home that night, Eddie Boland answers the phone. The president wants to talk to me. Christ, Eddie called the University Club. He called the Army and Navy Club. He called [ex-Representative] Fisher's office. He called the Democratic Club. We had never played before at the Metropolitan Club [they were ducking a pal who had been on a losing streak], so he never thought of calling me there.

I came in at three o'clock in the morning and he said, "Where'd you put the car?" I says, it's in the garage. I had come straight up to the apartment from the garage. He says, the Secret Service is sitting downstairs in the lobby. They been waiting for you all night. I says, the what? He says, about the *Star* article. I says, what about the *Star* article? He says, Christ, Johnson's called twenty-five times. Call the White House regardless of what time you come in.

The president went to bed at 11:45 P.M., leaving a message for O'Neill with the White House switchboard: Come see me in the morning.

Johnson aides say it often was hard to tell whether the president was really angry when he started shouting or whether he was just being his rambunctious, generally profane, self. But for sure, he could not abide the thought of someone turning on him for political expediency and with no forewarning. To Johnson, it looked as if O'Neill had done just that. Johnson had been angry; but the next morning he was sorrowful. "I can understand those assholes over on the floor opposing the war," he said to O'Neill, "but Jesus, you, my friend, to come out against me, I can't believe it. . . . Are you going to tell me you know more about this war than I do?"

O'Neill slowly explained the making of his decision, a story to be told dozens of times over the next few years. The groundwork had been laid in his own home where his five children were growing up, working their way through their teen years. Every Sunday, they and their friends gathered at the O'Neill house in Cambridge to gobble up food and politics. They didn't just listen, however; they talked. And they talked of their steadily growing unhappiness over the course of the war in Southeast Asia. Son Tom, then in college, and his two younger brothers would soon be eligible for the military draft. But at first O'Neill had stood by the president.

As a supporter of the war, O'Neill had frequently defended the president in talks with the younger generation. He was a popular speaker at colleges, not only in his own congressional district where there are twenty-two institutions of higher education, but at others around the country. As the Vietnam War heated up, it was inevitable that he would be asked about it wherever he went. Before each appearance, he was briefed by the Executive Branch experts to bring him up to date. They seemed to know what to expect and usually had all the "right" answers ready.

Early in 1967, he was invited to address a meeting of the Boston College Chapter of the Young Democrats in the auditorium of McElroy Commons. A young man named Pat McCarthy was there too. At twenty, he had dropped out of college and joined the army. He was visiting on campus that day in a break between boot camp and Officer Candidate School. McCarthy, who later graduated from Harvard Law School and went to work in the Advocates Bureau of the Small Business Administration, listened as O'Neill debated the Vietnam War with the students. O'Neill repeated, as he had many times in the past, that he had been briefed by everybody he could possibly be briefed by, from President Johnson on down. McCarthy stood up: "Have you ever been briefed by the other side?"

After the lecture that night, O'Neill said he got to thinking. No, he had not been briefed by the other side, not by anyone who would know anything about the situation. So he deliberately set out to learn all he could about the war.

A first stop was with Marine Corps Commandant David M. Shoup. To O'Neill's surprise, Shoup said he was opposed to continued U.S. participation in the war. He said the U.S. was fighting a war it couldn't win; what's more, it had no determination to win.

Next, O'Neill went to the Central Intelligence Agency. Actually, the CIA sought O'Neill out. Someone at the Agency had heard the congressman was rethinking his position on Vietnam. So a high-ranking CIA officer (all involved contend they remember no names) contacted a man known as an O'Neill acquaintance, John D. Walker, and asked him to set up a meeting with the congressman. Walker, then a senior United States intelligence officer for the Middle East, who was ostensibly assigned to the State Department, had worked with O'Neill's daughter, Rosemary, who was a State Department political and economic officer stationed on the Mediterranean island of Malta. Walker, due to go to Israel in June, had visited Malta earlier in the year. The briefing for Tip was set up in Walker's home on P Street in Georgetown. O'Neill described the participants simply as "all the head CIA fellas." Whoever they were, they told O'Neill a surprising story. They said that despite public statements from U.S. government officials on the war in Vietnam, it was, indeed, going badly. The word "unwinnable" was used repeatedly. But they said the big problem was that their messages assessing the war were not reaching the president. They said reports sent to the White House were snatched off the president's desk by national security aides who disagreed with the gloomy warnings. Some others argued at the time that it was not the CIA's role to give advice; the agency was merely supposed to gather facts. Still, O'Neill was bothered by the talk that day.

Maybe the president's military advisors didn't want to admit defeat.

A few days later, on April 27, 1967, O'Neill went again to the Walkers' home, this time for dinner. Among the guests that night was Thomas F. McCoy, a CIA officer assigned to "psychological and political matters" in the Far East. He had just returned from Vietnam. He too stated that the U.S. should get out of Southeast Asia. Unlike some critics of the war, McCoy said his objections were purely pragmatic. "We were involved in something that we weren't winning and could not win—without a declaration of war and a determination to go in and destroy North Vietnam." But he said the American people would not support such an all-out effort; they had no strong emotional interest in Vietnam, no stake in its future worth the risk. McCoy said he had written a CIA report recommending (as did Vermont Senator George Aiken a little later) that the United States pull out of Vietnam and that the president simply announce that he had achieved his purpose, which was to stop the north from overrunning the south. (Angry over President Johnson's war policy, McCoy left the CIA early in 1968 and went to work for the antiwar presidential candidate, Senator Eugene J. McCarthy, Democrat of Minnesota.)

In June 1967, O'Neill visited his daughter Rosemary in Malta. The Middle East had just erupted in a brief but violent six-day war between Israel and its Arab neighbors. A U.S. Navy communications ship, the *Liberty,* which had wandered too close to the action, drawing fire from Israeli planes, had put in at Malta. Although not traveling on official business, O'Neill made an informal inquiry of what had happened. But mostly he found he was talking about Vietnam. In his informal survey of opinions, he talked to the admirals of the Sixth Fleet. He talked to the embassy people, who assembled at Rosemary O'Neill's house. He talked to the U.S. ambassador to Malta, George J. Feldman. And the message he came away with was: "They kicked hell out of the [Vietnam] war."

Back in his Boston office that summer, O'Neill sat down with one of his young interns, law student Joseph McLaughlin, and drafted a statement to be sent to his constituents as a newsletter. Citing the war's "frightening cost" in lives and dollars, he said, "I cannot help but wonder whether this may not be too high a price to pay for an obscure and limited objective . . . in an inherently civil conflict." It was a difficult statement to write. O'Neill's political life had always been firmly rooted in party loyalty and unswerving support of Democratic presidents.

So it was that the man whose most recent House vote on the issue, in March 1967, had been to support the war effort, now in September, switched. On every Vietnam vote from that day forward, O'Neill voted with the doves. As he said in his newsletter and repeated to his president, O'Neill had come to feel that the conflict was an Asian problem. He said the United States should avoid further escalation of hostilities, stop the bombing raids in North Vietnam, encourage stronger democratic government in South Vietnam—and turn the whole thing over to the United Nations.

O'Neill told President Johnson that he was not bowing to pressure from "crackpot students" who had demonstrated against the war in Harvard Square and burned American flags, nor to the academicians (whom he called "acadamians") in his district who had long been opposed to the war. In fact, he was convinced that the pro-war sentiment was so strong in his area that he could be defeated for reelection. "Oh, Jesus," he said, "I ran through a hard period of time. People would cross the street when they saw me coming." Polls showed only 15 percent of the voters in his district agreed with him in opposing the war. (The Twenty-sixth Amendment, extending the vote to eighteen-year-olds, hadn't yet been ratified.)

When he finished talking, O'Neill remembers that President Johnson put his arm around his shoulder and told him that he understood, that in spite of O'Neill's decision, they would always be friends. Johnson would not quarrel with him once it was clear that the congressman's position was based on a conscientious assessment of the issue rather than on political expediency. "I said [there was] nothing political to it," O'Neill said. "It hurts me. I never had the academicians with me. I still don't have them with me."

Seven months later, Johnson, beaten down by criticism and unable to resolve the continuing conflict in Vietnam, went on national television to announce the suspension of the bombing of North Vietnam and, just incidentally, to announce that he would not run for reelection.

O'Neill's position on the war made him instantly popular with many antiwar groups and, over the next few years, as antiwar sentiment grew slowly, they stopped by his office regularly. He heard, he said, from the "concerned clergy," the "concerned students," the "concerned lawyers," even the "concerned Chamber of Commerce." Finally he said he told them they were wasting their time visiting him—his position was clear, he was already on their side. In fact, the entire New England congressional delegation was lopsidedly opposed to the war. The lineup was something like 24 to 2. To one group of high-ranking clergymen one day, O'Neill suggested they try to convert someone else, the Georgia delegation, for example. And he said the way to do it was to go to Georgia. "I can't convince a man from Georgia on the war," he said. "It has to come from home."

The interesting fact is they all went down to Georgia. That's a fact. The Baptist Convention was taking place. The first crack came when the Southern Baptist Convention in Georgia voted against the war and one of the elders or something was Jack Flynt and the first guy who came out against the war was Jack Flynt, and when Jack Flynt cracked, the whole delegation fell into line within three months. And we cracked the whole South.

Flynt, who retired in 1978 after twenty-four years in the House, quarrels with some of O'Neill's facts. He is a Methodist, for one thing. And he said he reached his antiwar position much the same way O'Neill did, by asking questions and by growing more and more skeptical of the administration's position. But whether O'Neill's ministers had anything to do with it or not, when Flynt finally converted in the spring of 1971, he was able to lead a number of war loyalists away from support of the long and bloody conflict. It was two more years, however, before a majority of the House caught up with a majority of the Senate to begin voting to cut off federal funds for U.S. troops to continue fighting in Vietnam. By that time, O'Neill was clearly the man out front on the issue.

If, as O'Neill said, he expected his Vietnam position to be politically unpopular at home, it turned out to be one of his more fortunate moves in Washington. It extended his appeal far beyond the poker-playing and big-city machine politicians to a new crowd of intellectuals and doves. More building blocks of leadership were fitting into place. It may be a cliché, but true, that much success in politics comes from being in the right place at the right time. O'Neill's stand on the war put him in the right place at the right time. In turn, this led to another break, engineered by the Democratic Study Group, which won him new support among the party reformers.

As the war issue heated up in 1969 and 1970, highlighted by a massive peace march on Washington and the news of the My Lai massacre in Vietnam, antiwar congressmen were searching desperately for a way to bring the war support question to the House floor for what they called an "up or down," or recorded, vote. They were, at first, a small band, and they had been repeatedly frustrated in their vote-gathering effort. They were convinced, however, that if House members were forced to stand up in public and vote yes or no on the war, they would vote no.

The only antiwar votes in the House those days were on procedural questions, which are always hard to explain to anyone unfamiliar with the arcane workings of Congress. Procedural votes are called on technicalities rather than on substantive issues. For example, one of the first attempts at an antiwar vote in the House came in 1967 on a supplemental appropriations bill for the Defense Department. It contained $4.5 billion for Vietnam. Representative George Brown, Democrat of California, wanted to add an amendment prohibiting the Defense Department from spending the money to carry out military operations in North Vietnam. But amendments were barred. So he made a motion to recommit the bill, with instructions to add the language. Such a recommittal motion does not actually send the bill back to the committee. If approved, the motion automatically sets a vote on the amended bill. But the key vote comes on recommittal, not Vietnam. Such motions usually lose. The House still wasn't ready for the Brown amendment on March 2, 1967. He lost, 371 to 18. It was a new high for the "doves," however. Two years later, they managed to get 55 votes against a resolution commending President Nixon for trying to achieve "Peace with Justice" in Vietnam. The count was rising. And in 1970, their numbers leaped to 153 on a motion by then Representative (later Senator) Donald W. Riegle, Democrat of Michigan, instructing House conferees to accept a Senate amendment curbing military operations in Cambodia, which had been attached to a military sales bill.

But war critics still were a long way from winning a majority vote in favor of pulling out of Vietnam. A major problem was that under House rules there were no recorded votes on amendments to bills. Thus, members of Congress could duck emotional questions like Vietnam simply by not showing up. Existing rules required only that House members file up the center aisle, first the "yeas" and then the "nays," and be counted by fellow members acting as "tellers." No one, except an occasional sharp-eyed gallery visitor, ever kept track of how anyone voted. The reformers' code word became "accountability." With no official record of votes, there was no way to hold congressmen accountable for the final shape of legislation.

DSG leaders and staff director Richard P. Conlon, working on a package of rules changes with the citizens' lobby, Common Cause, finally decided to press for recorded votes on amendments. Success in Congress depends largely on merchandizing. Legislative ideas have to be packaged so they appeal to large groups of people and to their representatives in Congress. Laws seldom are enacted unless Congress sees some national consensus for action. Thus, after the Arab oil boycott in the winter of 1973–74, bills marked "emergency" became the fad—emergency jobs, emergency standby conservation powers for the president, emergency housing, and so on. There was a general feeling that emergency action was called for, and many took advantage of it. In the 1950s, when Americans worried about falling behind the Soviet Union in the Space Age, backers of federal school aid pushed through the first big education bill by naming it the National Defense

Education Act. And in 1979, when both "foreign" and "aid" were unpopular, the foreign aid bill became the International Development Cooperation Act. It happens all the time. So, when Common Cause set out to fight for something oddly called "recorded teller votes," strategists hit on the word "secret." A campaign was launched against secrecy; few congressmen were willing to defend secrecy in government, not publicly anyhow.

While Common Cause mounted a nationwide publicity campaign against "secret" House votes, arguing for accountability, the DSG started looking around for a respected bipartisan team to lead the rules fight on the floor. First, they found a conservative Republican, Charles S. Gubser of California, who had arrived at a similar position from a different direction. He thought the House should at least have a roll-call vote on amendments defeated in the "teller" votes. At the same time, O'Neill, a member of DSG but not active in the organization, spoke up in the Rules Committee in favor of recorded votes. O'Neill had tried and failed to get a recorded vote in 1969 on the Nixon Administration's plan ("Safeguard") to deploy antiballistic missiles near U.S. offensive missile sites. O'Neill had become interested in the ABM issue, the most hotly debated topic in Congress that year, because the Johnson administration was talking in 1968 of a much wider system ("Sentinel") that would have included a base near Boston. Citizens there, fearing that such an installation would attract attackers rather than scare them off, protested vigorously, and O'Neill took up the anti-ABM campaign. It had meant bucking Democratic House leaders as well as the president. He lost on an unrecorded teller vote. O'Neill was convinced, however, that if House members had been forced to vote publicly, the ABM plan would have been defeated. So DSG leaders went to O'Neill with their plan: they would do all the work, organize public opinion by holding briefings with the press, supplying editorial ideas to hometown papers and lobbying among the House members, if O'Neill would join Gubser as cosponsor of the rules change. He said yes.

As usual, O'Neill can be given little or no credit for innovation, but he does get credit for his political instincts. "I'm not a reformer. The one thing in the world I don't want to be classified as is a reformer," he said in an interview. "I'm a professional politician, and I'm proud of it." The voting reform, like others that followed in later years, was an idea that O'Neill knew instinctively should be taken up, and he did it with skill. The recorded vote amendment eventually attracted 182 cosponsors and passed easily on a voice vote along with half a dozen other procedural changes aimed at opening up the congressional system to more public scrutiny. The new rule revolutionized the place. House members had to show up for votes or be listed as absentees. The first vote under the new system was a dramatic one. After years of support for federal funding of the multi-billion-dollar supersonic transport (SST) program, the House voted to end it on March 18, 1971, 217 to 204. As O'Neill walked to the well of the House that day with his green card signed and ready to add a yes vote on killing the SST, he muttered, "This'll probably be the end of me." Representative Henry Reuss, Democrat of Wisconsin, added, "Or the beginning."

A year later—on a recorded teller vote—the antiwar forces grew to 171 in a losing effort (with 229 on the other side) to end the war by October 1, 1972. But on May 10, 1973, they finally triumphed when the House voted 219 to 188 for an amendment prohibiting the Defense Department from spending any more money on military operations in Vietnam. Congress eventually set August 15 as the war cut-off date.

Within the next few years, however, the teller vote "reform" turned into something of a monster. The amendment process, with recorded votes possible on each motion, became a tool for harassment and delay. A congressman opposed to a particular piece of legislation would simply draft dozens of amendments and then proceed to call them up one by one and demand a record vote each time. Often, just the threat of such a tactic would sidetrack a bill. By 1980, O'Neill was saying mildly, "I think it's gotten out of hand," and a Rules Committee study was launched to seek a new reform of the old one.

O'Neill the politician was recruited by the DSG and Common Cause to lead two other liberal reform efforts in the early 1970s. One was a motion in the Democratic Caucus instructing the Foreign Affairs Committee to send to the House floor an antiwar resolution which had long been bottled up in the pro-war committee. The procedure worked but the resolution was ultimately defeated. The other was to provide for automatic Caucus votes on committee chairmen. Until then, the seniority system—in its time imposed as a "reform" in the 1910 revolt against the tyrannical Speaker "Uncle Joe" Cannon—was rigidly in place; the most senior member of a committee became its chairman. With the institution of Caucus votes, few chairmen were actually toppled but all were put on notice that it could happen to any one of them.

The DSG's Conlon explained the group's philosophy in asking O'Neill to take the lead: "We get the ideas. We think them through. We work with other members. Then we sit down and ask who's the best one to carry it out." All too often, reformers are viewed as wild-eyed radicals; when they insist on hogging the spotlight, they frequently lose. O'Neill and DSG were well matched for these early reforms. O'Neill needed issues to attract wider support in the House; the DSG needed a winner. Conlon, though not uncritical of O'Neill, is respectful: "When he sees the train is moving, he grabs the controls."

By this time, Congress was a year-round job. The ninety-first Congress set some kind of record, adjourning in 1969 on December 23, while in 1970 it ran on past the end of the year to adjourn the second session on January 2, 1971. O'Neill, with few legislative responsibilities and fiercely proud of Congress as an institution, had the time and the inclination to become involved in several efforts to strengthen the House and improve its national image. It helped to have Republican Richard Nixon in the White House, for it's always easier for congressional Democrats to assert themselves against a Republican president than against a Democratic one. Nixon, who had beaten one of the Democratic Party's best-loved leaders, Hubert H. Humphrey, in 1968, had the dubious distinction of being the first president since Zachary Taylor to fail to win control of Congress when first winning the presidency. Nixon soon developed a habit of trying to reverse the acts of Congress with vetoes or impoundments of appropriated funds. These actions, along with the realization that the United States had slid into a conflict in Asia without any declaration of war by Congress, provoked Congress into a gradual reassertion of congressional power, with O'Neill among the leaders. At stake were the kinds of issues that intrigued O'Neill: the Constitution gave Congress the power to raise and spend money and the power to declare war, powers that had slowly shifted into the hands of strong presidents. How could Congress counter that shift? O'Neill became a consistent and forceful advocate of bills to tip the balance back toward Capitol Hill, bills that eventually became the War Powers Act and the Budget and Impoundment Act.

For O'Neill, everything seemed to be dropping into place. His public image by the end of 1970 was a mix of old pol and liberal, reform-minded war critic. It was a smooth enough mix to assure him an easy reelection in the Eighth Congressional District. By then, those who had been angry with him for shifting on the Vietnam War, had begun switching themselves. And the super-liberals at the other end of his district, who thought he had been too slow to change on the war or who just didn't like his style, found themselves woefully outnumbered. Sam Brown, the former Harvard divinity student and antiwar activist, talked of running against O'Neill in the Democratic primary. But he was quickly dissuaded. "That's just about the silliest thing I ever heard," said one Democrat. "Tip can't be beat." In November, O'Neill was elected to his tenth term without opposition.

O'Neill had no glamorous illusions about his appeal to the voters, however, and told this story on himself several times:

There's a banquet in my state and I'm sharing the platform with our two senators who are, of course, famous. Afterwards, two hundred people come up and ask for Ted Kennedy's autograph. Two hundred come up and ask for Ed Brooke's autograph. And eighteen come up and ask me for a favor.

Although still close to Speaker John McCormack in this period, O'Neill had begun to move on a more independent course. McCormack, for one thing, continued to defend the Vietnam War. For that, and for other reasons, many felt McCormack was out of touch with the changing times. He was rooted in the New Deal liberalism of the 1930s and 1940s, and as he advanced toward age eighty, he drew more and more criticism from younger members. Richard Bolling, who had never shared the warm relationship with McCormack that he had with Rayburn, was one of the first to speak out openly against the Speaker. In October 1967, Bolling said McCormack had failed to provide the House with the kind of leadership needed to enact a strong Democratic legislative program. He called for McCormack's resignation as Speaker at the end of the next year. By that time, Bolling, as the unofficial philosopher of congressional leadership, had written two books on the subject. He made a compelling case for changes in rules and procedures—many of which were adopted over the next few years—to strengthen the House Democratic leadership, particularly the Speaker.

Younger members had trouble identifying with McCormack. He was twice as old as many of them. And he looked 150. Bony and deathly pale, with wispy white hair and an ever-present cigar dripping ashes on his dark three-piece suits, McCormack just did not seem like one of the boys. Many House members chafed at the image of a bland and aging House that McCormack projected.

One, Arizona Representative Morris K. Udall, even had the nerve to try to do something about it. Udall ran against McCormack for Speaker in 1969. He knew that in this hidebound institution, he had very little chance of upsetting the Speaker, but he felt it was a challenge that needed to be made. He even offered to step aside—if he got more votes than McCormack—to allow the Democrats to have a new and open election among all who might be interested. A witty and intelligent congressman with strong support among the younger members, Udall discovered that was not enough. He was asking his fellow Democrats to throw out an old man who had served as Speaker since 1962. It didn't work. McCormack won the nomination, 178 to 58.

The grumbling didn't stop, however. An angry Jerome Waldie, who later quit Congress to run unsuccessfully for governor of California, picked up the anti-McCormack theme and went public with it a year later. First, in a newsletter to his Sacramento area constituents, Waldie complained: "I no longer will remain a quiet, cooperative cog in a machine pretending that all is not as bad as it may seem—because, in fact, it is worse than it seems." Then, in a direct confrontation with McCormack, he sought a "vote of no confidence" against the Speaker in a Democratic Caucus. He protested that McCormack was unresponsive to the needs of the 1970s and that the House itself "sadly has become irrelevant."

Waldie failed to win much Caucus support. The Democrats voted 192 to 23 to table—thus kill— the resolution. But what Waldie did not know was that it no longer mattered. At that very moment, McCormack was being effectively defeated by his own trusted aide, Martin Sweig. McCormack's instinctive reaction to the growing criticism among House Democrats had been to announce he would seek a fifth term as Speaker. But, even as he did so, a federal grand jury was deciding in New York that Sweig and a Washington lobbyist named Nathan M. Voloshen should be indicted for perjury and influence peddling. Sweig had been McCormack's $36,000-a-year administrative assistant. McCormack, busy trying to run the House of Representatives, had given Sweig a free hand running the Speaker's office. It had become a hangout for men hoping that some of the power of the office would brush off on them, men like Voloshen whose clients did business with the government. Sweig was known as a man who could pick up the phone and, in a remarkable imitation of McCormack's Boston accent, call a government agency and say something like: "This is the Speaker . . . and I'd like to ask you to do a favor for a friend . . ." Other hangers on might try the same gambit, saying, "This is so-and-so calling from the Speaker's office." Eventually the world of influence and power collapsed around Sweig and Voloshen when they were found out. The two men were charged with trying to fix a case before the Securities and Exchange Commission. Sweig resigned from McCormack's office in October 1969. He was indicted in January 1970, convicted of perjury in July, and sent up a year later to begin serving a two-and-a-half-year prison term. Voloshen pleaded guilty to charges of conspiring to use the Speaker's office to influence matters before federal government agencies and then lying about it. He was fined $10,000 and given a one-year suspended prison term. McCormack, although apparently guilty only of sloppiness in running his office, announced on May 20, 1970, that he would not run again, either for the House or for Speaker. "My life," he kept saying, "is an open book. You know that."

Curiously, McCormack never really seemed to understand what had gone wrong, and his style in those last months was unchanged. Two months after Sweig was forced to quit, *Congressional Quarterly* reporter Alan Ehrenhalt watched in amazement as McCormack casually offered the use of his private office and telephone to G. W. Vaughan, a registered lobbyist since 1967 for the Union Camp Corp., a paper and paperboard company. Ehrenhalt reported that Vaughan came to the Speaker's office with the late Representative George W. Andrews, Democrat of Alabama, who introduced him to the Speaker as someone with a manufacturing plant in Massachusetts as well as Alabama. Andrews hesitated at first but McCormack insisted. So the two visitors used the phone while the Speaker left to preside over the House.

"You don't know who's using your name or who's peddling your name around," McCormack insisted later to reporters. "You always find out after the fact. It could happen to anybody."

O'Neill made a mental note. He would clean out the hangers-on from his office.

8

ON TO THE LEADERSHIP
LADDER

SEVEN MONTHS after McCormack announced his intention to resign as Speaker of the House, on December 22, 1970, Representative Dan Rostenkowski, the Chicago Democrat known as Mayor Richard Daley's man in the House, invited five of his fellow Democrats to lunch in the high-ceilinged room once known as the "Board of Education." Rostenkowski was chairman of the Democratic Caucus, and he wanted to work out some details in advance for the nomination of a new majority leader at the January Caucus session. The men he invited to lunch were the five announced candidates—Democratic Whip Hale Boggs of Louisiana, Udall of Arizona, James G. O'Hara of Michigan, Wayne L. Hays of Ohio, and B. F. Sisk of California. O'Neill wasn't even mentioned.

All five were veteran congressmen who felt they had waited long enough for leadership rewards and whose home districts were secure enough to enable them to spend more time in Washington on internal House politics. On a strict seniority basis, Boggs topped the list. He had been first elected to the House in 1940 as a twenty-six-year-old boy wonder from New Orleans. The next time around he lost, and went to war, returning to the House in 1947. Sisk, at sixty, was the oldest of the group and the most acceptable to conservatives. A native of Texas, he had, as a young man, moved to California, where he was elected to the House in 1954. His candidacy surprised many observers and was said to have been engineered by southerners unhappy with Boggs. Hays, fifty-nine, was the outspoken "bad boy" among the contenders, a globe-trotting member of the House Foreign Affairs Committee, in line, after twenty-two years in the House, to head the House Administration Committee. Hays was candid about his reason for running: he just thought he was smarter than the rest.

Politically, Udall and O'Hara were the most liberal; chronologically, they were the youngest and least experienced. Udall at forty-eight had been in the House ten years. O'Hara at forty-five had served fourteen years. Both were attractive, articulate, and popular among their colleagues. Of the two,

116

Udall worked the hardest on his majority leader campaign and appeared to be the frontrunner. He started with a core of younger members who had supported his ill-fated tilt with McCormack two years earlier. Some of his popularity no doubt was connected to his widely appreciated service in 1969 when he established an automatic pay-raise system that had lifted Congressional salaries from $30,000 to $42,500 a year without the embarrassment of a vote that might be interpreted back home as self-serving. (It worked only that one time, incidentally. Pay-raise critics found a way to force roll-call votes in future years as salaries took a giant leap to the 1979 levels of more than $60,000.) But Udall had a fatal flaw for a liberal Democrat, according to one significant outside force, organized labor. In 1965, he had voted against repeal of Section 14(b) of the Taft-Hartley Act that permitted states to enact right-to-work laws barring the union shop. Labor leaders have long memories and strong support in Congress. They were now backing O'Hara, whose pro-labor record was perfect and who, when it came time to step aside in the majority leader race, did not endorse Udall.

Rostenkowski started off the December meeting by announcing that he would not join the five as a sixth candidate. It was not because of lack of ambition; Rostenkowski had, in fact, toyed earlier with the idea of running for Speaker against the present Majority Leader Carl Albert. He simply recognized political reality. Any one of the five men in the room could beat him; all had been campaigning for months. One, Udall, had announced his candidacy the day Speaker McCormack said he would be stepping down. Rostenkowski said he would stick, instead, with his Caucus position.

The meeting went smoothly enough. The men were all professionals engaged in a special kind of political contest, vying for votes among their colleagues, gathering pledges of support from members of Congress anxious not to back a loser. There was speculation that some House members had already promised a vote to each one of them. Who could know for sure? The vote would be taken by secret ballot.

All the five could do at the December luncheon was protect themselves from any other "dark horse" candidates entering at the last minute. So, among the rules they agreed on was one limiting the contest to previously announced candidates who would be formally nominated at the opening of the January Caucus.

After the meeting, Rostenkowski ran into Tip O'Neill. "I want you to know we gave you a screwing," he said. "You're not as smart as you think you are."

"Why, Danny?"

"Because we just passed a resolution that any votes for a candidate will not be counted unless his name is put in nomination." And it was too late for that. If O'Neill had wanted to run for majority leader, he had hesitated too long.

I had been talking to people like [Hugh] Carey and other fellas. I knew I had a good following in the House. And if it became stalemated, I knew that on the first ballot, I'd get a dozen votes without my name ever having been put in nomination. Nothing formal, but there were twenty fellas who had said we will vote with you on the first ballot and then pick up a little more. We think we can do it.

The reasons for O'Neill's hesitation can be traced to some basic facets of his political personality. First of all, typically, he was reluctant to challenge the established order of things. Traditionally, Democratic House leaders moved up in an orderly line. The whip became majority leader, and the majority leader became Speaker. There was no question in 1971 that Albert would move up to Speaker. He was inoffensive if not dynamic, and he had served faithfully and quietly as McCormack's lieutenant. The question then for the Democrats in January was whether the whip, Hale Boggs, should be elected majority leader. Boggs had attracted criticism on a number of fronts. Conservative southerners objected to his liberal voting record. Some found him aloof and arrogant. But, perhaps more significantly, there were allegations of instability, that he drank too much or had some mysterious physical problem requiring medicine that made him act strange. Though articulate and amiable most of the time, Boggs would drift off into rambling incoherent discourses that caused some of his supporters to have second thoughts about whether he should move any further up the leadership ladder. By the time McCormack stepped down, the *National Journal* published a poll of House Democrats rating the leadership ability among the more prominent members. Boggs came in seventh behind former Representative Wilbur D. Mills of Arkansas, Albert, Udall, Bolling, O'Hara, and former Representative Donald M. Fraser of Minnesota, in that order.

By the fall of 1971, Udall seemed to be the front runner for majority leader. His projections, based on what he considered hard core commitments, showed him well ahead of the others. He figured he would have eighty-five first-ballot votes to fifty-five each for O'Hara and Boggs. The congressional November election appeared to boost his cause. The Democrats won a net gain of nine seats, making the party lineup 255 to 180. Of the thirty-three new Democrats, six had defeated older Establishment-minded members who would have been likely Boggs votes. No one conceded anything, however, and Boggs went to work on his image. First, he showed he could be charming and gracious, in a series of receptions for Democrats at his Maryland home. Then he showed he could work hard and ably, as the House stayed in session until past the end of the year.

O'Neill watched with interest. If Boggs was to be dumped for majority leader, O'Neill wanted to be in the running for majority leader himself. If not, he wanted to get on the next rung of the ladder as whip. The whip was to be appointed by the new Speaker and majority leader. O'Neill had already paved the way with Albert: on the day McCormack resigned and Albert announced his candidacy for Speaker, O'Neill had rounded up the signatures of Massachusetts Democratic congressmen in a letter endorsing Albert. It wasn't so much a gesture of admiration as it was a pledge of support for the regular order of things. O'Neill called it "Massachusetts-style" politics: you get written pledges.

O'Neill, however, had another problem. His roommate, Eddie Boland, was thinking of running for majority leader. O'Neill had promised him that as long as Boland might be a candidate, he would stay out of the way. Shortly after McCormack's announcement, Boston newsmen were saying that Boland was "quietly maneuvering" for the leadership post. He himself was quoted as saying, however, that it was too soon to say anything publicly. Boland's name had come up ahead of O'Neill's several months earlier when a group of liberal Democrats, trying to talk McCormack into retiring, suggested they would support Boland, one of McCormack's protégés, for the leadership. At that time, Boland was chairman of the transportation subcommittee on Appropriations while O'Neill was still only midway up the seniority list on the Rules Committee. Boland also was more attractive to the activist liberals because of his earlier ties to the Kennedy administration.

But summer passed and then autumn, and Boland never pursued his vote roundup actively. In Congressional politics, as in all politics, elections are won by those who go out and ask for votes. Boland hesitated, apparently hoping that the more aggressive candidates would falter and he would emerge as a logical compromise. Finally, in December, Boland announced he would not be a candidate and would support Udall. Although there was nothing in writing, Boland understood that he would probably be appointed whip if Udall won. By that time, it was too late for O'Neill to get into the race for the whip job. That fact, it turned out, was another lucky break for O'Neill.

Meanwhile, Boggs had gained in confidence as the Caucus date approached. He began using, very subtly, the office of whip as a lure for supporters in his campaign to be majority leader. Boland recalled one conversation. "Boggs said to me, 'You know, that whip job's wide open.'"

But Boland told Boggs he was committed to Udall. At the same time, Rostenkowski, who had had dozens of conversations with Boggs over various leadership-related matters during the previous six months, was made to feel confident he would be Boggs's choice for whip. They had decided not to announce anything publicly for fear of the appearance of bossism or political dealing. With a week to go before the Caucus, however, Boggs still felt he needed stronger support among Northeasterners. He called O'Neill, in an attempt to find out who he would support now that Boland was no longer in the running. O'Neill said he responded, as he often did over the years, with the story of Mrs. O'Brien and his first, unsuccessful, race for the Cambridge City Council when she had reminded him that everyone likes to be asked for their votes.

Boggs took the hint. He asked for O'Neill's support, and he got it. As Boggs hung up the phone after talking to O'Neill, he turned to his administrative assistant Gary Hymel and said, "I've just been elected leader. O'Neill can deliver more votes because of his personality and popularity among fellows not committed to anyone. It's all over. I've got it won." Boggs immediately sent O'Neill a list of twenty five Democrats to contact and try to win over.

On the first ballot the votes were Boggs, 95; Udall, 69; Sisk, 31; Hays, 28; O'Hara, 25. Hays and O'Hara immediately withdrew, with Hays endorsing Boggs. Boggs needed only 125 to win. The second ballot vote was Boggs, 140; Udall, 88; Sisk, 17.

Carl Albert was nominated for Speaker at the same session over only token opposition from Representative John Conyers, Democrat of Michigan, who managed to gather up only 20 votes to 220 for Albert.

Known as "the Little Giant from Little Dixie" because of his short stature and because he came from the southeast corner of Oklahoma, Albert had first been elected to Congress in 1946, the same year as John Kennedy and Richard Nixon. Unlike the other two, however, Albert decided to make his career in the House. He arrived with impressive academic credentials: he was a lawyer and a Rhodes scholar. He was almost immediately welcomed into the exclusive circle of Sam Rayburn, whose northeast Texas district was just across the state line from Albert's. Despite this benign guidance, Albert had had to wait twenty-four years to win the top prize of Speaker. Oddly enough, when he finally became Speaker, he seemed to lose all his steam. He had trouble establishing credibility among his colleagues, partly because he continued to support the Vietnam War long after most Democrats had backed off and partly because of his general image of indecisiveness. He wore an anxious look much of the time. He was hesitant to make decisions, distrustful of the press, uncomfortable in the spotlight. Always eager to please, he wanted to say yes to all sides. It was to get him into trouble as Speaker right from the beginning.

The morning after the Democratic Caucus, Albert, Boggs, and a few other House strategists met in Boggs' whip office (they wouldn't be formally elected Speaker and majority leader until the Ninety-second Congress convened the next day) to decide what next to do. Rostenkowski arrived late. He had suffered a surprise defeat in the Caucus when Representative Olin "Tiger" Teague of Texas was elected Caucus chairman. Rostenkowski found himself on the outside of the leadership group and he was anxious to nail down a commitment from Boggs for the whip assignment. The discussion that morning circled around the question and reached no decision other than to put off the announcement of majority whip for a couple of days. Boggs favored Rostenkowski, but Albert was flatly opposed to him. The public reason given later for why Rostenkowski did not get the whip job was that he had just been rejected by his own party for Caucus chairman. It would look strange if the elected leaders then turned around and rewarded him with something else. In truth, however, Albert opposed Rostenkowski for a simple political reason: the Illinois congressman, leader of his state delegation, had not supported Albert for Speaker. Rostenkowski's anti-Albert position came straight from Mayor Daley, no pal of Albert's, and harked back to the 1968 Democratic National Convention when Albert, as chairman, had been unable to control either the unruly antiwar crowds or the unruly Daley delegates.

While Albert and Boggs discussed their own strategy, there was talk among some of the younger Democrats that the whip should not be appointed at all, but should be elected. Recent history had shown that without fail the whip moved up to majority leader and then to Speaker. It didn't seem right that someone should be able to get on the leadership escalator without an initial vote by all Democrats.

As Albert left the breakfast meeting, reporters waiting outside started asking him questions. One wanted to know what he thought of the idea of an elected whip. He responded, quite casually, that he was not opposed and that, in fact, it might not be a bad idea at all. The word spread quickly: Albert would go for an elected whip. Knots of Democrats met in hurried meetings to decide what to do next. Wayne Hays might be a candidate, or Mo Udall, or the tough-talking Phillip Burton of San Francisco, who was in line to become chairman of the Democratic Study Group. Meanwhile, O'Neill and Hugh Carey sought out Hale Boggs for a meeting of their own.

The three of them quickly located the new Speaker and moved off into a small Ways and Means Committee hearing room just off the House floor. Boggs, O'Neill, and Carey were flabbergasted; they wondered whether Albert had been misquoted. O'Neill put into words what the others were thinking.

This is absolutely ridiculous. I cannot believe it. This is wrong. How do you know who's going to win? You have to have a man for whip from your own team. Furthermore, he's the fella that does the errands. He's the fella that does the checking. He's the fella that stimulates the members. He's the fella that gives you accuracy. He's got to be part of your team. He's got to be handpicked.

Albert frowned, upset at finding himself in the middle of a controversy even before his formal election as Speaker. But he could not stand up to the unanimous and outspoken views of the others in the room. He really had no firm position on the issue, anyhow; he would go along with whatever they decided. When Albert left this meeting, only twenty-four hours after he had backed the proposal to elect the whip, he was now saying, all right, we'll oppose it.

The discussion returned to square one: who was to be *appointed* whip? O'Neill once more thought of Mrs. O'Brien. He talked to his wife Millie: "Tom," Mrs. O'Neill is said to have told him, "you've been telling that Mrs. O'Brien story for thirty-five years. Why don't *you* go ask for that job?" O'Neill went to Boggs and asked. He knew that Boggs still favored Rostenkowski, but he wanted to make it clear that he was interested, too.

The Albert-Boggs stalemate over Rostenkowski persisted. Boggs still wanted to appoint Rostenkowski, but Albert said no. He said he favored Udall. Boggs said no. Finally, Boggs turned to his aide, Hymel, and asked him to draw up a list of any Democrats who would meet the requirements of loyalty and would provide geographic balance to a leadership team topped by Oklahoma and Louisiana. Hymel came back with a list of eight names, three from the East, three from the Midwest, and two from the West.

On Friday morning, Boggs took the list to Albert. Overnight, news stories were speculating that the frontrunners were Carey and O'Neill. Mrs. O'Neill called Tip from Boston and asked why he hadn't called her. She said she would have come to Washington for the occasion. O'Neill said he didn't think he'd win: "Huey Carey has his wife and thirteen kids in the gallery," he said, "so I have to presume Albert already has notified him to come over."

What O'Neill did not know was that some senior members of the New York delegation had complained to Albert and Boggs that Carey was overambitious, that he was trying to run the New York delegation and shove some of the older members aside. Albert took a look at Hymel's list, crossed out three names, and said any of the other five would be acceptable. In effect, however, he was choosing O'Neill. Boggs would be expected to eliminate the others for one reason or another, Boland and Udall, for example, because they had opposed him for majority leader. It probably also had occurred to Boggs that O'Neill, a big-city ethnic politician with liberal credentials, would be the perfect choice. The House Democratic leadership could satisfy two major blocs at once.

I went back over to my office. The telephone rang. It was the Speaker [Albert]. And he says, "Tip, Hale wants to talk to you. He wants you to be majority whip. Come on over right away. We want to announce it in front of television." I went over. I had on a blue shirt and a red tie. He says, "Ha, ha, you were expecting it. You were all dressed for television." But actually I wasn't expecting it.

Representative John McFall, Democrat of California, an assistant whip under Boggs, saw O'Neill a few minutes later in the hall and said, "Congratulations. Let's go over to the whip office."
"Ok," said O'Neill. "Where's that?"

For years, Democratic whips had done little more than stand and wait. Formally part of the leadership, they were third in line, and were always included in the functions reserved to House leaders, like regular White House meetings with the president. To that extent, they were members of the special club within the congressional club. But because they were appointed, not elected, there was a subtle difference in their standing among House Democrats. They could not act as a spokesman for the larger group, as the Speaker and majority leader could; they simply served at the pleasure of those two. It was like the difference between the owner of a company and a salaried—and trusted—aide to the owner. The whip's principal assignment was, and remains, to round up votes on major pieces of legislation. It is a two-way communications system: in the process of vote-counting, the whip is expected to pick up valuable intelligence on House moods and attitudes to pass along to the Speaker, his boss.

Until O'Neill became whip, the office was largely unstructured. As whip, Boggs had conducted weekly meetings with the dozen or so zone whips who represented various regions of the country. Each zone whip was assigned ten to twenty Democrats, usually from more than one state, to keep track of. But the Boggs meetings were more like informal coffee klatches than hard-nosed political strategy sessions. For most of the time Boggs served as whip, Lyndon Johnson was in the White House, and Johnson ran his own vote-counting system through the congressional liaison office. "I doubt," said McFall, California zone whip under Boggs, "that Hale ever really counted votes. Lyndon Johnson did it."

Tip O'Neill as whip was a natural extension of Tip O'Neill as Rules Committee member. He did the same thing, only in a more systematic way and with the added prestige and visibility of a member of the leadership. He was still taking care of his friends but the list of friends grew to include nearly all Democrats. His fascination with voter statistics and opinion polls had never lessened. As whip, he had an opportunity to extend this interest to the full House of Representatives. He soon became an expert in understanding the changing moods of the House. Operating with a small staff in two rooms and a hallway on the first floor of the Capitol, he soon reshaped the whip operation in his own image.

I took the whip organization and really made it into something. It had been nothing. We made the meetings on Thursday mornings attractive, first by giving them orange juice, donuts, and coffee, and, secondly, by having chairmen come down and explain the legislation, and thirdly, by insisting that Albert and Boggs be there. In the old days, the leadership never came. There was no incentive for anyone else to come.

O'Neill started off by naming two deputy whips, McFall, and Indiana Representative John Brademas. McFall had gravitated toward the Democratic leadership while McCormack had been Speaker. He often hung around the Speaker's office, helping out as needed. A pleasant, soft-spoken lawyer, McFall said his interest was in learning how the House and its leaders operated. He was one of a small group of House members who were willing to stay close to the House floor (despite the dullness of much of the debate) and act as one of the Speaker's lieutenants. He had been an early supporter of Albert for Speaker and was one of the names mentioned as a possible whip choice. McFall had also lined up the California delegation for Boggs. Brademas was picked for balance, both geographically and philosophically. He was viewed as one of the comers in the House, a relatively young (forty-three) and hard-working Democrat who had first been elected in 1958. Like Albert, he was a Rhodes scholar. He was one of the leaders on the Education and Labor Committee, which handled many bills important to the development of Democratic Party policy. O'Neill's aims by selecting these deputies were to establish closer ties with the Western congressmen through McFall and with the younger activists through Brademas.

O'Neill ran the whip office with an unlikely pair of professional staff aides. One was Leo Diehl, his oldest and closest friend from Massachusetts.

The day O'Neill was told he'd be whip, he called Diehl in Boston and said he wanted him to come to Washington to run the whip office. "I said, 'Geez, Tom, this is such a vast change for me, I'm in the tax department.' He said, 'Yeah, I figured you'd say that. So I already told the governor you've resigned.'" Diehl went to Washington and soon was ensconced in the spacious whip's office as O'Neill's administrative assistant. Assisting Diehl as legislative assistant was a pretty girl just out of college, Linda Melconian, who had worked while at Mount Holyoke College as an intern in Eddie Boland's office.

Remembering Martin Sweig and Nat Voloshen, O'Neill's first order to Diehl when he got to Washington was: clean out the hangers-on around the whip's office.

The old McCormack crowd that had followed him around for years thought they had a resting place when I became whip . . . for forty years, if anyone came down from Boston and didn't have a place to hang his hat, he'd hang it in McCormack's office. That was his style, and that was kind of my style. But after what happened [to McCormack], we didn't want to get involved anymore.

O'Neill was publicly embarrassed by this old easygoing style only once in those years. The Senate Foreign Relations Committee had been investigating the activities of U.S. lobbyists for foreign governments. On May 6, 1963, the committee summoned Martin Camacho, a naturalized American born in Portugal who had become a leader of the Portuguese community in Boston. Along the way, he also had become a close political ally of O'Neill. He could, as O'Neill explained later, deliver votes. In those early days of O'Neill's political career, an ethnic leader like Camacho could swing hundreds of votes just by passing the word in the close-packed immigrant neighborhoods. (As their children grew up in the United States and became more politically sophisticated, however, that was no longer the case.) Camacho was also a friend. It seemed only natural that when he came to Washington, he would go by O'Neill's office to "hang his hat." Camacho testified that he often used O'Neill's office phone, had O'Neill's secretaries write letters for him, drafted pro-Portuguese statements for O'Neill to deliver on the House floor, and even, on one occasion, used O'Neill franked (free-mail) envelopes to send out several thousand copies of a pamphlet reprinting the Camacho-drafted statements of O'Neill and others. "Yessir," Camacho told the Senate committee, "I used his office the same as if I were in my own office. That I used his staff the same as if I were in my own office, he will tell you that . . . Senator, I paid nothing." But Camacho wasn't just helping out some hometown constituents. What he hadn't told O'Neill was that he was working as a publicity agent for a group financed by the Portuguese government.

Fortunately for O'Neill, the story received little or no publicity.

Even so, O'Neill found it difficult to tell old friends they couldn't use his office. There were others, Peter Cloherty, for example. He had worked in John Kennedy's first House campaign, in 1946, and served in the state legislature. As a representative of a large construction company, he often went to Washington—and O'Neill's office. A secretary there remembered only that he had a beautiful singing voice. O'Neill was very fond of him.

O'Neill didn't want to offend any old friends but he also didn't want to run the risk of having a Sweig-Voloshen situation develop that could blast away his hopes for moving up the leadership ladder. Leo Diehl was the obvious architect of the new policy. "And so it worked," Diehl said. "They would come in and if I challenged somebody on whether to pick up the phone or something like that, they understood what I was talking about. They knew we [O'Neill and Diehl] had a close association."

There was a back room in the whip office where visitors could go and nobody would know they were around. Some of the old crowd of hangers-on who had been following McCormack and O'Neill around for years started congregating there when O'Neill was named whip. The first thing Diehl did was to take out the telephones. With the phones gone, there was little for them to do, no way to "conduct business," and they slowly drifted off.

Together, O'Neill, Diehl, and Melconian whipped the whip office into shape. "We turned the whip office into a real service organization," Ms. Melconian said. "We saw that information went from the leaders to the members of Congress, and vice versa." O'Neill, big and amiable, with a humorous anecdote to fit every occasion, soon became the focal point for miscellaneous problems and complaints, ranging from committee assignments to office space. At the same time, information began flowing from his office to House members in the form of weekly whip notices of upcoming legislation, assembled in packets with copies of the bills, resolutions, amendments, and, as available, Republican substitutes included. It was the first time the Democratic leadership had put together such information packets. There had been little previous communication between leaders and members. Rayburn wanted no such help; he ran the House with a handful of friends from the "Board of Education." McCormack had never thought of it; he ran the House out of his coat pocket, notes scribbled on scraps of paper, relying on men like McFall and O'Neill to keep him informed. Albert welcomed the O'Neill system and broadened the base of participation in

legislative decisions among House members. Future whips would expand
the O'Neill plan to include daily notices of bills due on the House floor each
day and regular summaries of Democratic legislative "accomplishments"
printed on pocket-sized speech cards for ready reference on home district
visits.

While whip, O'Neill never strayed far—legislatively or philosophically—from his home district. He was still a Tuesday-Thursday man,
and unlike most congressmen who move up to a leadership position, O'Neill
did not shift his base of operations to the whip office in the Capitol. Diehl
worked in the whip's office but O'Neill continued to work out of Room 2231
in the Rayburn Office Building. He had moved there from the old Cannon
Building in 1965, and he liked it. When Office Manager Dolores Snow
suggested moving to an office more convenient to the House floor, O'Neill
resisted: "We've had good luck here," he said.

Ironically, though the record shows that O'Neill seldom budged from a
proud provincialism during these years in Congress, one hometown
opponent, Jack P. Ricciardi, campaigned against him with the charge that he
was an "absentee congressman" who failed to initiate or sponsor major
legislation and who merely acted as a "rubber stamp" for more imaginative
colleagues. Ricciardi charged that the District had suffered a "decade of
indifference." O'Neill must have been amused at the charges, for few
congressmen spent more time than he on their home turfs. Nor was he
bothered by allegations that he failed to sponsor much significant legislation.
"In Congress," he said years later in a *Yankee* magazine interview, "I love
the maneuverability. I love the basic Democratic Party philosophy. I enjoy
the whip organization, the policy committee, the caucuses, better than I
enjoy the actual legislation on the floor itself. It's being able to set priorities
and find a way out of a dilemma."

In 1972, he would get a chance to test these political skills sooner than
anticipated.

In the early evening hours of Monday, October 16, 1972, wire service
machines clattered in the nearly empty newsrooms in Washington, D. C.
There was a brief item out of Anchorage, Alaska: "A light plane carrying
Democratic House Majority Leader Hale Boggs, 58, a veteran of 26 years in
Congress, disappeared tonight in a rainstorm on a flight from here to
Juneau."

The news reached Boggs's wife, Lindy, shortly before 9:00 P.M. when
Speaker Albert phoned and said he had just heard from the White House.
Federal aviation officials would do all they could, Albert assured her, to try

to find the plane. Over the next thirty-nine days, dozens of civilian and military aircraft searched the rugged Chugach Mountains and the rocky Alaska coastline—in vain. There were brief flickers of hope, a report here of a crash, a report there of a faint radio signal. Alaskans, hardened to the harshness of their land, told stories of men stumbling out of the wilderness months after a plane crash. But there was no sign anywhere of the Boggs plane, its pilot, or two other passengers, Representative Nicholas J. Begich and an aide. All had vanished without a trace. One by one, the searchers gave up and went home.

Boggs had been on a forty-eight-hour round trip to Alaska to make two fund-raising speeches for Begich, a freshman congressman. The trip was full of ironies and what-ifs. Begich, though new in Congress, was not in the kind of political trouble where the party's big guns ordinarily are needed to give a campaign lift. In the August primary, he had collected more than twice the number of votes of two Republican opponents combined. The experts said he'd be an easy winner in November. Also, it was an inefficient use of Boggs' time, a long, hurried trip over a two-day weekend break. When plans for the trip were first made, they had thought it would be more leisurely. Congress usually adjourns early in an election year. But this time, the Democratic lawmakers had been bickering with the Republican president—and among themselves—over spending ceilings and vetoes. The House worked past midnight Saturday, and Boggs caught an 9:00 A.M. flight for Alaska Sunday morning. He was due back in Washington Tuesday morning for what everyone hoped would be the last days of the Ninety-second Congress.

In Washington, after the first shock of the plane's disappearance and uncertainty over whether Boggs was dead or alive had passed, the inevitable political talk began: who would succeed him? It was awkward. No one wanted to offend anyone else: they especially did not want to hurt Lindy Boggs, who had been an active partner in Hale Boggs's political career and who was widely respected among House members.

Political scientist Robert L. Peabody of Johns Hopkins University has noted that traditional congressional leadership patterns of succession almost invariably are reinforced when a vacancy is caused by serious illness or death while Congress is in session. In their grief or shock, House members rally around something solid and familiar—the old way of doing things. In this case, the old way of doing things was to promote the majority whip to majority leader. Once again, the next rung on the ladder was clear for Tip O'Neill.

O'Neill was personally popular; his fellow Democrats thought he had done a good job in his twenty-two months as whip. As chairman of the Democratic National Congressional Committee, he had raised sizeable campaign funds and doled the money out evenhandedly (a nice political advantage of a DNCC chairmanship is that the checks are signed by the chairman); finally, in the closing days of the Ninety-second Congress, O'Neill had served as "acting majority leader," definitely a psychological advantage over the other candidates.

O'Neill worried about how to proceed. Two weeks went by with no traces of the Boggs plane or of its passengers. Should he go ahead and announce that he would be a candidate? Would that offend Lindy Boggs? If he failed to move, would that encourage others to get ahead of him? The old O'Neill formula was thwarted. He could not ask for pledges of support if he couldn't announce that he was a candidate for anything.

The break came election night, November 7. With Boggs and Begich still unaccounted for but not declared dead, the two were elected to the Ninety-third Congress. Boggs was unopposed; Begich won 56 percent of the vote over Republican Don Young, who later won the seat in a special election. O'Neill watched the returns on television in his office, picking up the phone from time to time to congratulate a winner. During the evening, Gary Hymel and Boggs's oldest son, Thomas Hale Boggs, Jr., came by. They said they understood his problem and would help. They arranged for O'Neill to talk to Lindy Boggs the next morning. In her gracious way, she told O'Neill that they should both be practical, that if the roles had been reversed, Hale Boggs would want to get started on the new campaign.

O'Neill wasted no time. With Gary Hymel by his side and three secretaries putting in telephone calls around the country, O'Neill launched his campaign. Pointedly, to each Democrat he mentioned that young Boggs was with him, giving him the Boggs family stamp of approval.

With each call O'Neill said he was, as he put it, "leveling with them." He told them Boggs might be found alive—"if it is the Lord's will and I hope that it is"—but, if not, he said the Democrats must have a leader. He promised Lindy Boggs that if her husband were found alive, he would gladly step aside. By dinner time, O'Neill had 63 firm commitments of the 121 needed to win in the Democratic Caucus. "I'm so amazed at the support I'm getting," he said. "It's beautiful."

He added 46 more commitments the next day and 11 on Friday, bringing the total to 120. It was getting harder as O'Neill moved from the list of Democratic regulars, the main source of his strength, to the outer wings of the party, the Southern conservatives and the ultra-liberals.

The winning vote was delivered over the weekend by Boggs's top assistant, Gary Hymel, an astute politician in his own right. At a reception for Lindy Boggs in New Orleans, Hymel convinced Representative F. Edward Hebert, dean of the Louisiana House delegation and chairman of the Armed Services Committee, that he should be on the winning side and pledge his vote to O'Neill. With Hebert signed up, the rest of the delegation soon followed.

On November 13, just a week after the election, O'Neill issued one of his rare press releases. The news in it came as no surprise. It announced he was a candidate for majority leader.

Although strong support from the Louisiana delegation seemed to close off the possibility of a challenge from conservatives, Representative Sam Gibbons, fifty-two, a liberal Democrat from Florida, announced that he would run as a "rallying point for members who want to open up the system." He protested that he was not running against O'Neill, he was running for a position that would be vacant if Boggs were not found. He sought to appeal to liberals, and he talked of the need for strengthening the Democratic Congress in a Republican administration. It was not enough. O'Neill had preempted the liberal reformer's issues just enough to make Gibbons's campaign hopeless. On December 29, Gibbons withdrew.

At the Democratic Caucus the day before the new Congress convened, O'Neill was elected majority leader without opposition. Carl Albert was nominated for a second term as Speaker over only a token challenge from Conyers, repeating his effort of two years earlier. Again, Conyers used the opportunity to criticize the Albert leadership style, or lack of it. He charged that Albert had let too much congressional power erode. The vote was 202 to 25. The Democrats were not yet ready for a change.

The only significant Caucus fight came on the question of whether the third leadership position, the whip, should be appointed or elected. Many of the same members argued for an elected whip this year as they had two years earlier. Potential candidates, led by Phil Burton and Sam Gibbons, already were lining up. After an emotional debate, the Caucus decided by a vote of 123 to 114 to allow Albert and O'Neill to pick their own whip. They chose McFall, with one deputy whip, Brademas.

As leaders of the House Democrats, O'Neill and Albert were a strange-looking pair, the nervous little man from Oklahoma and the big amiable Irishman from Boston. Politically, they were in tune, but personally, they were miles apart. In the next couple of years, it would be hard for

O'Neill to stand in Albert's shadow, although, as a loyal team man, he knew he must. There would be times, however, when events demanded prompt action and O'Neill would assert himself with a hesitant and unsure Albert—on the resignation of Spiro T. Agnew, for example, and the impeachment of Richard Nixon.

9

MR. LEADER

E SWEPT into the Capitol with a regal air, a tall, nattily dressed figure, trim in a well-tailored gray suit that blended with his gray hair slicked back. All was in order. Trousers sharply creased. Not a hair out of place. His stride was confident, a man who knew his way around and who could get what he wanted. He was surrounded by the trappings of Washington power, a chauffeured limousine, aides carrying brief cases, Secret Service agents with buttons in their ears wired to a worldwide communications system. But this day, none of it would matter. On this day, he would fail. Vice-President Spiro T. Agnew was trying to duck the law.

It was the afternoon of September 25, 1973. Agnew, picked as his vice-president in 1968 by Nixon from the relative obscurity of the Maryland governor's office, had phoned House Republican leader Gerald R. Ford earlier and asked him to set up a meeting with congressional leaders. Ford called Albert, who sent an aide to find O'Neill and others in the leadership. Agnew arrived promptly. The others straggled in to Albert's office, just off the House floor. Agnew looked out of place, a little stiff with the baggy-pants congressional set.

The congressmen knew Agnew was in trouble. The news of an investigation by the U. S. Attorney in Baltimore, George Beall, had been reported publicly in August. Beall was looking into allegations that Agnew, first as Baltimore county attorney and later as governor and vice-president, had accepted kickbacks from architectural and engineering firms improperly awarded state and federal contracts. On August 8, Agnew had appeared before a nationally televised press conference to deny all charges, declaring he would be cleared. But Beall persisted. U. S. Attorney General Elliot L. Richardson assured Agnew that no charges would be presented to the grand jury without his, Richardson's, approval. Irrefutable evidence continued to pile up, however, and finally, in mid-September, Richardson said Beall would take the case to the grand jury on September 27. Despite continued support from President Nixon and repeated statements that he would not resign, Agnew was beginning to get desperate. In the search for another way out of his troubles, he turned to Congress.

Albert opened the meeting. He said the vice-president had something to discuss, and Agnew plunged into his tale of what he called harassment by an ambitious young district attorney, son of a former senator and an Agnew friend. O'Neill doodled on a note pad and remembered that he had met the senator, J. Glenn Beall, when he had first come to Washington. Another son, J. Glenn Beall, Jr., had served one inconspicuous term in the House and had been elected to the Senate himself in 1970. They were all prominent Maryland Republicans together, Agnew and the Bealls.

Agnew now talked about the Constitution. He was, after all, the Vice-President of the United States. It would be unconstitutional to try him for a criminal offense, a felony, while in office, he argued. He and his lawyers had drafted a letter that was a formal request that the House investigate the charges compiled by George Beall.

Outside in the marble hallway, word spread quickly that Agnew was in Albert's office to argue some kind of special plea. Aides moved in and out of the office, refusing to answer questions, inviting others inside: House Judiciary Committee Chairman Peter W. Rodino of New Jersey and the committee's senior Republican, Edward Hutchinson of Michigan, first, then Republican Senate Leader Hugh Scott of Pennsylvania and Barry Goldwater, the senator from Arizona, who had been the GOP presidential nominee nine years earlier. After a while, Albert emerged, looking worried. He brushed past reporters and went to the House floor. Without elaboration, he said, "I have a communication from the Vice-President of the United States." With that, he handed the three-page letter to a clerk, who read it into the official record of House proceedings. There was no further action, no discussion.

In his letter, Agnew asked the House to conduct a full inquiry into the government's charges "in the dual interests of preserving the Constitutional stature of my office and accomplishing my personal vindication." By wrapping himself in the Constitution, Agnew was, in short, trying to maintain that he was somehow different from other men because of the office he held. The letter agreed that the Constitution did not permit the government to prosecute a sitting president or vice-president. As a precedent, he cited the 1827 House investigation that had cleared Vice-President John C. Calhoun of charges of profiteering on an army contract during earlier service as Secretary of War. Thus, Agnew contended, the House was the proper place, the only place, for his case to be considered. "I shall, of course, cooperate fully," he said. "As I have said before, I have nothing to hide."

Albert returned to his office without saying anything more to anyone. The politically sensitive task of deciding what to do with the Agnew letter remained. The discussion was dominated by the Republicans at first. They were sympathetic to his plea and thought the House should go along. They spoke of fairness and "due process of law" and began to discuss the strategy of how the inquiry should be conducted.

O'Neill recalled wondering what was going on. Wasn't it clear that Agnew was trying to block the grand jury proceedings? Did he think he was above the law? As the lawyer-congressmen talked of legal niceties, O'Neill the politician looked squarely at the politics. A House inquiry could drag on for months. President Nixon himself seemed to be sliding into deeper and deeper trouble over Watergate. He had fired his top aides, ordered new reports on the cover-up, changed his own story a couple of times. In mid-July, the Senate Watergate Committee, headed by Sam Ervin, Democrat of North Carolina, had learned of a secret White House tape-recording system that had preserved every word of conversations between Nixon and his men. And now there was a scramble by law authorities to try to get the tapes. The cover-up was unraveling. Why should Congress save Agnew? What if Nixon was forced to resign and Agnew went to prison? By law, Speaker of the House Albert, a Democrat, would be president. In addition, there was something about Agnew that convinced O'Neill he was lying. O'Neill finally suggested that the Republicans leave the room. The decision would be made by the Democrats.

O'Neill declared he was opposed to granting Agnew's request. Albert and Rodino were noncommittal. They wanted to talk to others, sleep on it. The group decided to meet again in the morning. Outside in the hall, Albert told reporters, "We don't have any idea of what we will do." He hurried down the hall to his other office and closed the door.

O'Neill, however, did not hesitate. "We shouldn't act until the courts around here act," he said. ". . . We can impeach, but I don't see that we have an obligation to make an inquiry on his behalf. If the courts say he is not indictable, that's a different matter." It was the first time O'Neill had spoken out publicly at odds with the Speaker. As majority leader, he had until now avoided any act that could be interpreted as upstaging Albert. He had been very careful. He had refused, for example, repeated requests to go to the television gallery to deliver comments on the particular issue of the day. But this time, he could not keep quiet. All his political instincts told him that Agnew's plea should be denied.

The next morning, as it often happened, O'Neill was running late. Gary Hymel, who had become his administrative assistant after Boggs's disappearance, went on ahead to Albert's office and was startled to find the Speaker and Parliamentarian Lewis Deschler studying a typed statement announcing Albert's intention to go along with the Agnew request. Hymel ran downstairs to the dining room where O'Neill was having breakfast, and told him what was happening. O'Neill, despite his size, can move. He grabbed the phone behind the restaurant's candy and cigarette counter and dialed the Speaker's office. Albert was calm. "Peter [Rodino] and I have it all worked out," he said, "but you can come up if you want to."

Deschler sat in on the meeting, as he did at most leadership sessions. He had been House parliamentarian since 1927 and was viewed with a mixture of awe and fear for his iron grasp of House rules. He had enormous influence. There were no written precedents. Deschler had them all in his head; few, therefore, could argue with him. As a political conservative, he often was at odds with younger House members. Deschler apparently had drafted the press release giving Agnew what he wanted. O'Neill said no. He could be as tough as Deschler. When the meeting broke up, the often indecisive Albert had turned around. Minutes before the House went into session at noon, Albert read a new statement to reporters: "The vice-president's letter relates to a matter before the courts. In view of that fact, I, as Speaker, will not take any action on the matter at this time." It was, Jerry Ford said, "a Democratic [party] decision. I don't think there's anything we can do. . . ."

In his book, *How the Good Guys Finally Won*, Jimmy Breslin quotes O'Neill talking to Diehl:

You know, Leo, if the guy would've said to us, 'Look, I've got a family. I'm afraid of going to the can.' Geez, that's all you have to tell me. I don't want to see any man go to jail. I don't have it in me. Maybe something could have been done for him. Give him some kind of hearing so he could kill a little time and then disappear. But the way the sonofabitch lied to us. And he acted as if it was our duty to believe him. He's got to be kidding. I don't want to be played for a sucker.

On September 27, Beall began presenting evidence to the grand jury in Baltimore. While Agnew went public, appealing to the American people and attacking the press for printing damaging news leaks from the grand jury, his lawyers went behind the scenes to bargain for a plea that would keep him out of prison. On October 10, a deal was cut. Agnew resigned the vice-presidency and pleaded no contest to a single charge of income tax evasion. He was fined $10,000 and sentenced to three years unsupervised probation. Nevertheless, he was bitter. He claimed it was Tip O'Neill's fault.

"Gentlemen," Senate Democratic Leader Mike Mansfield said in the charged atmosphere at the Capitol the next day, "the government is still functioning. The line of succession has been broken only momentarily."

Congress was about to do something it had never done before, vote to confirm or deny a president's choice to fill a vacancy for vice-president. It was the first test of the Twenty-fifth Amendment to the Constitution, ratified in 1967, which requires, in case of a vacancy, confirmation of vice-presidential nominees by majority votes in both the House and Senate. Nixon had chosen Congressman Jerry Ford.

The Democratic congressional leaders promised a thorough inquiry into Ford's qualifications for the job. They said they must not err, as Nixon had, and approve a man with hidden flaws in his past. "In the light of recent experience," Rodino said, "we will conduct the most searching kind of inquiry. I don't see any urgency for going ahead without taking the kind of time necessary to do a thorough job." He noted, almost as an afterthought, that a Constitutional line of succession remained intact: the Speaker of the House was next.

O'Neill denies there was any conscious effort by Democrats to stall on the Ford nomination. At the same time, there was no denying the fact that Albert was next in line and many Democratic cloakroom gossipers dared to speculate that he could be president. As early as June, O'Neill was advising Rodino to "get ready. . . . This thing [a Nixon impeachment] is going to hit us, and you've got to be prepared for it." Ironically, however, with eager Democratic presidential aspirants spotted all over Capitol Hill, the idea gave Albert the jitters. He wanted no part of the political speculation that surrounded him. He was forced to pause and contemplate the suddenly real possibility that he could become president of the United States, and he wondered aloud whether, with a nation torn by the emotional turmoil of Watergate, he would be able to govern effectively. Albert talked it over with his aides and friends. He wanted to be sure to do the right thing. Would the country support a Democratic president if it appeared he had anything to do with impeaching his Republican predecessor? He was reminded that Americans had rallied around Harry Truman and Lyndon Johnson when they had stepped in for stricken presidents. But that was different, Albert said; in

1974 the talk was of impeachment. Albert was apprehensive. The Secret Service agents dispatched to his side the minute Agnew had quit made him doubly nervous. Suddenly, he lost his privacy. They wouldn't even let him drive his own car. He didn't like it at all.

Events of the next few weeks were to add to his discomfort. The most dramatic moment came on a Saturday, October 20. Nixon, under court order to surrender the White House tapes to U. S. District Court Judge John J. Sirica, had been stalling. He came up with a suggested compromise, offering typed transcripts of the tapes. Special Prosecutor Archibald Cox said transcripts weren't enough, and before the day was over, in what was called the "Saturday Night Massacre," Nixon had Cox fired. Attorney General Elliott Richardson and his deputy, William Ruckelshaus, promptly departed. One resigned and the other was fired. Immediately, there were angry demands for the House to start impeachment proceedings against the president.

The word *impeachment* frightened a lot of people, especially Rodino. But there was no stopping the insistent cries for some kind of action by the House. On October 5, the American Civil Liberties Union had already called for impeachment of Nixon. Four days later, Rodino approved the printing of a document, largely historical, of "selected materials" on impeachment. Judiciary Committee Counsel Jerome Zeifman had been quietly assembling the materials for some time. He did not have to be convinced. He thought the committee should move ahead with the impeachment inquiry.

O'Neill was spending a long weekend at his Cape Cod summer home when the Saturday Night Massacre occurred. Albert, in Washington, phoned him and the two agreed to say nothing right away. Albert suggested they meet at the Capitol Monday, a federal holiday, Veterans' Day. The House was not in session that Monday and the Capitol was quiet, except for Albert's office. The House leaders met, trying to figure out what to do. The Saturday Night Massacre had loosed an enormous outpouring of public rage. National reaction was almost entirely negative. Dozens of congressmen were at work drafting resolutions calling for the impeachment of Richard Nixon.

Albert hesitated. "In my opinion," he said, in a cautious statement issued by his office, "the president's action Saturday was unfortunate. It seems to me to contribute to divisiveness among the American people at a time when the leadership of the nation should seek unity. For the Congress to act in a reckless or hasty manner would further engender disunity." But the force behind the impeachment demands was too great. Albert couldn't stop it.

When the House reconvened the next day, eighty-four impeachment resolutions were introduced.

They were not the first. The first impeachment resolution had come much earlier, in mid-summer, drafted by Representative Robert Drinan, the Jesuit priest from Massachusetts who had been the first and most insistent Congressman to say that Nixon must go. Drinan, a man of very strong views, was convinced Nixon was lying about Watergate. But there were additional crimes, he felt. He suggested impeaching Nixon for waging war in Southeast Asia without congressional approval. His resolution was not specific. It simply said: "Resolved, that Richard M. Nixon, President of the United States, is impeached of high crimes and misdemeanors."

Under House rules, an impeachment resolution is privileged, which means it can be called up at any time for a vote without necessarily going through the committee process. Albert and O'Neill had felt it would be premature to vote on impeachment in the summer of 1973. They feared if the resolution failed the vote would be seen as vindication for Nixon. Cloakroom rumors had it that the Republicans would force a vote on the resolution to make their president look good. O'Neill discussed Drinan's resolution with GOP Leader Ford, who said Nixon wasn't worried. Why bother with a vote? There would just be another resolution the next day. "They never really dreamed what was going to happen," O'Neill said.

Three months later, it was a different story. O'Neill said he had never seen such an avalanche of angry telegrams as came in over the weekend of the Saturday Night Massacre. Western Union lines were jammed. Extra help was needed to run the switchboard. On October 23, Nixon, clearly recognizing he had badly miscalculated public reaction to his tapes decision, reversed himself and said he would give the court nine of the tapes. It was a conciliatory gesture but it was too late. Within days, gaps were discovered in the tapes, and impeachment was discussed openly on Capitol Hill.

Like Albert, O'Neill issued a statement. Unlike Albert, however, he suffered no doubts. He questioned Nixon's ability to continue to run the country and said the impeachment inquiry should begin. "He has left the people no recourse," O'Neill said on the House floor. "They have had enough double-dealing. . . . The case must be referred to the Judiciary Committee."

The Judiciary Committee already had one assignment before it, the confirmation of Jerry Ford. Since October 10, there had been no vice-president. With impeachment now being advocated by more and more people each day, the pressure on Albert increased. "Some of the Democrats in the House wanted me to steal the presidency from the Republicans," Albert said in a 1979 interview with the *Washington Star*. "I could have named a select committee of really rough people and they could have pushed Nixon around. But we did it the right way. Pete Rodino and I worked it out, and nobody else had a damn thing to do with it." Albert did not want to be president. His only ambition in life, he said, was to be Speaker of the House.

On November 27, the Senate voted 92-to-3 to confirm Ford as vice-president. The House followed December 6 with a 387-to-15 vote. An hour later, Ford took the oath of office at a joint session of the House and Senate. Nixon watched from the balcony.

Afterward, O'Neill stood in the Speaker's lobby gabbing with a small knot of reporters when someone commented that the ceremonies had been very impressive. O'Neill, with an Irish deadpan, replied, "And you won't see anything like it again—for two or three months."

O'Neill had known Nixon from the earliest years of his vice-presidency. Theirs had been, to put it mildly, a curious relationship.

Nixon used to play cards at the University Club. He tried to be one of the guys but he didn't know how. When he became vice-president, he never went back to the University Club. So, when every now and then he'd call up and say he'd like to play, we'd have a Wednesday night game or a Tuesday night game and we'd go to Al Carter's house. [Carter, a former Republican Congressman from California, was then a lobbyist for a West Coast electric utility company.] One night I says, "I'm sick and tired, Mr. Vice-President, of reading what a great poker player you are. You're one of the lousiest poker players I ever saw." He says, "When I'm playing with Kluczynski and Fisher and you sharks, maybe, but when I was in the Navy, I was pretty good." And I says, "Whaddya mean? You were playing with those farm boys who had never played poker in their lives." One night Al Carter called me: "The vice-president's going to be here. He wants to talk to you about Massachusetts politics." So I went down there and the vice-president says, "They tell me you know Massachusetts politics better than anyone else, and if you know Democratic politics, you know Republican politics. I don't want to go with the old guys who've been around a long time. Give me the names of some young fellas I ought to take into my organization." "Well," I says, "you're wasting your time to start off with. Kennedy's going to be the Democratic nominee [in 1960] and you won't have a chance of carrying Massachusetts." He says "Kennedy's got no chance, I'm running against Johnson. You're not going to be able to stop him." So I suggested Brad Morse, able and talented, a member of Congress, or John Fisher, a tremendously able guy, an assistant Secretary of Commerce. Both had been administrative assistants to [Senator Leverett] Saltonstall. Fisher's an eloquent talker, historian of Lincoln, smart, sharp, knows how to get things done. Also, there's a young Boston lawyer, Chuck Colson, now there's an able guy. He wrote Colson's name down. That's the first time he had heard of Colson.

Politically, it was easy for O'Neill to favor impeachment. Nixon had never been popular in the Eighth Congressional District of Massachusetts. There were few Conservatives there and fewer Republicans. Letters into O'Neill's office during the spring and summer of 1973, as White House aides went to trial in Washington and the Ervin committee quizzed them on national television, ran strongly in favor of forcing Nixon out of office. Privately, O'Neill agreed. Publicly, he continued to say it was too early to talk of impeachment—until the Saturday Night Massacre. From then on, there was no question in his mind: impeachment proceedings must move forward.

Rodino and Albert, always more cautious, although for differing reasons, reluctantly went along. Rodino, the son of Italian immigrants, had only become Judiciary Committee chairman that year. He followed a strong and dynamic chairman, Emanuel Celler of New York, and had been somewhat intimidated by him. Rodino's twenty-four-year House career had been lackluster. On Judiciary, his assignment had been to handle the steady flow of special bills dealing with immigration and naturalization.

Rodino was stubborn. He insisted on finishing one case, the Ford confirmation, before even beginning to think of another. It began to look as though there would be no committee action on anything dealing with impeachment before the end of the 1973 session of Congress. The session was running late, tied up in a dispute over how to handle the current energy crisis (resulting from an Arab oil embargo). Many House members, anxious to see some sign of life in the Judiciary Committee, started complaining to O'Neill. He seemed the logical person to go to. They had been disappointed in Albert's indecisiveness and in his reluctance to take the lead on other issues, House reforms, for example, and the Vietnam War. There were complaints that Albert was out of touch with his own constituency, the Democrats in the House. O'Neill's door was open.

I can remember people coming in and saying, "Hey, when is that committee going to move?" After every weekend, they would come back and say, "Geez, what are we going to do about this thing? It is reaching tremendous proportions. We're doing nothing." And, as the majority leader, it was my obligation. I don't think the Speaker ever spoke to anyone about it. I wasn't looking for glamor or anything like that. It's not my style. Every time Zeifman came in, he'd say, "This thing's falling apart. There's no inclination to move, no head or tail." He [Zeifman] had an ally in [Texas Representative] Jack Brooks. Peter used to get furious. He said he was having a tough time getting an attorney. I said, "Hey, if you want names, I'll give you names." I gave him a list of mostly Harvard law professors. Every time I'd give him a name, he'd have an excuse. This one's a member of the ADA [Americans for Democratic Action], or this, or that. Peter had an excuse.

Finally, O'Neill went up to Rodino one day on the House floor. He told Rodino the committee must sign up a special impeachment lawyer before Congress adjourned for Christmas and the members returned to their home districts. Rodino protested. He said the matter had to be approached with care. He complained that O'Neill's list of prospective lawyers wouldn't do. "You don't understand," Rodino complained. "You're not a lawyer." O'Neill reasoned with him, cajoled him. The two sat in the House chamber, side by side in the leather-covered chairs arranged in a semicircle facing the Speaker's chair, Rodino, small and trim; O'Neill, big and rumpled. It was hard to say no to O'Neill. He could be very persuasive.

On December 16, Rodino brought a special guest to meet members of the Judiciary Committee. He was John Doar, a tall, thin lawyer with black curly hair, a Republican who had headed the Justice Department's Civil Rights Division under Attorney General Robert F. Kennedy. He was Rodino's choice to handle the impeachment inquiry, and he was instantly acceptable to the rest of the committee. On December 20, Doar's appointment was announced at a news conference. On December 22, Congress adjourned for the year.

The rest is history. Doar, a fine legal craftsman, painstakingly assembled the evidence against Nixon under the tightest security in offices made available to him at what had been the Congressional Hotel across the street from the House office buildings. Not everyone was content with the pace of the inquiry. Too slow, some said. Even when Doar began presenting the enormous Nixon file to the Judiciary Committee in closed-door session, there was grumbling that Doar was, of all things, too even handed. He simply laid all the information out. In the end, however, Doar's approach was devastating to Nixon. Finally leaving aside the carefully neutral professorial role he had played for months, Doar summed up: "Reasonable men acting reasonably, would find the president guilty" of misusing the power of his office. It was July 19. Nixon had resisted cooperating with the committee every step of the way. In a final act of defiance, he had refused to give Doar the documents sought in four last subpoenas.

Still Nixon insisted he would not resign. But the numbers were against him. The counting on impeachment began in the House as early as May when Nixon released the first transcripts of White House tape recordings.

Americans were as shocked by the crudeness and awkwardness of the language as they were by the meaning of what was said. No matter what the reason, public sentiment had overwhelmingly turned against Nixon. The evidence from his own tape recordings pointed to obstruction of justice, and maybe more. It remained only for Congress to decide whether that was an impeachable offense.

Toward the end of May, Tip O'Neill, ace head counter, said there would be a minimum of 206 "sure" Democratic votes and 40 from the Republican side for impeachment if the issue came to the floor that day. It would take 218 to pass.

Although O'Neill, in measuring the House, depends a great deal on hunch, or intuition, or some kind of political sixth sense, he has also developed a healthy respect for facts. He might not always recall those facts accurately once deposited in his head. A decimal point could slip a notch. But the thrust would remain. Take polls, for example. O'Neill is fascinated by polls. One pollster, William R. Hamilton, began dropping by the O'Neill office in 1972. Every election year, he did a poll for the American Federation of State County and Municipal Employees (AFSCME) on marginal congressional districts, the ones most likely to switch one way or another. Hamilton got into the habit of briefing O'Neill on the same data. In April, 1973, Hamilton conducted a national sampling of attitudes toward Nixon. He concluded that by a margin of 43-to-29, Americans would support congressmen who voted to impeach the president. The rest didn't care. When broken down by party, the figures showed that 50 percent of the Republicans would vote *against* a congressman inclined to oppose impeachment and only 7 percent of the Democrats would vote *for* a congressman inclined the same way. In June, Hamilton packaged his results into a forty-page booklet and went up to the Capitol to see O'Neill. No one had commissioned this poll, but Hamilton thought someone might be interested. O'Neill was. He took a summary of the figures and put it into his pocket. "Hey," he'd say to other congressmen as they walked the halls or lounged around the cloakroom. "Didja see this poll yet?"

At the other end of Pennsylvania Avenue the atmosphere was grim, but Nixon remained unyielding. Strange things were happening. Watergate was bearing down on Nixon while he tried to change the subject. Foreign affairs was his strong suit. He wanted to talk about foreign affairs. O'Neill remembered a visit to the White House at the time by House and Senate congressional leaders. Secretary of State Henry A. Kissinger was to brief the congressmen on the status of peace negotiations in the Middle East.

Inexplicably, Nixon started to discuss Russian history. He talked for twenty-five minutes, going back to the tsars and the Russian Revolution, to Lenin and Trotsky. "He talked and talked," O'Neill said. "Nobody else said a word." Finally, Nixon stopped and, with a quick apology, turned the meeting over to Kissinger. But just as Kissinger was beginning, Nixon broke in again and rambled on about Russia for another half hour. Everyone was uncomfortable. The House leaders had to leave in order to open a 10:00 A.M. session. They never did get briefed by Kissinger.

Coming back in the car, George Mahon [Appropriations Committee Chairman] says, "Didn't the president act very strange this morning? Wasn't that an odd meeting?" Doc Morgan [Foreign Affairs Committee Chairman Thomas E. Morgan of Pennsylvania] says, "Geez, the guy is paranoid. I suppose if we had gone through what he has gone through, we'd be the same way." We came back and I was worried. I called [Senate Democratic Leader] Mike Mansfield and I says, "Mike, what did you think of that meeting? It was odd." I says, "Mike, I'm worried about the nation." He says, "Don't worry. Everything's all right. Alexander Haig [Nixon's chief of staff] has good control." So I was happy that someone was watching the Ship of State. I was confident that no buttons would be pushed. Haig was always a tough guy. I've always had great respect for him.

The tide for impeachment could not be stopped. On Saturday, July 27, in the early evening, the House Judiciary Committee voted 27-to-11 in favor of the first article of impeachment, obstruction of justice. It was a solemn and dramatic moment as each member carefully weighed and explained innermost thoughts. The normally bustling hearing room fell silent as the roll was called. When it was over, Rodino quickly adjourned until Monday. It went easier the second time. The committee voted 28-to-10 for a second article charging Nixon with misuse of presidential powers. On July 30, a third article was approved, contempt of Congress for refusing to answer committee subpoenas, 21-to-17.

The next day, Ford got together with some old friends to do something he liked best, play golf. He had signed up for a foursome at the Pleasant Valley Classic in Sutton, Massachusetts, with O'Neill and two local men, Dave Stockton, a former Classic winner, and Dick Hanselman, executive vice-president of the Samsonite Corporation. A number of other congressmen were also in the tournament and they all gathered in Washington to fly to Massachusetts on the vice-president's official plane. Ford was late. As the others waited, they discussed the topic of the day, impeachment. "Les," O'Neill said to GOP whip Leslie C. Arends of Illinois, "you know impeachment's going to hit very soon. The votes are there." O'Neill declared there wouldn't be more than twenty votes for Nixon in the Senate if the House, acting as a sort of grand jury in the impeachment process, sent the case to the Senate for trial. "Oh," said Arends, "you don't know what you're talking about."

As Ford's limousine pulled onto the field, his press aide came to the congressional group on the plane and admonished them not to talk of impeachment. "The press corps traveling with us will ask what you've been talking about," he said, "and we don't want you to say you've been talking about impeachment." Ford got on the plane and apologized for being late. He had been out of town, he said, and his wife, Betty, had insisted that he stop by the new vice-presidential house at the Naval Observatory on Massachusetts Avenue. The Fords would be the first to live there. Until then, there had been no special residence for vice-presidents. Ford said his wife had been picking out curtains and furniture and wanted his advice before making any final decisions. O'Neill broke in. "What the hell are you bothering with that for? You'll never live in the house." Ford, skirting the hot topic, admonished him: "No more of that talk. Let's get going."

As the plane took off for Boston, Arends went with Ford into the vice-president's special section in the front of the aircraft. He closed the door.

I could hear the conversation. He says, "Jesus, Tip really is an expert at counting the House, and he says this thing is all over, that you're going to be president, and that the votes to convict are in the Senate. He knows what he's talking about." Jerry says, "No way. The votes aren't in the Senate."

None of the group played golf well that day for some reason. Ford drove off sharply to the left and O'Neill sharply to the right, reversing their political positions. They joked about it, bantered with the press, and seemed relaxed. Their scores were not revealed.

Back in Washington, reality came down hard. On Thursday, August 1, Haig called Ford. He said it was urgent. "I want to alert you that things are deteriorating," Ford recalled Haig warning. "You'd better start thinking about a change in your life." Nixon had been forced to turn over sixty-four more tape recordings to Judge Sirica. They would show, Haig said, that Nixon knew about the Watergate cover-up six days after the break-in and that he'd been deceiving the American people ever since.

On August 2, former Nixon counsel John Dean was sentenced to one to four years in prison for his role in the Watergate cover-up. He had pleaded guilty to one count of conspiracy to obstruct justice. In hearings before

Senator Ervin's committee, he had blown the whistle on others on the White House staff.

On August 3, a report from congressional auditors at the General Accounting Office said Nixon would lose his $60,000 annual federal pension if he were impeached and convicted—but not if he resigned.

On August 5, transcripts of White House conversations were released revealing—as Haig had told Ford—that Nixon knew of the break-in and cover-up on June 23, 1972, and had withheld evidence of his role from both his own lawyers and his supporters on the House Judiciary Committee.

On August 6, House support for the president virtually collapsed. House Minority Leader John J. Rhodes of Arizona and all ten Judiciary Committee members who had opposed articles of impeachment earlier said they would vote at least for one article, obstruction of justice.

On August 8, Nixon gave up. In a television broadcast to the nation, he said he would resign as president the next day.

On August 9, Ford was to be sworn in as thirty-eighth president of the United States. At 2:45 P.M., Ford called O'Neill to ask him to attend the brief White House ceremony. "Are wives invited, Jerry?" O'Neill asked. "The reason I'm asking is that I've already told Millie to pack and get down here." "Wives were not invited," Ford said, "but they are now."

At the Capitol, O'Neill released a statement commenting on the new president:

While we are close personal friends and I have great respect for his honesty, integrity, and ability, our political philosophies are diametrically opposed. I wish him every success in bringing our politically torn country together. He can expect cooperation from Congress, and I trust he will cooperate with Congress and the rest of America in the days ahead.

On the telephone to Ford, he was less statesmanlike: "Christ, Jerry, isn't this a wonderful country," Ford recalled him saying. "Here we can talk like this and you and I can be friends, and eighteen months from now, I'll be going around the country kicking your ass in."

Eighteen months later, or maybe even earlier, O'Neill was telling reporters that Ford was "a good golfing partner, but he doesn't know how to govern the country."

10

ON TO SPEAKER

I
T'S HARD to plan ahead for history. Events have a way of happening
haphazardly. If you're lucky, these events, like the pieces of a
puzzle, may fall into place, and you will come out ahead. Thus it was
that during his four years as majority leader, O'Neill saw his uncanny
luck take bizarre turns until there he was, reaching for the ladder's
top rung, with no one in his way. O'Neill had been thrust forward by the
demands for congressional leadership during the Nixon and Agnew crises.
Forces for change within the House had found him a receptive ally and the
resulting procedural reforms ultimately strengthened the office of Speaker.
In an effort to reverse Congress's downward slide in public opinion polls,
O'Neill had helped Congress pass laws limiting presidential budget and
war-making powers. At home, O'Neill's political base was so secure that he
required little campaign time and money to get reelected. That left him time
and money for Washington politicking, a fact of some importance. Finally,
events totally beyond his control had eliminated two of O'Neill's strongest
potential rivals for leadership. It would be easy to credit O'Neill's
poker-playing shrewdness with the steady upward course of his political
career. There is a certain neatness to the image of a man playing his cards
well, outfoxing the rest with his ability to keep track of all the numbers in the
deck, triumphantly flipping over the one card from his own hand that will
win the pot. But it takes luck—in poker and in the House of Representatives.
O'Neill has had very good luck.

O'Neill is also smart, politically smart. He may not be an intellectual but
he is intelligent, a thoughtful and caring man who reads a lot and has a
remarkable memory. His taste in books runs to historical novels and political
biographies rather than to heavy philosophical tomes. O'Neill can absorb
vast quantities of information, reach conclusions quickly, and state his views
precisely. He has no trouble making decisions and he is willing to admit,
often with a smile of mock innocence, when he is wrong.

Although the dramatic high point of O'Neill's years as majority leader
was the fall of the Nixon-Agnew administration, institutional changes were

being adopted in the House which were to be of much greater long-range impact within the narrow world of congressional operations.

Two of the most significant changes, dealing with the budget process and with war-making powers, concerned Nixon particularly and the presidency in general. Although it is difficult to measure these things, both changes represented victories for Congress at a time when Nixon was at his weakest. Preoccupied with Watergate, he could only lash out angrily at Congress.

When O'Neill was elected majority leader, he had immediately announced two Democratic legislative priorities: to end the war and to write a law that would force the president to spend the funds appropriated by Congress. Nixon, using (and O'Neill would say, abusing) his executive power, had refused to spend billions of dollars in congressionally approved programs, particularly in education and welfare programs initiated by the Democrats.

With a significant push from Congress, Nixon was finally to end the war, but antiwar sentiment in general simmered on Capitol Hill until a new law, the War Powers Act, aimed at stopping future such wars was adopted. Nixon vetoed the bill as unconstitutional and a dangerous intrusion on presidential power. Congress, in turn, took another vote and enacted the bill over his veto.

Throughout most of 1973, Nixon, despite his Watergate troubles, held the support of enough senators and House members to sustain eight vetoes. The ninth came on war powers. The bill provided that a president must consult with Congress before going to war and must not commit troops to battle unless war has been formally declared or the United States has been attacked. War-weary congressmen felt strongly that the legislation was needed to avoid future Vietnams. Still, the House override vote was close, 284 to 135, only four more than the two-thirds needed to enact legislation over presidential objections. The Senate swept the Nixon arguments aside easily, 75 to 18.

Gaining control of the budget process was more difficult. Nixon's first term had ended in a lively sparring match with Congress over spending. There was a great deal of support for some kind of legislation to limit the president's power to impound funds. In the process of discussing what to do to curb the president's power, however, congressional leaders began to consider changes in their own appropriations system. The Constitution clearly gives Congress the responsibility to raise money through taxes and to decide how that money should be spent. But as the federal budget inched into the hundreds of billions of dollars, it had become too complicated for Congress to handle effectively. Several dozen committees and subcommittees were involved at some point in authorizing programs or providing money. There was no way for Congress to view the budget as a whole.

In 1973, a special Senate-House study committee came up with a solution: create two new committees, instruct them to set budget ceilings, and then require Congress to stay within those ceilings. If Congress wanted to add a new program, it would have to cut somewhere else. O'Neill became a vigorous advocate of the new proposals, which eventually became law in 1974, coupled with an additional provision aimed at stopping Nixon from impounding funds once appropriated—the initial sore point. Any proposed impoundments had to be submitted to Congress for approval.

O'Neill counted the budget and War Powers acts as work well done. As he saw it, both set Congress onto the path of reversing processes that had gradually been eroding congressional prerogatives and powers and had helped plunge Congress to the bottom of the public opinion polls. He felt the power and prestige of Congress was literally at stake.

Some of O'Neill's optimism was soon to be shaken by events. Within six months of Nixon's resignation, the *Washington Post* was reporting that less than a year after Congress had laid low the imperial presidency of Richard Nixon and seemed on the way to asserting a new brand of congressional government, the House still could not effectively express its own majority sentiments.

"The House yearns for long-term solutions—and winds up in stalemate," *Post* reporters William Greider and Barry Sussman wrote. "It tinkers with reform—and further complicates its ability to act. It finds consensus on some issues—then sees its own will frustrated by events, by institutional obstacles, by the veto of minorities and other power centers."

Greider and Sussman weren't simply holding a finger to the wind. They had conducted an unusual four-month survey of House members using roughly the same techniques as national opinion pollsters, combining old-fashioned reporting and modern computerized research. The survey offered no remedies, but simply reflected the current condition of the House as seen by its members.

Greider and Sussman found, for example, that the freshmen weren't the only Democrats unhappy with Speaker Albert's leadership style. The newcomers merely were more open about their discontent, demanding a meeting with Albert to present their gripes and talking with reporters afterwards. In fact, the *Post* poll showed that 54 percent of veteran House Democrats also were "dissatisfied" with their leadership.

Although O'Neill was part of that leadership, he himself was not personally held responsible for its ills. For him, there were lessons in

Albert's troubles. Most of the freshmen complaints could be solved easily by a Speaker who made himself more accessible to the members and better able to keep the House on a sensible work schedule. How to hold together a majority for Democratic programs and cope with the harassment of delaying tactics from a belligerent minority would take a little longer.

O'Neill's consistent defense of the House as an institution, as an equal partner with presidents and Supreme Courts, continued to win him friends, however. Having cast his lot with House service as the ultimate goal of his political life, O'Neill was determined to do all he could to enhance its standing with the American people. Whether by accident or design—and it may well have been design; O'Neill is not totally without guile—this position also enhanced O'Neill's own standing in the quiet maneuvering for position within the House leadership. No one was certain how long Albert would want to serve.

Time magazine described O'Neill in early 1973 as "perhaps the best liked man in the House." Still, O'Neill worried. Was that enough to make him the undisputed challenger when Carl Albert stepped down? Good politicians run scared. O'Neill was leaving nothing to chance. He did not want to appear to be breathing down Albert's neck. O'Neill was, after all, as loyal as anyone could be to the established order of things. He would never challenge Albert for Speaker. At the same time, Tip O'Neill was no fool. He couldn't afford to let any potential rivals take advantage of that loyalty and move out ahead of him should Albert retire. He knew that it was not enough to carry the title majority leader and to be liked as a clever story teller; he had to be seen by his colleagues as the single most logical choice for Speaker. One way to reach out to all House Democrats was with money. Tip O'Neill, as he had done before, went into the fund-raising business.

O'Neill was not new to the art of friendly political fund-raising. He had never needed large campaign contributions himself for his own reelection efforts, so it had seemed quite logical to him that he should pass along donations that came his way. This quiet practice had drawn public attention for the first time in 1971 when James Polk of the Associated Press (later with NBC News) revealed that in 1970 O'Neill had used a "hidden committee" in Washington, D. C., to raise $12,000 without revealing the names of donors. There was nothing illegal about it under District law. O'Neill simply had routed campaign contributions through a "D.C. O'Neill Committee" to avoid making names of contributors public as required by Massachusetts law. "You know the law. You don't have to report it down there," O'Neill said candidly when approached by Boston reporters. "In fairness to the friends who contribute to our campaign, we do them a service by sending it to the

Washington committee and then transferring it to the Boston account." That "service," he explained, was to keep his contribution list secret, and thus protected from harassment by other fund-raisers.

It was the last time O'Neill used a hidden committee, however. Always willing to respond to changing political mores, O'Neill routinely released to the press the names of all contributors in any of his future money-raising efforts.

As majority leader, O'Neill had switched his fund-raising hats. He had been chairman of the Democratic Congressional Campaign Committee during his years as whip and, as such, staged one big fund-raising dinner a year. After his election as majority leader, he set up a Thomas P. O'Neill, Jr., Congress Fund. He raised $76,000 in 1974 and $73,000 at one $1,000-a-plate dinner in 1975. The largest contributions came predictably from the most affluent lobby groups, large corporations and labor unions. When critical news accounts suggested these were "fat cats" trying to buy favor with the Democrats, O'Neill shrugged it off. He said he never paid attention to who gave the money, just to how much was there.

It is hard to believe that O'Neill, the master of detail, could have such a casual attitude toward money. More than likely, his statement is only partly true. He certainly knew who the Democratic party's big donors were and, largely because of their generosity, his door was open. He probably did not care how much they gave so long as there was enough money to go around. The money was then handed out in equal amounts to Democratic candidates who needed help. More than 85 candidates benefitted from this Tip O'Neill largesse in 1974. One donor list included unions of railway clerks, laborers, seafarers, teamsters, hotel and restaurant employees, and the AFL-CIO itself, plus business political action groups of insurance men, General Electric, and the Pullman Company. In 1976, O'Neill raised more than $150,000 and gave it out to 182 Democratic Congressional candidates without regard to philosophy or seniority. Columnist Jack Anderson added it up in 1976 and concluded that O'Neill had raised a total of $267,870.

The question of whether such contributions bought influence with O'Neill is a difficult one. Whether he studied the lists of contributors or not, he always knew who the big donors were. The question then becomes: does the AFL-CIO, or the Seafarers, or General Electric have easy access to O'Neill because of campaign contributions or because they represent large numbers of people? Take the case of James P. Wilmot, chairman of the congressional campaign unit's dinner committee and a $1,000 contributor to O'Neill's fund in 1974. Wilmot, a New York businessman involved in real estate development and commuter airlines (Page Airways), among other things, was having trouble getting a decision from the Department of Housing and Urban Development (HUD) on an environmental impact statement for one of his apartment enterprises. Wilmot called O'Neill, who promptly picked up the phone and called HUD Secretary Carla Hills, asking her to speed up action on the report. "Did I make a call for him?" O'Neill snapped when asked by reporters about the incident. "Yes, he's my friend. He said he was being pushed around by the department. An inequity and an injustice was being done. I'd do it for anyone." The project was approved. In 1975, Wilmot and several members of his family and friends, each gave $1,000 for a total of $8,000.

Or philanthropist Mary Lasker, a stalwart in Democratic fund-raising drives—including the Tip O'Neill campaigns—over the years. When Mrs. Lasker wanted to find a way to increase federal funds for cancer research, she went directly to Tip O'Neill. O'Neill responded in his usual straightforward manner. He invited the congressmen and federal health officers most involved in developing health programs and appropriating money to a luncheon in his office—with Mary Lasker. She made her pitch and cancer research got the money. "Sure," said O'Neill. "I'll open doors for anyone. Then it's up to them to sell their product. . . . Nobody ever asked me for anything and nobody ever gave me anything. They know better. They'd get thrown out on their ass."

O'Neill sounded defensive as he made this statement. It was obviously a sore subject—doing favors. The simple act of making a phone call for a friend or a supporter could be seen as a payoff. But these little favors are very much a part of the O'Neill operating style, and the man is not a crook. If someone tried to offer O'Neill an outright bribe, he probably *would* get thrown out of the office. But no one would offer. They'd find other ways to reach his sentimental Irish heart—or pocketbook—with other signs of personal and Democratic party loyalty, occasional tips on business deals, frequent campaign contributions, favors for friends. . . . In O'Neill's world, it's all called politics, and it's an honorable profession.

After O'Neill was elected majority leader, he had moved his base of operations to the Capitol Building, where he stayed. From then on, he spent little time in his congressional office in the Rayburn Building. So it was from the Capitol, in a large, handsome, first-floor office facing the Mall, that O'Neill ran for Speaker. If he wasn't in his office, he was on the House floor or in the Democratic cloakroom. He was always available. He would listen to complaints, tell stories, lend a hand. And, as occasion demanded, he would stand up on the House floor to champion Democratic programs or attack the Republicans.

O'Neill made no secret of his partisanship. He had grown up a Democrat and would remain loyal to his party through all kinds of troubles. He firmly believed it was the political group that offered the best course for the United States—toward better health, more jobs, safer communities, cheaper housing, higher wages—noble goals even if often elusive. "The party of the people," as he often said, "and not of big business and special interests." He did not hesitate when confronted with a Republican proposal; he opposed it without question. "I'm a very partisan person," O'Neill said frankly. "I always have been and I always will be."

Representative John J. Rhodes, Republican of Arizona, who succeeded Jerry Ford as House Republican Leader, did not find O'Neill's partisanship endearing. "Tip can be impossible to deal with," he said, "if you are in the minority." Rhodes even wrote a book about his frustration dealing with O'Neill and the Democratic majority, called *The Futile System.* With a Republican in the White House and Democrats in control of Congress, Rhodes proposed something he called "consensus government." It would have drawn congressional Republicans into the decision-making process. He proposed that the president and congressional leaders of both parties sit down at the beginning of the year and lay out plans where they could agree and focus legislative activity on those areas. Thus, Rhodes argued, deadlocks between Congress and the president would be avoided. Rhodes was not surprised when O'Neill said no. He recalled O'Neill's comment: "Republicans are just going to have to get it through their heads that they are not going to write legislation."

Although Rhodes said he enjoyed being with O'Neill at social gatherings, he sounded bitter about his legislative plan. "My consensus proposal never had a chance to work because Tip O'Neill would not let it work. He would much rather stand up on the Floor and deliver a partisan attack on the president for vetoing a bill than sit down with the president early in the legislative process to help avoid a veto."

O'Neill's partisanship is not so rigid when it comes to individuals. He likes John Rhodes and enjoys playing golf with Jerry Ford. One of his closest friends in Washington is Representative Silvio Conte, Republican of Massachusetts. A graduate of Boston College a dozen years after O'Neill, Conte had served a term in the state legislature with O'Neill before the latter went to Washington. Conte followed six years later. Like O'Neill, Conte is a good talker with an infectious sense of humor. The two men worked together with state legislators on redistricting plans in the 1960s aimed (successfully) at preserving winning majorities in their districts. When Millie O'Neill moved to Washington in 1977, the Contes and the O'Neills became regular bridge partners (O'Neill largely gave up playing poker with the boys), and close friends.

The Ford-O'Neill relationship offers a special insight into how Congress often works. Friendship and partisanship are isolated political realities where the harsh words of public debate seldom spill over into private conversation. They respect each other as politicians upholding the generally conflicting positions of their separate political parties. When Ford became president, he did not shy away from vetoing bills prepared and adopted by his old Democratic friends and O'Neill did not hesitate to condemn Ford's positions as shortsighted. But they remained friends.

In his autobiography, Ford tells of the time he was urging Congress to enact a huge tax cut—$28 billion—and balance it with an equally large cut in federal spending. Congressional Democrats assailed the plan as preposterous; programs like welfare and Social Security, the so-called "uncontrollables" of the federal budget, would have to be reshaped. "We're not gonna let you have it," Ford reported O'Neill told him. "There's no way you're gonna get it through." And then he added, "How's your golf game, Mr. President?" Ford commented on the conversation: "I expected that from Tip, a fierce partisan, but also a valued friend. He could be scathingly critical of my policies—and often was—but there never was anything *personal* in his attacks."

They were, after all, professional politicians. As the 1976 elections neared, Ford said he knew he would have trouble with the Democratic Congress. O'Neill, certain to be Speaker in 1977 and anxious to help elect a Democratic president in 1976, "wanted to make me look bad," Ford wrote matter-of-factly. One way to do that was to stall congressional action on Ford's plan for dealing with energy crises such as the one that followed the Arab oil embargo in the winter of 1973–74. Congress delayed acting until late 1975 and then, rejecting Ford's ideas, enacted its own energy-saving plan (including a mandate for greater fuel efficiency in U. S. automobiles). Ford advisers urged him to veto the bill, but he didn't. He knew 1976 would be a very partisan year; he didn't want to give the Democrats a chance to attack him for blocking efforts to reduce oil and gas consumption.

There was one Ford act, one of his most controversial, that O'Neill did not quarrel with, at least not publicly. That was the unconditional pardon of former President Richard Nixon. As a private citizen living in San Clemente, California, Nixon was vulnerable to prosecution for his role in the Watergate scandal. Even while president, on March 1, 1974, he had been named as an "unindicted coconspirator" by the federal grand jury that indicted seven former Nixon aides, including John Mitchell, the one-time U. S. Attorney General. Nixon associates were discussing the possibility of a pardon even before he resigned. To go to trial was one of Nixon's greatest fears. No deal for a pardon had been worked out in advance, Ford maintained. He decided to go ahead with the pardon a month after becoming president because he felt a trial would drag out the painful agony of Watergate for another year and a half. He wanted it ended.

When Ford called congressional leaders to tell them of his decision, he said no one gave him any argument, except O'Neill. "Jesus," he recalled O'Neill saying, "don't you think it's kind of early?" But Ford said when he explained that he felt this was the only way to get on with the business of running the country, O'Neill said, "Okay, Mr. President." And O'Neill stuck by his support of Ford despite the strong anti-pardon sentiment in his own district. It was time, O'Neill agreed, to try to close the book on Watergate.

As majority leader, O'Neill was responsible for keeping track of legislation and the schedule for votes on the House floor. Typically, however, his interests focused more on the politics of a bill than on their substance. But conscious of the fact that his job included legislative leadership, O'Neill made an occasional stab at mastering legislative detail— and, also occasionally, he got things screwed up.

One day, for example, he asked Gary Hymel to put together a list of the major bills coming up in the following year so he could discuss them with two reporters coming to his office that afternoon. When the reporters arrived, they were surprised to hear O'Neill tell them, at some length, of how Congress would move quickly on an area of great need, prison reform. He spoke of the terrible conditions in prisons, and so on. As the reporters left, Hymel chased them down the hall. "Hey guys," he said, "I'd appreciate it if you wouldn't use that stuff about prison reform. I had written 'pension reform' on the list." They laughed and agreed to hold off. It was generally understood that O'Neill handled the politics and left legislative details to others.

Even with the extra work of the majority leader office, O'Neill maintained close ties to his home district. He continued to fight for the Navy Yard, met with anti-abortion groups, attended testimonial dinners and a few funerals, received honorary college degrees and managed to claim partial credit for passage of a new mass transit bill that would pump $600 million into public transportation facilities in Massachusetts. (Years later, ex-Speaker

Albert said he thought O'Neill still spent too much time in Massachusetts during his majority leader term.)

In these years, with the increased demands of the majority leader's office cutting into his time, O'Neill and his wife again talked of moving the family to Washington. Mrs. O'Neill even went on a Washington house-hunting trip but was horrified at the high prices and decided to stay in Cambridge. Congressional pay was then $42,500 a year. She didn't move to Washington until O'Neill became Speaker.

It was a time of growing federal financial involvement in state and local affairs, and O'Neill slipped easily into the new world of federal grantmanship. It wasn't all that different from the old days when politicians handed out jobs to their constituents. You just substitute the new language of grants, loans and subsidies for the old language of jobs. Hundreds of millions of dollars poured into Massachusetts and into the Eighth Congressional District. Federal dollars built the Route 128 beltway on three sides of the city and then the federal government put money into the research and development industry that spun off from the universities in O'Neill's district and settled along the beltway. Downtown, federal dollars built skyscraper office buildings in Scollay Square where there had been only a venerable burlesque house and a seedy hotel, and federal dollars rehabilitated the decaying market place and rundown buildings of Faneuil Hall. There were low-cost housing, and parks, and sewage treatment grants. By the late 1970s, Massachusetts was collecting more than $2 billion a year in federal money (although some state officials still complained they weren't getting their fair share). "I've gotten more federal public works and other construction projects into my district than any other in the country," O'Neill said. "It takes work. You don't think these things happen by accident, do you?"

On November 5, 1974, a nation weary of Watergate scandals and disenchanted with government in general, sent seventy-five new Democrats and seventeen new Republicans to the House of Representatives. The worst Republican fears had been realized. Thirty-six GOP incumbents had been defeated, compared with only four Democratic losses. The new members were young, independent, liberal, and intent on shaking up the institution. They were determined to be seen *and* heard. The reform movement, slowly growing over the previous six or eight years, was ready for them.

For too long, it was felt, committee chairmen had ruled the House virtually without challenge. Lower ranking members were left with little more than a duty to ratify the decisions of their seniors. The Democrats took a small step away from the seniority system in 1973 when they decided that the Caucus should be able to vote on committee chairmen. Although some chairmen were very unpopular—District Committee Chairman John L. McMillan, of South Carolina, in particular—no effort to defeat any chairmen was launched at that time. The mere idea of allowing all Democrats to vote on each chairman had had an impact, however: the chairmen became friendlier.

In a series of Democratic caucuses before and after the new Congress convened on January 14, 1975, the freshmen made their presence, and their votes, felt. First the Democrats shifted the power of committee assignment from the Ways and Means Committee to the new Steering and Policy Committee headed by Albert, O'Neill, and other House leaders. Then, the freshmen decided that if they were to vote on committee chairmen, they should get to know them a little. So they invited the chairmen to separate caucuses. The chairmen cut short their Christmas vacations and went, virtually hat in hand. There was power in seventy-five votes, and the freshmen of 1975 knew it.

O'Neill was not quite ready for the revolution that followed. Later, he would come around to see how some of the reforms, especially the shift of committee appointment power, would strengthen his own hand as Speaker. But in December 1974 and January 1975, he was still enough of an establishment man to suspect that some of the reformers were going too far.

When the steering committee met to nominate committee chairmen, O'Neill offered a resolution to rename all the incumbents. Representative Jonathan Bingham, Democrat of New York, objected. He said the committee should vote on each by secret ballot. Bolling backed him up. The first to lose was Banking Chairman Wright Patman of Texas. In his place, the committee nominated Representative Henry Reuss (D-Wisconsin) instead. Then, Representative Frank Thompson (D-New Jersey) was substituted for Representative Wayne Hays (D-Ohio) as chairman of the House Administration Committee. All the rest were renominated but some of the votes were close. When the issue moved to the full Caucus, the freshmen were ready. Two others, Armed Services Chairman Hebert and Agriculture Chairman William R. Poage (D-Texas) joined Patman on the ouster list.

At the same time, Wayne Hays was reinstated over Thompson, not because Hays was popular and Thompson unpopular, but because Hays fought for it and Thompson held back. Hays had openly built a power base on the House Administration Committee by handing out a steady stream of new perquisites (attacked as "perks" in the press) for members, such as more federally financed trips back home, more money for newsletters and phone calls—the tools of successful reelection campaigning—in a way that did not require a House vote. The perks just flowed, and House members were appreciative. The new members had not experienced this largesse but they were told of it, and promised more. Although often criticized as a bully because of his impatience with the low-ranking and often slow-moving House employees under his committee's jurisdiction, Hays was also appreciated as an articulate and able politician. He enlisted another tough character, Phil Burton, in his campaign to hold the chairmanship. Burton, an intense and tireless politician, had formed a power base of his own in the Democratic Study Group and had won friends among the freshmen for helping in the 1974 elections, both with political advice and with money. When the votes were counted, Hays won, 176 to 109.

O'Neill played his Caucus role carefully. He didn't want to alienate anyone, the old bulls or the young tigers. In a private breakfast meeting, he assured Hays he had voted for him in the steering committee; then he made a special trip to the freshman caucus to show he was sympathetic to their problems and aims. He wanted all of them on his side. Just after the 1974 election, Carl Albert had told O'Neill confidentially that in two years the Speaker's office could be his.

His Irish luck was at work again. Before the year was out, two of O'Neill's strongest potential rivals for power were eliminated by their own failings. Strange twists of fate that began at 2:00 A.M., Monday, October 7, 1974, when Fanne Foxe jumped into the Tidal Basin.

On that particular night, Mills, the very model—publicly—of a sober-sided congressional gentleman, and Fanne Foxe had been partying at a downtown bar and were on their way home to Arlington where both had apartments with their respective spouses in the same building. Suddenly, the car stopped near the Tidal Basin, and Foxe jumped out and plunged into the chilly waters. When police came and fished her out, they reported that Mills had cuts on his face and appeared drunk. As events unfolded over the next few months, it turned out that Mills was, indeed, drunk often. He was an alcoholic. And in the harsh glare of national publicity, Mills admitted he was an alcoholic, quit drinking, left Congress, and became actively involved in Alcoholics Anonymous.

As chairman of the Ways and Means Committee, Mills invariably had been described as the most powerful man in Congress. He kept a tight hold on the committee. All staff aides were hired by him. All legislation was considered by the full committee (no subcommittees) with him as chairman. He was known as a tax-writing wizard who could steer hideously complex bills dealing with subjects such as income taxes, Social Security, and Medicare, through the House with skill. He was viewed with a respect approaching awe for his ability to "read" the House and to know just exactly the right time to call up a tax bill—and pass it. He had been in Congress a very long time, entering in 1939 at the age of thirty, a bright young man from Kensett, Arkansas, by way of Harvard Law School. Over the years, Mills had developed the Ways and Means Committee into an independent power base, his power strengthened by the fact that Ways and Means Democrats sat as a committee on committees to make all Democratic committee assignments.

Mills served one more House term (after the Fanne Foxe incident) but was forced to give up his committee chairmanship. He said he could no longer handle the intricate details of tax legislation. Albert and O'Neill seized the opportunity to shift the power of committee assignment away from Ways and Means and onto the steering committee controlled by the Speaker. With Mills gone, the days of one-man control of the Ways and Means Committee were over. More members were added to the committee. Subcommittees were created. Tax bills were opened up to floor amendments. And the size of the staff was tripled. His fellow Democrats sympathized with Mills but were also embarrassed by him. He was instantly non-powerful, a rather sad figure shifting gears from writing the nation's tax laws to evangelizing against booze.

Next came the Elizabeth Ray affair taking out another rival power-broker, Wayne Hays. Hays was one of the House's most power-conscious members. He understood it. He used it. And, in the end, he abused it. There's no denying he was brainy, but he was also arrogant and perfectly willing to verbally abuse anyone who couldn't fight back.

On Sunday, May 23, 1976, the *Washington Post* carried a front-page story by reporters Marion Clark and Rudy Maxa. For nearly two years, they wrote, Hays had kept Elizabeth Ray on his payroll at $14,000 a year with no duties other than to serve as his mistress. "I can't type, I can't file. I can't even answer the phone," Ray said in her small unmarked office on the fifth floor of the Longworth Building. "Supposedly, I'm on the Oversight Committee. But I call it the Out-of-Sight Committee."

Hays tried to bluster his way out of this mess. "Hell's fire," he said, "I'm a very happily married man." But the story wouldn't go away. The House Ethics Committee, the Justice Department, and the FBI all became involved in the case, looking into whether Hays violated the law by using federal funds to support a mistress.

Albert and O'Neill were in England when the Hays story broke. They

were on an official and largely ceremonial trip to "accept" the loan of the
Magna Carta for America's bicentennial celebration. When they returned,
Albert was undecided about what to do. O'Neill wasn't. The image of the
House, the institution, was being tarnished, he said. In a stormy meeting in
the majority leader's office, O'Neill bluntly told Hays he had to step down
immediately from chairmanships on the House Administration committee
and the Congressional campaign committee, where he had succeeded
O'Neill. "I know a man is innocent until proven guilty," O'Neill told
reporters, "and I hope for his sake Hays is vindicated. But a man in public
office must be like Caesar's wife, above suspicion. There is a double standard
for public officials, and in this goldfish bowl we live in, we have to adhere to
it. In fairness to his colleagues, and for the decency and dignity of the
House, he must step aside."

Hays gave up by inches. On June 3, he said he would resign from the
campaign committee. On June 18, he gave up the Administration Committee chairmanship. On August 13, he announced he would resign from the
House, after thirty years in Congress.

In the middle of the Hays scandal, Albert announced publicly what
O'Neill had known for half a year—he would not run again. He was tired and
wanted to go home to McAlester, Oklahoma. To no one's surprise, O'Neill
announced that he would like to be Speaker. In a letter to all Democrats, he
said, "I have a record of proven accomplishments for the Democratic
Party. . . . I earnestly solicit your support in the Caucus and on the floor in
January." The outcome was never in doubt. There was no opposition.

11

MR. SPEAKER

THEY came down from Boston, three planeloads full and some by car. They had names like Sullivan and O'Rourke and Malloy and Kelly and O'Hara and, of course, O'Neill. They crowded into the cool marble elegance of the Capitol's Statuary Hall where larger-than-life sculptures of past heroes stand silently along a gently curving wall. Metal folding chairs, hastily gathered from meeting rooms around the building, were lined up in a semicircle facing a television set. The group fussed with chairs and coats and chattered happily in the accents of Somerville and North Cambridge and Charlestown. They were state and local public officials, housewives, lobbyists, friends, and, according to Walter Sullivan, who seemed to be in charge, "a lot of priests." They had just decided to come to Washington, uninvited but welcome, this January day in 1977, to see their old friend Thomas P. O'Neill, Jr., sworn in as the forty-seventh Speaker of the United States House of Representatives. O'Neill, spruced up in a new three-piece suit, his usually unruly mop of white hair neatly slicked back, greeted the visitors warmly, hugging men and women alike. They were his people and he loved them. Then, as he left for the House floor to take the oath of office, the group settled back to watch it all on television. They were very proud.

With his family looking on from the visitors' gallery and his constituents packed into Statuary Hall, O'Neill was formally elected Speaker over Republican Leader John Rhodes. All Democrats voted for O'Neill (the only time they *all* voted together in the Ninety-fifth Congress); all Republicans voted for Rhodes. Tradition dictates that this is a light-hearted competition, the outcome never in doubt. The minority party leader—a Republican, in recent years—presides briefly, long enough to introduce the winner and hand over the Speaker's gavel. "This is a habit I would like to break," Rhodes the biennial loser quipped. But, as befits a victory celebration, Rhodes struck a friendly note: "Mr. Speaker-elect, you are my friend. We came to Congress together about a hundred years ago. We will retain that friendship through the next two years. . . . I also want to say, Mr. Speaker-elect, that once upon a time I wrote a book, and in that book I said you were the most partisan man I ever knew." He paused briefly. "I am expecting you to work for the next two years to prove what a liar I am." Finally, expressing the constant Republican dream of winning control of Congress, Rhodes predicted O'Neill would be "the greatest one-term Speaker the House has ever had." Everyone laughed and Rhodes stepped down to the minority table on the west side of the chamber.

(Two years later, when O'Neill was elected to his second term, he gave Rhodes the gavel to keep. He said that was the only way the Republicans would wrest it from him. "I understand," O'Neill said with a smile, "that he [Rhodes] has his eye on the Speaker's seat. I can assure you that is all he will have on it.")

The mood grew serious that January day as O'Neill delivered his first speech to the packed House chamber. "Few men," he said softly, "have the good fortune to see their dreams realized. But, thanks to you and thanks to the people of the Eighth Congressional District of Massachusetts, I am about to assume the highest office that I have ever aspired to."

O'Neill then spoke of favorite themes, of party responsibility and of partnership with a new Democratic president. There was a warning, too. Congress would not be a rubber stamp for White House programs. This was a new day. A congressional budget system was on the books and had been pronounced workable. A War Powers Act had been signed into law and would stop any president from making warlike moves around the world— without the consent of Congress. After years of bowing to strong Democratic presidents and bickering with Republican ones, Congress was, O'Neill said, "reasserting its rightful place in our scheme of government." He was optimistic. New Democratic leaders were in the White House and in Congress; with a little luck, they would get things done together.

In this speech, O'Neill set a theme for his own administration that he repeated over and over: ethics. He warned the hesitant in Congress and he promised the American people that he would push for enactment of the strongest possible ethics code. "We must restore faith in the federal government by proving that it can operate efficiently and honestly," he said. "We must bolster public confidence in Congress by adopting and living by a tough code of ethics."

It was not idle talk. O'Neill was deeply concerned that Congress had fallen in national public opinion polls. Only about one American in five expressed any faith in the integrity of public officials. Government in general and Congress in particular had been bloodied by the Watergate and Korean scandals and by a steady stream of stories of Congressional misbehavior. O'Neill was convinced that only Congress could correct its own bad reputation. Typically, having recognized the problem, O'Neill moved quickly on an issue where others had been working for years. But there was no resentment: he was a welcome ally.

"I was surprised and pleased," said David Cohen, president of Common Cause. "We did not discuss it specifically with him. We were glad to see him out front." Common Cause, the 250,000-member citizens lobby, had been urging Congress to tighten its rules of conduct for years. Two major Common Cause proposals—public financial disclosure and a limit on outside earnings—became the heart of the new House ethics code.

O'Neill, with his "old pol" manner and a past reluctance to release publicly a list of his own personal finances, seemed an unlikely ethics reformer. He was not, in fact, any more a "reformer" in 1979 than he had been in 1970 when he led the fight for recorded teller votes on the House floor. He would never be the type of reformer who would bleed and die and march on Washington for a cause. He was a practical politician. "I think Tip's move on ethics" Cohen said, "had something to do with the question of how you show you're serious. How do you do something with distinction to show you're serious about the institution?"

O'Neill's first major move on ethics had come at the caucus of new freshmen Democrats on December 4, 1976. The forty-seven newcomers were less aggressive than the bumper crop elected in 1974, but, still, they wanted to assert themselves. Together with the second-termers, they represented nearly half the total number of Democrats in the House. The freshmen turned down an invitation from the sophomore group to join forces in what could be a powerful alliance, preferring to go their own less flamboyant way.

The freshmen did, however, invite the leadership candidates and committee chairmen seeking renomination to come talk to them. In O'Neill's case, there was no opposition for Speaker. A fight was being waged for his old job, majority leader, so O'Neill seized the opportunity to march straight to the head of the parade on ethics. He was tough. He attacked the "special interests" in business and industry who tried to buy influence with Congress. He criticized the existing House ethics code as "toothless." He talked of congressional power and prestige and the post-Watergate moral climate in which voters were sending new and younger faces to Congress each election. "The American people," he concluded, "believe too many public officials go unpunished."

Back in his office, he mused about the way things had changed in his time:

The whole ballgame is different. Ethics has changed politics so. Sam Rayburn, in days gone by, well, he would call the United States Attorney and say, "Come up to my office." And they'd come and he'd say, "Lookit, you're investigating so-and-so." "Yes." "Well, I want you to stop it. Understand?" Or with the Internal Revenue Service, he would say, "That case has been kicking around three years and it can either go criminal or it can go civil and I want an answer by five o'clock and I want it to go civil." Now, I couldn't make a call like that for myself, let alone for anyone else. Or, Sam could call up the chairman of a committee and say, "I want you to put a dam in for so-and-so," or he'd call the Army Corps of Engineers and say, "Start digging that canal Monday. I'll put the money in for it next year, but we need this fellow [in Congress] and it's going to help him in his election." These things are all gone.

On ethics, as with other issues, O'Neill spent little time on specifics. He wanted a tough ethics code and he wanted it adopted quickly. He believed it was essential that the code contain a limit on how much money a Congressman could earn from outside businesses. There had been a great deal of criticism, especially from Common Cause, of members of Congress who tried to do two things at once, running a congressional office while at the same time running a hometown business or law firm. O'Neill, himself, bowing to that pressure (and increased demands on his time in Washington) had given up his insurance business in Cambridge. Other Congressmen complained, however, that O'Neill was asking too much. For some, it would mean giving up as much as $100,000 in outside income. O'Neill proposed a compromise. Maybe he couldn't pick up a phone and have a dam built in their district. But he could figure a way to balance off some of the loss in outside earnings with higher federal pay. Except for one relatively small cost-of-living raise, congressional salaries had not gone up since 1969. In the years from 1969 to 1976 non-farm earnings were up 70.1 percent, the consumer price index for urban wage earners and clerical employees was up 60.5 percent, and executive pay in private industry up 52.5 percent.

Congressional discontent about personal finances seemed reasonable to O'Neill, but he did not think the answer was for congressmen to go home and make more money as lawyers or businessmen; he thought they should make more money as congressmen. It was clearly a full-time job. Members should be paid accordingly.

So he linked the two: ethics and pay. Go along with the ethics code,

O'Neill told his colleagues, and we'll find a way to raise congressional salaries.

Two days before O'Neill spoke to the Democratic freshmen in 1976, Peter G. Peterson, chairman of President Ford's Commission on Executive, Legislative, and Judicial Salaries, was reaching the same conclusion—that Congress (as well as all other federal officials) should receive significant pay boosts and that a new strict code of ethics should be adopted. "If we continue down the path of the past eight years, in which the politics of survival have required no pay raises at all," Peterson said, "we must accept the implications of a government of only the rich or only the young and untried or, more likely, a government of those who are willing to compromise themselves with political money. The costs of such a government reach beyond the costs of a salary increase; they are incalculable and, to a free people, unacceptable." Peterson, board chairman of the New York investment banking firm of Lehman Bros., Inc., had been Secretary of Commerce in 1972 and 1973.

President Ford agreed. Higher pay, he said, would help restore public confidence in national leaders by attracting more qualified persons to government service. Senate leaders also agreed. In a report by former Iowa Senator Harold E. Hughes (1969–75), Congressional salaries were described as "seriously inadequate." Hughes suggested raising them to $65,000—and adopting a stiff ethics code.

O'Neill's task was not as easy as it may sound. No congressman wants to vote publicly on raising his own pay and in every political group there is at least one person so philosophically opposed to pay raises that he or she will try to force the others to vote against any raise.

The Ninety-fifth Congress had Representative Charles E. Grassley (R-Iowa), thin and pale and very serious, to fill this role. Grassley was willing to spend hours each day, his watchful eye fastened on the Democrats, to make sure no one slipped a pay raise past him.

Actually, there should have been relatively little difficulty getting the pay raise enacted. Under a 1967 law, pay increases for all top government jobs had been made automatic. The president was to name a panel every four years (Peterson's was the latest) to study the economics of federal pay and cost-of-living percentages and recommend new pay levels if justified by the statistics. Once submitted to Congress, these higher rates would go into effect almost immediately unless vetoed by either House or Senate.

The automatic pay plan put together initially by Mo Udall looked good on paper. It seemed to guarantee regular pay increases while sparing Congress the embarrassment of voting to enrich itself. But the plan fell victim to politicking, working smoothly only once, in 1969, when President Johnson forwarded the 1968 pay panel's recommendations to Congress before leaving office. Congressional salaries went from $30,000 to $42,500 a year.

Four years later, President Nixon delayed naming the pay commission until so late in 1973 that the recommendations failed to reach Capitol Hill until 1974, an election year. It is always difficult for Congress to vote itself a pay raise; it is impossible in an election year. The recommendations were killed in the Senate.

The next year, advocates of a raise managed to sneak through an amendment adding Congress to the federal civil service cost-of-living escalator and that, too, worked once: pay went to $44,625 a year.

In 1976, another election year, Congress voted to pass up any more cost-of-living increases.

The paradox in all of this is that congressmen continually complained that their salaries were not keeping up with inflation. The gripes were all the same: most had to maintain two homes; constituents expected them to contribute to favorite charities and pick up the check at lunch; like everyone else, they had to send children to college, meet mortgage payments, buy a car. By 1977, the gap between congressional salaries and the Peterson Commission recommendations was 29 percent, a politically impossible figure for a nervous Congress to accept publicly.

The new pay scale, $57,500 (and $75,000 for the Speaker, vice-president, and Chief Justice), was due to go into effect February 20, but Grassley and his backers were poised to try to force a vote. For his part, O'Neill was poised with a fast gavel to try to stop them. O'Neill was anxious to get moving on an ethics code. But he had promised the representatives a pay raise in exchange. O'Neill had worked out a strategy: Avoid a pay raise vote before the February 20 deadline and then delay any follow-up votes (on appropriations bills, for example) for as long as possible so that any anti-pay vote would mean a substantial rollback. By mid-summer, he figured, members of the House would have grown accustomed to the larger paychecks and would be willing to oppose any Grassley cutback move.

It worked. Grassley failed to force a vote in February, only succeeding in July. Even then, he was outmaneuvered by the new Speaker of the House. O'Neill and Udall had worked out a procedure that packaged congressional pay with raises for all top federal government employees and the judiciary. A no vote would have killed higher salaries across-the-board. As added insurance, O'Neill gave the House a chance to cast a politically more attractive vote a day earlier on a bill denying any further pay raises (including cost-of-living increases) in 1977 to anyone who received the February raise. The bill passed, 397 to 20.

The next day, when the Grassley amendment was voted on, O'Neill made an unusual personal plea. "Do the decent thing for your fellow colleagues," he asked, "and vote against the Grassley amendment."

Representative Pat Schroeder (D-Colorado) who opposed the pay raise, complained that the Speaker and his allies had twisted arms. "This was made out to be the macho vote of the year," she said. "You were told you were weak and cowardly if you didn't vote for it. There were none of us who didn't get leaned on."

O'Neill accepted Schroeder's complaint as a compliment. He did, indeed, lean on as many House members as possible. He had made a promise: that if the House would approve an ethics code, there would be a pay raise. His word was at stake.

O'Neill supporters were urged to show up early for the vote so the pro-raise count could get off to a fast start. With a little luck, O'Neill reasoned, that would create momentum and the others would fall into line. Udall called it "judgment day." As the bells sounded for the vote and the electric tote board lit up to record the votes, O'Neill forces jumped out to a quick lead and never lost ground. When all had voted, O'Neill won, 241 to 181.

Next, O'Neill turned to the ethics question. There had been no single jarring event, no congressional Watergate, that had made Congress suddenly ethics conscious. It was a series of ripples over the years: John Dowdy (D-Texas) convicted of perjury in a bribe case; Senator Daniel B. Brewster (D-Maryland) convicted of accepting money to influence his votes; Martin Sweig and Nat Voloshen, convicted for actions casting a cloud over House Speaker McCormack's office; the Wayne Hays sex-for-pay scandal; the Wilbur Mills public bout with alcoholism; Richard Hanna of California, convicted in the Korean influence-buying case (and the only congressman to serve time in prison for his part in the Korean affair); several others accused of improper acts in the same case; Representative Robert L. F. Sikes (D-Florida) censured by the House for conflicts of interest in some Florida financial deals; Gulf Oil revealing it had handed out more than $5 million in illegal contributions to congressmen over a ten-year period; an aide to Representative John Young (D-Texas) echoing the Hays scandal with a charge that her boss, too, had hired her primarily as a mistress; Joe D.

Waggonner, Jr. (D-Louisiana) and Allan T. Howe (D-Utah) picked up for soliciting "prostitutes" who turned out to be police decoys. . . .

The press called it the "post-Watergate morality." It meant the old ways wouldn't do for the 1980s.

The Senate was the first to move, adding a provision for public disclosure of personal finances to a bill providing federal money for presidential election campaigns. The public disclosure section was dropped later in conference with the House. The Senate soon tried again, adding ethics rules and financial disclosure to a larger piece of legislation growing out of the Watergate scandal (providing, among other things, for a permanent special federal prosecutor), but that bill died in the House Judiciary Committee.

With some gentle prodding from O'Neill, the House was moving in the same direction, but at its own measured pace. After the Hays affair hit the front pages, a task force on office accounts from Hays's own House Administration Committee recommended that a new panel be created to take a long and careful look at all House financial matters which had been dominated so long by Hays himself. As often happens on Capitol Hill, the man who suggested the creation of a new committee wound up at the head of it, Representative David R. Obey, Democrat of Wisconsin.

Obey, intense, hard-driving, was sent to Congress at the age of thirty in a 1969 special election to fill the seat of former Representative Melvin R. Laird, who had moved on to serve as President Nixon's Secretary of Defense. A man of strong convictions but with a cool analytical mind, Obey approached his task in much the same way he might prepare a doctoral dissertation or the reorganization of a failing corporation. He started with a bipartisan commission of eight House members and seven private citizens. They were divided into task forces, with hired staffs including political scientists, opinion research experts, and computer analysts. The groups set about doing a top-to-bottom review of House operations, discovering, to no one's surprise, that the House was an administrative and legislative nightmare. Unfortunately, by the time the commission's ambitious proposals hit the House floor, the steam had gone out of the reform movement. Modernization of the House was put off for several years. The Obey commission, however, had better luck with its package of ethics reforms.

By the time the post-election caucuses of December, 1976, were underway, O'Neill was convinced that an ethics code should be adopted quickly in the new Ninety-fifth Congress. He had vowed he would be a strong Speaker. Recognizing that the old ethics committee—the Committee on Standards of Official Conduct—had been ineffective, he backed moves to strengthen it by limiting members to two terms and by appointing new members of stronger backbone. And, then, just to make sure that the ethics code stayed on track, he said he would name a special ethics committee to take up where the Obey commission had left off—and write the new rules into law.

To the revitalized *old* ethics committee, O'Neill gave the difficult assignment of investigating current news stories that an unknown number of members of Congress might have accepted illegal campaign contributions and gifts from Tongsun Park. The House had drawn criticism for failing to act on the charges. O'Neill backed a resolution offered in the Democratic caucus by Representative Toby Moffett (D-Connecticut) directing the ethics committee to start work. "Because there is a cloud over the House," O'Neill said, "it is my desire to go as quickly as we possibly can on this Korean matter and see if we can straighten it out." It was a pesky topic that was to plague O'Neill for much of the next year, but he wanted to get moving. Failure to act on these allegations within the House could damage the entire ethics campaign.

O'Neill's ethics drive nearly faltered on a wholly separate question: whether the veteran Bob Sikes, first elected to the House in 1940 and censured for financial misconduct in 1976, should retain his chairmanship of the military construction appropriations subcommittee in 1977. O'Neill sided with Sikes, accepting the Florida Democrat's argument that he had been (1) punished already and (2) reelected since then, in 1976. Therefore, Sikes said and O'Neill agreed, it would be a version of double jeopardy to punish him again. Furthermore, the voters, who are the ultimate judges, had sent Sikes back to Washington.

True reformers, like Common Cause and the more outspoken liberal Democrats, found the O'Neill position inconsistent. If you are in favor of a strong ethics code, then it should be applied to everyone, they reasoned. If a man did something ethically wrong in the eyes of his fellow legislators, then he should not enjoy one of the special rewards of the majority party, a chairmanship.

For O'Neill, his position may have had something to do with his religion—Roman Catholics confess and forgive—and with his reverence for the institution of Congress and the regular order of its procedures. Publicly, all he said was: "Sikes has been dealt with by Congress. His punishment was severe when he was censured. The people saw fit to send him back by an overwhelming vote." Of himself, he said, "Tip O'Neill, yeah, he forgives."

Even O'Neill's own nominee to head the special ethics panel to codify the new rules, Representative L. Richardson Preyer, (D–North Carolina) a quietly respectful and respected former federal judge, spoke out against O'Neill's defense of Sikes. "If we are not prepared to enforce the code of ethics," he said, "then it's a futile exercise to write one."

When it came time to vote, the count was decisive. Sikes lost 189 to 93, and Utah Democrat Gunn McKay was elected chairman of the subcommittee.

It was lucky for O'Neill that Sikes lost. It would have been seen as a potentially fatal flaw of leadership if O'Neill and his Democrats had winked at misbehavior while pushing for a new and stronger code of ethics. Saved by his friends, O'Neill turned to Obey. In a personal appeal to the Obey commission, O'Neill urged it to draft the new code of ethics by early February. "Go all the way," O'Neill told Obey, "I still mean that." Timing was important. He wanted the ethics code adopted at the same time as the new pay raise went into effect.

On February 7, the Obey Commission issued its proposals:

—Nearly total public financial disclosure.

—A ban on private unofficial office accounts, known all too often as "slush funds," with an off-setting increase of $5,000 in official office accounts.

—A limit of 15 percent of congressional salaries (or $8,625 when at the $57,500 rate) on outside earnings.

—A $750 ceiling (later lifted to $1,000) on fees for making speeches or writing magazine articles.

—A ban on the use of campaign contributions to pay off personal debts. (Majority Leader Jim Wright of Texas disclosed in January that he had converted $98,501 of 1976 campaign contributions to pay off old debts.)

—A $100 limit on the value of gifts accepted from lobbyists.

—A ban on franked (free-postage) mass mailings within sixty days of an election.

—No "lame duck" junkets, that is, no tax-paid travel by House members after the election in which they were defeated or retired.

A resolution embodying the Obey commission proposals was divided into three parts and sent to three committees—Standards of Official Conduct (ethics), House Administration, and Rules—with orders to report back promptly.

The ethics committee, by then firmly loyal to O'Neill, was first to report. Then, the House Administration Committee, after a fierce fight with Republicans opposed to increasing the office allowance and amid cries of "railroading" and "arm-twisting," came through narrowly, reporting the bill 13 to 12.

The arm-twisting was done by O'Neill, but only after Obey had threatened to quit as chairman. That night, after the House Administration Committee battle, O'Neill put his arm on Obey's shoulder and said, "Once you bite a fella in the ass, you don't let go."

But there was still the Rules Committee—and more trouble.

On paper, the Rules Committee was an arm of the leadership. Its assignment was to clear bills for floor action, setting such procedures as the number of amendments allowed and the number of hours of debate. Since 1975, the Speaker alone had named members of the Rules Committee. Not even the Steering Committee was involved in the process. At age seventy-four in 1975, Representative James J. Delaney (D–New York) had become chairman of the Rules Committee. Although a northerner, Delaney was as conservative as some of his southern predecessors. But he had promised Albert and O'Neill that if named chairman, he would not block leadership requests for action. Behind him on the committee were ten generally liberal Democrats and only five Republicans. The lineup appeared to be solidly with O'Neill.

Until they got to the subject of money.

Representative Claude Pepper (D-Florida) made $100,000 a year from his Miami law firm. Representative Morgan Murphy (D-Illinois) declared he took in as much as $60,000 from his law firm in Chicago. Representative Shirley Chisholm (D–New York) who had attracted national attention in 1972 as the first black woman to talk of running for president, was very big on the lecture circuit, earning much more than the proposed $8,625 limit. Representative B. F. Sisk (D-California) dabbled in real estate in Washington and objected to public disclosure. Eleven Democrats minus four is seven. Five Republicans plus four is nine. O'Neill and his ethics bill were in trouble.

On the morning of Wednesday, February 23, just days after the new pay raise went into effect, O'Neill invited the Rules Committee Democrats to his office for breakfast. What followed, said one of the guests, was a "rather heated" exchange. He went over a lot of old ground: ethics, salaries, loyalty. His position had been bolstered by a Lou Harris poll released by the Obey commission showing that both the American people and a majority of the members of Congress endorsed the commission's recommendations. Among other items, 54 percent of the public and 64 percent of the House members thought congressmen should give up any private careers. They felt Congress should be a full-time job. To O'Neill, a most persuasive finding was that only 22 percent of the Americans polled said they had confidence in Congress and thought it could mend its ways.

February 23 was Ash Wednesday. That fact alone would be of no particular significance except for an incident one of the Rules Committee members recalled later. The breakfast prepared in the House restaurant and served in the Speaker's office included bacon. For O'Neill, Ash Wednesday was a fast day—no meat. As he angrily confronted the balky Rules Committee Democrats, he spotted the bacon, picked it up, and threw it aside without breaking his oratorical stride. He did not pause to mention bacon; O'Neill was talking of loyalty and duty. He told the Democrats they served on that particular prestigious committee at his pleasure and he could just as easily assign them to someplace like the Post Office or District committees. Tomorrow. "He almost pleaded," said one Democrat. "I haven't seen anything like this for some time in Congress."

As O'Neill told Michael J. Malbin of *National Journal,* "I says, 'Lookit, I've committed myself as the leader of the party to the strongest ethics bill in the history of the country. And I'm asking you, the Rules Committee, as the one handpicked committee that's appointed by the Speaker. You're my handpicked people. Now, I've been able to get this through the Obey commission without any difficulty, and I would expect that I would be able to get it through here.' "

He got his way. Some Rules Committee Democrats still opposed the ethics code's limit on outside earnings, but they dutifully voted to send the resolution to the House floor for a vote. In exchange, they won a small concession. There would be an opportunity for a separate vote on the earnings question.

When the measure reached the House floor on March 2, 1977, O'Neill was ready. As the bells rang to signal key votes, O'Neill studied the computerized vote monitor, noting how the tally was going and who still hadn't voted. As the afternoon wore on, the House rejected all substantive amendments (Morgan Murphy's move to strike out the limit on outside earnings lost 344 to 79) and, in a major personal triumph for the new House Speaker, finally voted 402 to 22 for a strong code of ethics. It was a battle O'Neill could not afford to lose, a test of who would be in charge in the House. The *Washington Star* headline the next day summed it up: HOUSE VOTES ETHICS CODE AND A NEW HILL STRONGMAN IS BORN.

The crucial vote came on a motion to open the ethics code to further amendment. Bolling, acting as floor manager, argued against the motion. "The only way to pass this piece of legislation," he said to a chorus of boos from the GOP side of the aisle, "is not to allow it to be unraveled." By then, it had become a partisan political issue. The Republicans charged the Democrats with imposing a "gag rule." They did not like many parts of the proposed code of behavior and protested that there should be a chance to amend it. But the O'Neill forces stood firm, and the pro-amendment motion was defeated 267 to 153. Only fifteen Democrats deserted him. As O'Neill left the floor to return to his office, he turned to an aide and said, "I want their names."

Tip O'Neill gestured toward his outer office where a large loose-leaf book lay on a table.

Do we keep a daily record? The answer is yes. Do we keep the percentages? The answer is yes. All I have to do is go out and get the book and I can tell you how many times each Democrat has voted with the Speaker's preference and how many times he has voted with the party view—and how many times he has voted wrong. Sure, we have a record on that. For example, I know that [Arizona Democratic Representative Bob] Stump voted with us only once last year. For Speaker. Never gave us another vote. And [Georgia Democratic Representative Larry] McDonald gave us only one vote other than for Speaker. He voted twice with the Democratic Party. . . . We keep a daily record. We know how each Democrat voted on labor, conservation matters, everything. It's all indexed. . . . Stump is complaining, of course, that he doesn't have a major committee.

O'Neill wanted to be a strong Speaker of the U.S. House of Representatives, much as he had been a strong Speaker of the Massachusetts House of Representatives, and he was off to a fast start. Early assessments in 1977 ranked him far above his predecessors, Albert and McCormack, and some speculated that he might even surpass the legendary Rayburn in overall effectiveness—if he played his cards right.

But the game had new rules. New forces were at work in Congress in the late Seventies. The reforms of the past decade, while making tools available for the use of a shrewd, strong Speaker, also made the House more difficult to manage. The reformers had given with one hand and taken away with the other.

Thus, thanks to recent changes, O'Neill had firm control of the Rules Committee, which guided the flow of legislation to the House floor. And he had firm control of the Steering and Policy Committee, which made committee assignments and developed party policy. Arcane-sounding procedural changes had given him firmer control of overall legislative scheduling and had weakened the once unchallenged power of committee chairmen.

At the same time, however, the Congressional "democratization" of the

1970s, flowing from activist entities like Common Cause and the Democratic Study Group and abetted by the enormous turnover in the House, had diffused the old power centers and left the House harder to manage. Instead of two dozen autocratic old bulls at the heads of full committees, there were scores of ambitious younger members at the heads of new subcommittees.

The new political style was independence. The younger members were described as "independent" in the effort to understand why the House had become politically unpredictable. Big-city Democratic bosses no longer could deliver a bloc of dutiful votes on an issue. It was no longer sufficient simply to "pass the word" before a vote and see the Democrats fall in line. This new breed asked questions. They had to be convinced.

Further, changes in election financing laws had altered political influence both in home districts and on Capitol Hill. The new (1974) Federal Election Commission had ruled that private corporations could set up political action committees to raise money among employees and hand it out to political candidates—much as labor unions had done for years. With that ruling, PACs sprung up by the hundreds and dollars flowed by the thousands. A congressional candidate, accustomed to seeing most campaign donations come from the major political parties, labor unions, and such broad-based groups as the American Medical Association, began to collect money from all over the place. As a result, party influence on individual congressmen was weakened while the impact of dozens of special interests was strengthened.

In Washington, these special interests often came together in single-issue lobby groups concerned over one piece of legislation and not a congressman's overall voting record. Traditional vote bargaining became more difficult. Newer members might vote, for example, against a farm bill, not realizing that they might need support later from the rural states on some urban clean-up legislation. Lobbyists for the clean-air act didn't care how a member voted on food stamps.

O'Neill watched it all, and adjusted accordingly.

If nothing else, after forty years in politics, O'Neill understood power. He understood that it was a combination of little things, of seizing initiatives, of moving quickly to reward and punish, of keeping track of how fellow Democrats voted. "Well," said O'Neill in a long interview with *Yankee* magazine, "what is power? Power is when people assume you have power. That's when you have it." Jimmy Breslin, studying O'Neill during the impeachment period, concluded that power is an illusion: "mirrors and blue smoke."

O'Neill is a powerful Speaker because he has been assertive. If he could not rule with an iron hand as he did in Massachusetts, he could still rule. He recognizes that times change, and he has hired a skillful staff and strong lieutenants who complement his leadership style.

As Speaker, O'Neill simply has built on the strengths of a political lifetime. He has accumulated a reservoir of popularity and fewer rivals than any House leader in decades. Everyone likes him. He knows it and he builds on it. He is available to anyone with a question or a problem. He has worked carefully to hammer together majorities for key votes. Sometimes it worked. Sometimes it didn't. He keeps looking for new ways to impose old standards.

There's no way I can impose party discipline. There is no party discipline in America today. In this day and age, it is completely different from the Rayburn days [of one-man rule]. I meet with the Freshman Caucus. I meet with the Sophomore Caucus, the Black Caucus. I meet with the Democratic Study Group. I meet with the Middle American Caucus. I meet with the Farm and Rural Caucus, the New England Caucus. I meet with their executive committees. I meet with the freshmen twice a month, the sophomores twice a month. Now, when I have legislation coming along, how do I handle it? I put together an ad hoc committee. . . .

On December 13, 1976, the Organization of Petroleum Exporting Countries (OPEC) met in Qatar, a small Arab country on a peninsula jutting out into the Persian Gulf. Delegates were to decide how much to raise the price of oil (not whether to raise the price, just how much). After haggling back and forth, an increase of 5 percent was agreed upon, with another 5 percent to follow later.

In the United States, Americans burned more oil than ever in 1977. Nearly half, an average of 8.8 million barrels of oil a day, was imported despite the higher prices. President Carter saw the dwindling oil supplies and increasing prices as a major crisis and asked Congress to do two things: create a new Department of Energy, and adopt a comprehensive package of energy tax, conservation, and decontrol legislation. The first was easy. A DOE bill was signed into law that summer. The second took a little longer.

Concern over energy policy was not new. It had reached the level of a national debate during the Arab oil embargo of 1973–74 and had simmered inconclusively during the Ford administration.

Oil shortages and prices were subjects that O'Neill was quite familiar with. New England, with its heavy dependence on imported home heating oil, was hard hit by each new crisis. In December, as the OPEC ministers were mulling over world prices, O'Neill suggested that the House set up a separate committee to handle energy issues then scattered among half a dozen committees.

Although the idea sounded logical, it required every ounce of O'Neill's diplomatic skills. First of all, the chairmen of those six committees and the energy subcommittees on each of the full committees were—to a man— opposed. Each feared a loss of his power with the loss of authority over any part of such an important issue as energy policy. Each realized that only one could be chairman of the new committee.

O'Neill moved carefully. He decided against creating a new permanent committee, setting up instead a special panel just to handle energy legislation in the Ninety-fifth Congress. It was considered a stroke of genius. All involved in energy matters were named to the new committee but still retained authority over various pieces of the Carter energy package in their separate roles on other committees.

But in fact, O'Neill was in charge. Under authority only recently extended to the Speaker, he was able to set deadlines for each committee to finish its part of the package and then another deadline for the special committee to put it all together. He announced that the House would pass the bill before taking off for an August recess, and while many observers, especially members of the press, scoffed, he did just that. The bill passed.

It is a mark of O'Neill's skill that he could put together such a committee and make it work. Two years earlier, when Carl Albert had tried a similar move, he was thwarted by the chairmen of standing committees that shared energy jurisdiction. The feuding caused the Democratic energy program to collapse. O'Neill, however, picked carefully, waiting until Minority Leader Rhodes had named his twelve members, then chose thirteen Democrats with the aim of assuring a 19-to-18 vote on what John Rhodes has termed "everything that counts."

The Speaker's energy strategy had another goal: to draw younger Democrats into the inner circle. One of them was Representative Philip R. Sharp (D-Indiana), a star of the Ninety-fourth Congress's freshman class. Sharp was named to the ad hoc committee as a representative of the House Commerce energy subcommittee. A former university professor, Sharp had caught O'Neill's eye when, as a first-termer, he had drafted a successful floor amendment to the Clean Air Act, setting fuel efficiency standards for new American-made automobiles.

"I remember," Sharp said in an interview, "Tip called a caucus of the Democrats on the ad hoc committee. We met in his office and he gave a very strong statement against parochialism. He said, 'You're put on here to represent the national interest, not just regional.' I understood, there was a general expectation, that we were going to have to bite the bullet."

When it came time to organize for a House floor vote, O'Neill again turned to Sharp to head a task force to round up reluctant supporters. "He was always strong, urging us to work," Sharp said. "He made it very clear he considered passage of the bill important. There was no question where the leadership stood."

Sharp figured O'Neill called on him because he was a worker, willing to do some of the running around that older members might decline. He accepted enthusiastically. It offered an opportunity, Sharp said, to see how the leadership operated. "We were actually drawn into the task of getting things done," Sharp said. "We all get tunnel vision around here, you know, focusing on our own special interests. The leadership's problems are phenomenal, just phenomenal. The Speaker's constantly being buffeted."

O'Neill's use of task forces like Sharp's was no accident. He had been thinking of ways to bring younger members into internal House operations for years:

What I have found is that there is too much frustration in the Congress of the United States. There's a tremendous amount of ability, a tremendous amount of talent. The truth of the matter is that there are so many guys who don't have spots to get rid of that frustration. So, every major piece of legislation that comes through here I put together an ad hoc committee. With Phil Sharp, Butler Derrick [D–South Carolina]. I don't have a helluva lot more than that to offer. If they want to go to Europe, will I sign a slip? Sure I'll sign a slip. If there's something that comes along that sounds good, sure I try to help them. I don't have anything else to give them.

It's the old Tip O'Neill in a new world.

Hey, that's the only way I've got to repay these guys for going along. Y'know, you ask me what are my powers and my authority around here? The power to recognize on the floor, little odds and ends. Like men get pride out of the prestige of handling the Committee of the Whole, being named Speaker for the day. And those little trips that come along, like those trips to China, trips to Russia, things of that nature. . . .

And I have an open-door policy. Rare is the occasion when a man has a personal fund-raiser or is being personally honored that I don't show up at it. I'm always accessible. These are parts of the duties and the obligations of the Speaker, and it shows the hand of friendship. That's what it's all about.

Early in 1980, O'Neill's ethics campaign and "post-Watergate morality" received another jolt. Seven House members and a senator were snagged in an undercover operation run by the Federal Bureau of Investigation and code-named ABSCAM, for Arab scam. FBI agents, posing as wealthy Arab sheiks, offered the congressmen large bribes in exchange for high-level help on business and immigration matters. Some took the money; some did not. All were tarnished and in the minds of many Americans the old notion that politicians are all crooks was confirmed.

O'Neill was gloomy. "Am I shocked? Yes, of course I'm shocked," he said. "I naturally feel the institution has been hurt. But I have great confidence in the bulk of the members of this House." He shrugged. "I want to clean it [ABSCAM] up and let the cards fall where they may."

12

TRIALS WITH
THE PRESS

THE BELLS ring three times in quick succession, a sharp jarring sound heard everywhere on the House side of Capitol Hill. It is the signal that the House will convene in fifteen minutes. It also means that Tip O'Neill is about to meet the press.

I look at myself as an easy-going fella. I'm willing and ready to meet anyone openly. I have an open-door policy with the press, and I'm ready to talk frankly on the issues.

Sometimes. But not always. As Speaker, O'Neill certainly has been more open than his predecessors. But he has remained thin-skinned and suspicious of reporters as well. Still, in much the same way that voters can deride "politicians" in general yet love their own congressman, O'Neill excoriates the press in general while warmly embracing individual reporters.

The daily (when the House was in session) press conferences were friendly for the most part, dominated by an O'Neill skilled at bantering. He soon discovered that a prompt response to questions and a little bit of candor mixed with charm would win over most reporters—as it won over most members of the House. His most dazzling performances, came, however, when ducking questions.

Mary Russell of the *Washington Post* once asked, for example, whether O'Neill had tried to block a Justice Department inquiry into an alleged numbers (gambling) operation in one of the office buildings. O'Neill didn't want to answer. He didn't want to discuss the subject at all for fear of giving new life to what he felt was an unattractive story. So he launched into a long reminiscence about a time he had gone to a Maryland race track and run into the late J. Edgar Hoover, director of the FBI. Hoover offered O'Neill a ride back to Washington. When they arrived, Hoover discovered he had taken the wrong car. Everyone laughed. No more questions.

On another occasion, the question dealt with a complaint by O'Neill about trying to dislodge a Republican holdover at the Civil Service

Commission. Would the Carter reorganization plan alter this "spoils system?" a reporter asked.

Q: "Who are you?" O'Neill demanded.

A: "Miles Benson" [of Newhouse News Service].

Q: "Who do you work for? the *Boston Herald?*"

A: "No."

Q: "Next question."

O'Neill had no intention of commenting in any way that would enable someone to use the words "spoils system," not publicly. Moreover, he didn't want to be put into the position of evaluating a plan he knew little about.

Once when the *Boston Globe*'s Rachelle Patterson tried to ask O'Neill about his personal finances, he shot back: "Do you work for the *Boston Globe* or some high-school paper?"

And when sharp-tongued Sarah McLendon demanded: "Did you have anything to do with shoving out Jay Solomon [from being head of the General Services Administration]?" O'Neill said only: "Hey, stop it, willya?"

Sometimes, he could respond to questions in such a way that reporters wouldn't know what the answer had been. On gas rationing, for example, O'Neill was asked in the spring of 1979 whether he favored some kind of rationing to conserve gas. He seemed to say yes, but then again maybe he didn't. He talked about the injustice of high prices and he said he would favor "what's best for the country" and would go along with "whatever the experts say" without advocating anything specific.

O'Neill really had the press spinning during the period in September 1979, when Senator Edward M. Kennedy emerged from his non–presidential candidate status to "maybe." There were news stories each day trying to interpret Kennedy's stronger and stronger hints that he would, indeed, challenge Carter for the Democratic presidential nomination.

Lacking a definitive word from Kennedy, the reporters converged on O'Neill, who meets with the press daily as a matter of routine. It makes him the most accessible politician in town, and because he was from Massachusetts, reporters assumed that O'Neill knew what Kennedy was up to. They were wrong. At first, O'Neill said, "I don't think Kennedy can be denied the Democratic nomination if he were to run." That was interpreted, in the shorthand of deadline reporting, as O'Neill support for Kennedy against Carter, which bothered O'Neill, the old party loyalist. He was not ready to urge Kennedy to run.

Then, only a few days later, O'Neill said he didn't think Kennedy would run. "The nominee will be Jimmy Carter," he said. "I think if [Kennedy] were a candidate, he'd be out there organizing." This was interpreted as inside dope that Kennedy would not run, by the ever-eager reporters. O'Neill was described as a close personal and political ally of Kennedy and, therefore, on the inside track. Apparently, not so.

Kennedy then told reporters himself that perhaps they ought to listen to him rather than O'Neill. The next day, O'Neill revised his statement. "I would have to say he [Kennedy] is giving it consideration," he said. And with that, he shut up.

And the press conferences continued. . . .

If reporters ran out of questions, O'Neill would fill in the empty space. "Any more questions? Don't just stand there like Stoughton bottles." Stoughton bottles? "Dr. Stoughton's elixir, or something like that. You have to ask Eddie Boland. I don't know whether you drank it or rubbed it on your chest. Every Irish home had them. They'd use up the elixir and line the bottles up on the mantel, right next to the Virgin Mary."

And on one St. Patrick's Day: "The top o' the mornin' to ya'." Silence. "I can tell there's not an Irishman in the crowd. You're supposed to say, 'And the rest of the day to you.'"

Another morning, reporters heard O'Neill on:

Cards: "I am not a gambler. I engage in games of skill." Pause. Chuckles. "I am a good poker player and a good gin rummy player. Gin rummy is about 2 percent skill. On a slow plane to Boston, that can pay the fare."

Whiskey: "I never drink before five o'clock. I never drink alone, and I never drink if I have any work to do. When I stop drinking beer, I can lose weight fairly easily. I like a glass of white wine now and then."

His wife: "She beat me forty-one out of the last forty-two times we played backgammon. I wouldn't bet her even a quarter on a game."

On more serious topics, reporters generally find O'Neill a reliable source. His batting average on predicting House votes is high, and he shares this information freely. He generally has been willing to discuss what goes on at White House meetings with congressional leaders and to use the press conferences as a forum for pushing Democratic party programs. If not always eloquent, he can be forceful. By controlling the tone of the press meetings, he manages to deflect unwanted questions without making reporters angry. For the most part, they like him and vice versa.

One exception involved Stephen Wermiel of the *Boston Globe*. It wasn't that the two men disliked one another; it was that Wermiel once wrote a story O'Neill didn't like. Nor was Wermiel pleased with O'Neill's reaction, which effectively closed the O'Neill office to him for about a year.

In the spring and summer of 1975, Wermiel, then assigned to the *Globe*'s

Washington bureau, wrote that O'Neill had waffled on the politically sensitive hometown issue of school busing. As Wermiel said later, he was just reporting the facts: O'Neill had told one Boston group that he opposed busing and told another that he would "reluctantly" support some pro-busing moves. He promised that he would help clear the way for a resolution to amend the Constitution and restrict court-ordered busing. He had not said he would vote for it, according to Wermiel, just that he thought others should have a chance to vote. Thanks to Wermiel, O'Neill attracted some unwanted criticism.

The next time Wermiel went to O'Neill's office, the congressman came out and angrily said, "I trusted you [he had let the reporter sit in on meetings] and you broke faith with me." The order went out: No more Wermiel interviews. O'Neill would deal with other, more friendly, *Globe* reporters. He cannot understand why any Boston reporters should be critical. He thinks they should be proud that someone from their town is Speaker of the House and he was hurt, even offended, when his motives were questioned.

Most politicians advise against tangling publicly with the press. The person with the typewriter and printing press usually has the last word. If a slight—or even an error—is ignored, it's likely to go away. But a politician who succumbs to outrage and goes public with it, may make heroes of little people and mountains of molehills. Tip O'Neill knows this, but sometimes.

For example, Doonesbury is a comic strip, a very funny satirical one. Its author, Garry Trudeau, may be the sharpest political commentator of the day. In June 1978, he got around to Tip O'Neill with a pair of daily comic strips lampooning O'Neill for allowing Korean rice-merchant Tongsun Park to throw birthday parties for him. A reporter for the *Los Angeles Times* called O'Neill's office before the strips were printed and suggested they might be libelous. After eliciting the O'Neill attitude, the reporter wrote up the story. "They set us up," O'Neill said bitterly of the *Times*. "They asked us confidentially what our views were and then they ran a front-page story [reporting O'Neill's indignant reaction to the comic strip]. That's setting you up."

O'Neill's views of the cartoons, relayed to Trudeau by Gary Hymel, were that they were unfair and unfactual and should be changed or withdrawn. The offending comic strips ran intact in five hundred newspapers. The *Los Angeles Times* story was also picked up in a number of newspapers. To top it off, more than two hundred readers took the time to clip a small coupon from the second cartoon and send it to O'Neill as a protest of his Korean connection. "Dear Tip," read the coupon. "Yes! I would like more information on the following: (check one or more)."

What followed was a list of the six congressmen named in stories about Korean influence-peddling and a final box that said: "Yourself." The coupon had a line for signatures and addresses under the slogan: "Yours for a Clean Congress."

Trudeau's editor said the columns provoked more response than usual because O'Neill himself "got hysterical. We only get a lot of response if the celebrity overreacts." Trudeau took another swipe at O'Neill in December, but this time it was ignored.

Most of the time, O'Neill and the Washington press corps get along fine. In his years as majority leader and a leading contender for Speaker, the major news publications glowed with admiration for him. Not a single word of criticism appeared in the February 4, 1974, *Time* magazine cover story. Headlines in the *Chicago Tribune* and the *National Observer* reflected widely held views: "A Master Politician's Silent Rise to the Top" and "Tip O'Neill: An Old Pol Spots the New Issues." So it struck him as particularly cruel that a newspaper in his own backyard would launch, as the *Boston Herald American* did, in 1977, a major investigative effort to determine whether O'Neill's business dealings violated federal conflict-of-interest laws. The *Herald* stories came in clusters, and one contained serious errors. But they were printed. The articles went on for months, leading nowhere. The kindest thing to say is that the *Herald* was overzealous. Some, even among *Herald* reporters, called the stories irresponsible. Leo Diehl said the whole campaign was malicious.

Separate threads of the story began in an Allston, Massachusetts, sterilizer equipment company, a Washington, D.C., bar, the corporate board rooms of the Hearst publishing company and the *Herald* newsroom. Key figures included a gregarious social-climbing Korean, a big Irish congressman who couldn't say no to a pal, a gadfly Massachusetts Republican convinced that all congressmen are dishonest, and an editor anxious to rescue a troubled newspaper from a steady decline in advertising and circulation.

To begin more or less chronologically, one must begin with the *Herald* itself, and its crosstown rival, the *Boston Globe*. For nearly a generation, the *Globe* had been climbing steadily in circulation, advertising revenues, and size. Over the years, Boston's other newspapers closed or merged. The *Boston Post* died in 1956, the evening *Traveler* in 1967. Its morning editions then combined with the 121-year-old *Herald* to become the *Herald Traveler*.

Hearst entered the Boston newspaper market in 1904 with the *American*, which thrived for years, buying out less hardy rivals as first the *Advertiser* failed and then the *Record*. In 1972, the *Herald Traveler* lost a long legal battle to keep control of its principal source of revenue, television Channel 5, and Hearst moved in to buy out the financially troubled paper. The resulting *Boston Record American and Herald Traveler/Sunday Advertiser* soon was shortened to a more manageable *Herald American*. At that point, revenue losses were averaging $3 million a year.

In 1975, Hearst brought in a new publisher, Robert C. Bergenheim, with a mandate to revitalize the paper and reverse its declining circulation and advertising revenues. By trimming deadwood and unnecessary costs, Bergenheim did manage to show a profit the first couple of years. But the downward slide couldn't be stopped. Deficits returned and circulation fell. The *Herald* seemed to be in a painfully losing contest with the *Globe*. As *Herald* circulation fell an average of 5 percent a year, *Globe* circulation rose by about 5 percent a year.

In true Hearst style, the *Herald* grabbed for readers by focusing on the most sensational aspects of news. They tried everything. Bold black headlines featured murders, three-alarm fires, daring rescues, disasters, scandals. Nothing worked. The paper still was losing money. Rumors persisted that the Hearst Corporation, which was run by businessmen interested in making money, after all, would sell out or close down. Hearst executives discussed the problem time and again in the next few years. The decision was to stick with the paper, allocate more money to build it up, and hire a top-flight editor to try to reverse the trends.

William F. McIlwain was their man. McIlwain had worked on newspapers in North Carolina, Virginia, New York, Canada, and New Jersey—in that order—over the years. In midcareer, while an editor at *Newsday*, he had acknowledged that he was an alcoholic, had checked himself into a state hospital in North Carolina to kick the habit, and had emerged a sober man. He wrote a book about it all, *A Farewell to Alcohol*, and, after a tour as a writer-in-residence at Wake Forest University, returned to newspaper work. He was widely respected as a gifted editor. He was a Nieman Fellow at Harvard University in 1957. One former colleague described McIlwain as a "Gothic Southerner" who did everything by indirection, or example. "Instead of writing a memo saying, 'This is what we're going to do, 1-2-3-4,'" he said, "McIlwain will kind of nudge people in the direction he wants to go. It's a trial and error process. He'll say he likes one thing and doesn't like another until you get the message." McIlwain joined the *Herald* in March 1977.

While the *Herald* was still looking for an editor, a Massachusetts Republican, William A. "Battlin' Bill" Barnstead, already was looking for O'Neill's scalp. Barnstead worked out of a small cluttered office in a company he headed, Consolidated Stills & Sterilizers, in Allston. He was a Republican, a very conservative one to judge by the articles and letters from people like Ronald Reagan and Philip Crane he has tacked onto his office walls. He was proud to say, however, that in 1974 he was the first chairman of a Republican state committee to urge President Nixon to resign.

Barnstead had run against O'Neill in 1976 and 1978 and intended to do so again in 1980. He didn't expect to win, since the district is so heavily Democratic. But he felt someone ought to challenge O'Neill: "He's a shining example of what's wrong in Washington." So, Barnstead offered himself. He was not quiet about it. Words flew from his mouth. Xeroxed news clippings, pamphlets, and letters were stuffed into file folders and offered haphazardly to all visitors. It's all there, he said, the story of Tip O'Neill. "He's a hack, a political hack. . . . I wouldn't call him a crook, but I wouldn't call him honest."

The way Barnstead attracted attention in 1976 and 1977 was to "leak" (if a leak can be something given out so flamboyantly) anti-O'Neill documents, innuendoes, allegations, tips, to any member of the news media who would listen. Most political reporters shrugged him off as a biased and unreliable source. He himself says, "I'm a John Q. Citizen who doesn't have a chance. The reason I run for office is to get attention."

After the 1976 election, reporter Richard D. Lyons of the *New York Times* went to Boston to write a story about O'Neill, the man who was then certain to be the next Speaker of the U.S. House. Among those he interviewed was O'Neill's Republican opponent in the most recent campaign, Bill Barnstead. Barnstead loaded Lyons up with anti-O'Neill literature. Included was something about an O'Neill interest in a downtown parking lot and some Xerox copies of documents allegedly showing O'Neill business activities.

Lyons, under pressure to write a story quickly—O'Neill was to be nominated for Speaker by House Democrats the next Monday—said none of the Barnstead material made much sense to him, nor did he have time to double-check it. His assignment was not to investigate past business dealings, however; he was to find out O'Neill's current financial condition, his net worth.

O'Neill had resisted giving Lyons a detailed report at first. He said the information was not readily available. But Lyons insisted, until O'Neill finally telephoned Lyons with rough estimates, in round figures, of a net worth adding up to $125,000. It was his first public disclosure of personal finances. "There are people who think I've made a lot of money in public life," O'Neill told the reporter, "but it just isn't so."

Lyons discussed the Barnstead charges with O'Neill but did not report them in detail in his story. He simply wrote that O'Neill denied involvement in the business deals as outlined by "some of his political foes in Boston." O'Neill had told Lyons, among other things, that he had invested $5,000 in the Bristol Nursing Home in Attleboro, Massachusetts, in the 1960s. "The operation went bankrupt," he said, "and the total return on my investment was five dollars."

The Lyons story was carried on the national *New York Times* wire service and was featured on the front page of the Boston *Herald American* where the nursing home paragraph caught an editor's eye and was filed away for future reference.

In Washington, the thread of O'Neill's trial by press leads next to a Capitol Hill bar on June 23, 1977. Although details are predictably scarce, the story that circulated around Congress went like this: two reporters were having an after-work drink with a friend, a former Capitol Hill employee. The reporters convinced the friend that she should call the House ethics committee, formally known as the Committee on Standards of Official Conduct, with a tip they had picked up from a questionable source. She called the committee and said that she had heard that Tongsun Park, a wealthy Korean businessman, had paid the rent on a house in Georgetown shared by Tip O'Neill and Eddie Boland. The fact that O'Neill and Boland did not live in Georgetown apparently made little difference, and the committee staff decided to look into the anonymous tip as they looked into every other piece of information dealing with Park who, by then, appeared to be something other than a friendly Korean businessman. There were charges that Park had handed out hundreds of thousands of dollars to congressmen in an effort to buy favors for his government. O'Neill became suspect because he had been the guest of honor at two lavish Park parties. The committee also was studying whether birthday gifts given O'Neill at those parties violated the House code of conduct rule against accepting gifts from foreign governments.

The fact that the ethics committee was investigating the rent tip was leaked to the press later in the summer. The allegation became a banner headline run across the top of the page in the *Boston Herald,* and was featured in most major newspapers across the country. O'Neill, relaxing at his home on the Cape, was shaken. "It's the headlines that hurt you back home. The young twenty-year-olds don't read the whole story. Talk about McCarthyism. . . ." Several days later, in a less flashy story, ethics committee sources were quoted as saying the staff had determined—from studying O'Neill-Boland check stubs—that in fact they had paid their own rent all along, $287 a month for eleven years.

But O'Neill had been forced into a defensive position. He turned over all his papers to the House ethics committee, urging a thorough investigation of everyone involved. He insisted over and over that he had done nothing wrong, that he hardly knew Tongsun Park, and had never talked about Korean government matters with him.

Hey, I've met a thousand guys like Tongsun Park in my life. He wasn't a friend of mine and I wasn't a friend of his. So somebody throws a party and somebody else takes credit for it. That's the way it goes. . . . I've met the guy maybe five times in my life. The first time he was an undergraduate at Georgetown and somebody brought him by the office and said he was in some small business for himself. I says something like, "Isn't that wonderful? Only in America." Then I saw him a couple of times after he became established in business. I've been to Korea [in April 1974] and never once did Tongsun Park mention one word about his business or mention one word about Korea.

On December 10, 1973, Park had invited O'Neill to a party at the George Town Club, which he had founded and partly financed. Two congressmen, William E. Minshall, Democrat of Ohio, and Richard D. Hanna, Democrat of California, were listed as cohosts. O'Neill said he went because he made it a practice to drop by parties given by colleagues as often as possible. Twenty-two other congressmen also attended. During the party, Boland casually mentioned that O'Neill had celebrated his sixty-first birthday just the day before. Park promptly announced to everyone that it was a birthday party and sent a friend out to buy a gift from a shop down the street (a set of pewter lamps priced at $263.55 and worth about $40, O'Neill said). Eighty-six persons attended the party. The bill was $1,978 plus gift. The party was not considered unusually lavish.

The next year when O'Neill's birthday rolled around, Park again sent out invitations, this time for the Madison Hotel on December 16. O'Neill said he understood that although Park was host, the party really was a get-together of friends to celebrate his birthday, and the retirement from Congress of

Minshall and Hanna. President Ford was to be a guest of honor but cancelled at the last minute. There were 140 persons at the 1974 bash. The bill was $5,597.86 plus gift, a golf bag and a set of clubs.

At the time, no one criticized O'Neill for attending the party; in fact it attracted very little attention. It was just part of the Washington scene. Lobbyists and social climbers are always giving such parties and people-loving politicians like O'Neill go to them.

Before the next birthday season, however, details of Tongsun Park's hidden role as an influence buyer for the Korean government had begun to emerge. The first hints appeared in a news story by reporter Ronald Kessler in the *Washington Post*. Kessler had been hearing rumors for months that perhaps Park's activities in Washington were a cover for something else. But he hadn't been able to nail down any illegality. On July 27, 1975, Kessler wrote: "Tongsun Park, a South Korean businessman who regularly entertains many of the top leaders of the U.S. government, is one of Washington's most accomplished power brokers." All O'Neill had to read were the words: "who regularly entertains many of the top leaders of the U.S. government." That was the end, he said, of any contact he might have had with Park.

Martin Nolan of the *Boston Globe* has said that Park used to try to impress visitors by dawdling in the hall outside O'Neill's office and then stopping the congressman to chat on his way in or out. O'Neill was always affable and it may have looked as though they were buddies. But, more than likely, they probably were—as O'Neill insists—only casual acquaintances. After the Kessler story, Diehl stopped even the hallway encounters.

One item in the ethics committee's O'Neill inquiry concerned O'Neill's son, Tom, who was by then lieutenant governor of Massachusetts. It turned out that in 1973 Tom O'Neill had served on a board of directors with Park for something called McLaughlin Fisheries in Ireland. Both Park and young O'Neill testified they didn't know the other was on the board. An O'Neill aide said, "Tommy didn't know Tongsun Park from Fenway Park." The company had been organized by an old O'Neill friend, Francis X. McLaughlin, a former Secret Service agent and unsuccessful candidate in 1953 for the Boston City Council. McLaughlin told the committee that neither Park nor Tom O'Neill had put any money into the business or taken any out of it. Tip O'Neill became involved only when a question was raised as to whether he had honestly answered the ethics committee questionnaire when it asked: "Have you or any member of your immediate family . . . had any commercial business dealings with Tongsun Park?" O'Neill had answered no. The committee concluded he probably was telling the truth; certainly, no O'Neill made any money from the venture.

One of the more bizarre O'Neill-Park stories involved allegations that O'Neill had accepted "sums of money" from Park. The informant for this allegation was a man named Jack Kelly. He had told his story, in fact, to several reporters, who were convinced of the man's reliability, at least at first. Among other things, Kelly said he had worked as a financial adviser to Park and, on one occasion in 1971, had cashed a $20,000 check for Park to take on a visit to O'Neill. Kelly said he drove Park to the airport where he bought a ticket to New York. He said Park intended to drive from there to Nantucket to spend Thanksgiving with the O'Neills. (O'Neill's house is in Harwichport on Cape Cod, and besides, Nantucket is an island.) Only after careful investigation did the committee learn that Kelly was a drunk, down on his luck and trying to make some money off peddling a story about a prominent person. There was, indeed, money changing hands, but the name of the man involved was "Neil," short for Cornelius Gallagher, a former Democratic congressman from New Jersey, not O'Neill. Gallagher served time in federal prison for income tax evasion after being charged with taking kickbacks from a number of persons, including Park.

It took the ethics committee a year to unravel the Korean story as it related to O'Neill. House investigators chased down all leads, even listening to a tape recording of one Tongsun Park party, before clearing O'Neill of any wrongdoing. It may have been "unwise," the committee staff report concluded, for O'Neill to accept those two birthday parties, but it was not illegal. "I always knew in my heart and my mind," O'Neill said, "that I never did anything unethical."

Nevertheless, for O'Neill, it was a very bad year. The published stories of his relationship with Tongsun Park were painful enough. But the *Boston Herald* was still on his trail. The paper's Washington reporter, Chris Black, was being pressed to write what she called "the ultimate Koreagate story." The *Herald* was anxious to break a big story. "It just couldn't be done," Black said after she left the *Herald* in frustration (and went to work for the *Globe*). "Once you got beyond the little parties and things, it just wasn't there. I really researched the thing and browbeat all the investigators to make sure. It just wasn't a story."

The *Herald American* is located in a relatively new building on a sleazy edge of downtown Boston where the subway becomes an elevated. On an October day in 1977, as Tip O'Neill struggled in Washington to hold President Carter's energy program together and tried in vain to marshall the votes for a controversial package of House procedural reforms, *Herald* Editor McIlwain called a few of his top reporters together with Assistant

Managing Editor Charlotte Hall and Political Editor William Lewis. (Lewis soon would be shifted to reporting and replaced by Wayne Woodlief, the *Herald*'s Washington correspondent, who had been called to Boston for the meeting.) The time had come, McIlwain said, to take a systematic look at O'Neill and his friends. Up to then, there had been scattered stories, the *Times* item on the nursing home venture, a longer piece in Boston's underground paper, *Phoenix*, which repeated many of the Barnstead allegations, and, finally, the Tongsun Park stories. Barnstead had dropped off packets of anti-O'Neill files at a number of other newspaper offices, including the *Washington Post* and the *New York Times*. If anyone were to get the story, McIlwain wanted it to be the *Herald*. "It was not really a 'Get Tip' thing," said one reporter, "but more like a get-there-before-anyone-else. There was no planned conspiracy to pin Tip's scalp to the wall. McIlwain just had the notion that anyone who had been around Boston politics as long as Tip had, probably had been into some shady stuff. He couldn't believe that he had not."

McIlwain denied expressing such thoughts. "I've been an editor thirty-six years," he said after quitting the *Herald* in 1979 for the *Washington Star*. "If I made judgments that way, I wouldn't have been very good at my work." The O'Neill stories grew out of information gathered and checked out by *Herald* reporters, he said. If anyone said anything disparaging at editorial conferences about O'Neill's looks or Boston politics, it would have been "in whimsy or joking around."

McIlwain believed in chains of command. Most of the time, he dealt with sub-editors who dealt with the reporters. Thus it was that Chris Black remembers Charlotte Hall, who had worked with McIlwain on the Bergen, New Jersey *Record*—and followed him to Boston—as the one who pushed her for O'Neill stories. The attitude around the *Herald*, Black said, was that you only have to look at O'Neill to know he's a crook: "The guy has to be crooked. If we look hard enough, we'll find it."

Hall denies that any such opinion was voiced, or even thought. "To say that we were out to get Tip O'Neill is a complete mischaracterization," she says. "We received tips that we thought bore looking into. One of the roles of the press is to scrutinize the conduct of high public officials. When a paper receives such tips, it has an obligation to the public to try to determine the facts. . . . Accuracy and fairness are my two highest ideals."

No matter what anyone actually said at the *Herald*, newspaper reporters, especially investigative reporters, would not be shocked to hear that someone somewhere in the organization pressed for a story because he or she simply had a hunch that something was amiss. It is this kind of basic underlying skepticism of public officials on the part of the press that has produced prize-winning exposés for years. City Hall reporters wonder about the public works department. National reporters wonder about the federal government's contracting procedures. Economics reporters wonder about complex interrelationships in the financial world. They pour over documents, official and unofficial. They thrive on tips and leaks. They exult when the pieces fit together.

The difficulty comes when the pieces don't fit together or, as in the case of the *Boston Herald*, where the pressure to produce a story is so intense that a reporter presents an incomplete or inaccurate story, or presents as a "story" something that isn't. One *Herald* reporter has cited the "competitive situation" for the paper's rush to print O'Neill stories, "to beat the opposition, to get in ahead of the *Times* or the *Post*, or especially the *Globe*. . . . We would have been a lot better off if we had assembled things gradually, checked them out thoroughly, and put together a major takeout. Instead, we did it in bits and pieces. As they say, if you go after the king, you've got to kill him. We were firing slingshots at his ankles."

Chris Black feels that the *Herald* editors found O'Neill's brand of politics hard to comprehend. "What they never really understood," she said, "was that Tip cares more about power than about money. . . . You know how Tip is, he's loyal to his friends."

During this period O'Neill frequently came under attack by William Safire, conservative *New York Times* columnist and former Nixon speechwriter. Several of these *Times* "essays" hammered at the Tongsun Park affair and accused O'Neill of inspiring a coverup of the House investigation. At one point, Safire got through to O'Neill by telephone and asked him some pointed questions about the time he had interceded for James P. Wilmot with the Department of Housing and Urban Development.

The memories of O'Neill and Safire concerning that conversation are totally different.

O'Neill remembers that Safire opened the conversation by saying, "This you, Mr. Goodguy?" a reference to Breslin's book, *How the Good Guys Finally Won*. Safire maintains he used the phrase in a column but never addressed the Speaker that way. But the real difference concerns their parting exchange.

According to O'Neill, Safire told him, "Let me tell you something, Mr. Goodguy. I'm going to chase you until the day you die." O'Neill said he slammed down the receiver, but not before replying, "Mr. Safire, you can kiss my Irish ass. How do you like that, you horseshit, you?"

Safire said this version of their exchange was a total fabrication on O'Neill's part but one O'Neill had probably repeated so often to reporters and friends that he believed it to be true. "It's pure fiction—he made it up," Safire said. "I wouldn't ever say anything like that. It's not in my character to even phrase something like that."

In a way, O'Neill brought some of his woes on himself. His loyalty to old friends runs deep and tends to be blind, trusting, unshakeable. It goes back more than forty years to Barry's Corner, Boston College, and his days with the state legislature. It is virtually indestructible.

Thus it was that everywhere O'Neill went he was trailed by old cronies, the kind of Boston Irish characters found on the fringes of Massachusetts politics for generations. He got them jobs, sometimes on his own staff, often on the federal payroll, both in Washington and, as the federal government expanded into regional outposts around the country, in Boston. He was godfather to their children. He listened to their problems. He remembered all their names and the names of their wives, brothers, uncles, children. He went to their weddings and wakes and testimonial dinners. He embraced them all and if they asked a favor, he said yes. He always said yes. An O'Neill friend could do no wrong.

To wit: O'Neill steadfastly refused to criticize Boston aide Jim Rowan for dabbling in half a dozen businesses while on his congressional payroll at $33,000 a year. Among other enterprises, detailed by the *Herald* in another front-page story, Rowan was a bank director, an insurance broker, a restaurant operator, and a partner in a securities investment fund. "I don't know anything about Jim's business," O'Neill stated. "All I know is that Jim is an honest guy. He's been with me twenty-six years and I have absolute faith that nobody paid James Rowan a dime for anything illegal." Of the *Herald* stories, he said, "I guess it's Barnstead feeding stuff to the papers." Rowan, in his own defense, said he worked a full schedule in O'Neill's Boston office, handling his own businesses in off hours. "I like to work," he said. "There are some who like to work. I like to work."

When another old friend, Robert T. Griffin, was threatened with joblessness, O'Neill went directly to President Carter. Griffin, as thin and pale as Rowan is stout and ruddy, dates back to his Boston College days with O'Neill. He had come to Washington ahead of O'Neill, in 1949, to join the newly formed General Services Administration, the housekeeping (and buying) agency for the federal government. In 1961, he had become head of the property management section. Over the years, he had kept close contact with his old friend, Tip O'Neill, as he worked his way up to deputy director of GSA. At about the time Carter became president, news of widespread

fraud in GSA contracting began to emerge. Griffin, subordinates complained, had tried to thwart both internal investigations and JusticeDepart-
ment inquiries until finally he tangled with Carter's new GSA chief, Jay
Solomon. Solomon acted quickly. He fired Griffin. Griffin, with equal
speed, went directly to his old friend, O'Neill, who was furious. He'd had no
advance warning that Griffin would be ousted. He had, in fact, been
boosting Griffin for the top job. O'Neill protested directly to the president
that his friend had been treated shabbily. A bitter feud threatened to upset
the often delicate O'Neill-Carter alliance, so Carter moved to ease the
tension by giving Griffin an equally high-paying ($50,000 a year) job in the
White House assigned to the obliging chief trade negotiator and presidential
troubleshooter, Robert S. Strauss. One of Griffin's duties was to help
persuade Congress to ratify new trade treaties. As a result, he was often seen
in O'Neill's office.

O'Neill could be persistent in his efforts for his friends. O'Neill lobbied
both Carter and the U.S. Senate to name a former aide and good friend,
John W. McGarry, to a Democratic seat on the Federal Elections Commission. It took a year and a half, but O'Neill prevailed. McGarry was an old
friend dating back to the 1950s when he had worked in O'Neill's office.
Later, after McGarry opened a law office in Boston, he commuted
occasionally to Washington to work on O'Neill's special elections committee,
which was recreated every two years to examine contested elections. In the
1970s, he was back in Washington again as a consultant to the House
Administration Committee (a three-day-a-week, $38,000-a-year job), help-
ing to write the law that created the FEC. O'Neill felt this experience
qualified McGarry as a logical man for the job of commissioner. When the
Democratic Party reclaimed control of the White House in 1976, O'Neill
went directly to Carter and suggested McGarry for an FEC appointment.
The name was submitted to the Senate for confirmation in November 1977,
and attracted criticism almost immediately. Common Cause opposed
McGarry because of his close ties to House members—the group doubted
he would be able to maintain the necessary "arm's-length independent
enforcement capacity." Republicans raised questions about his personal
finances. At lengthy Senate Rules Committee hearings, discrepancies arose
between his personal finances and the financial statements he had filed with
the House—he had failed to include money earned by severing his
connections with a Boston law firm. Safire bluntly called him a "party hack"
and "Tip's gopher" (slang for a flunky, or someone who performs menial
duties, as in "go fer" a cup of coffee). Thanks to a GOP filibuster, the
Ninety-fifth Congress adjourned without acting on the McGarry nomination.

Carter, again pressed by O'Neill, then named McGarry as an interim appointee, thus allowing him to start working at the FEC even without Senate action. The outgoing commissioner, Neil O. Staebler, a one-term Democratic congressman from Michigan (1963–5), protested the appointment in vain and threatened to sue. Common Cause backed him up. Its president, David Cohen, criticized Carter for making a "political payoff" to O'Neill. But the court upheld the president's power to appoint. After the dust settled, McGarry went to work at the FEC and the Senate quickly confirmed him without a roll-call vote.

In each of these cases and many more over the years. O'Neill acted unhesitatingly, instinctively. Friends, qualified by friendship and loyalty, needed help. It was the old loyalty rooted in close-knit neighborhoods and nourished in the clubbiness of politics. O'Neill refused to share the public criticism of his friends; he had no private doubts. He would never understand why others—the investigative reporters from out of town—could not understand such a simple straightforward philosophy. Thus, when John A. Shea needed a helping hand, O'Neill was there.

John Shea was administrative assistant to the public relations director and chief liaison between the governor's office and the Speaker. Everything in those days was patronage. He had charge of all the patronage in the state when I was Speaker of the [Massachusetts] House. Do you think I was friendly with him? Ha, ha. He was an honorable decent guy. You know, he got indicted for influencing the legislature. By Eddie Brooke (then Republican state attorney general. later senator). Three years later, it was thrown out of court. Brooke never called it up. The court said there was no evidence. I never heard of anyone working for the governor's office indicted for trying to influence votes in the legislature. That would be like indicting Frank Moore [Carter's liaison chief on Capitol Hill] for trying to influence Congress. Anyhow, they paid him [Shea] back salary and he invested in this nursing home.

The *Herald* continued to be interested in Tip's career. The first two stories appeared a day apart at the end of October 1977. One proved nothing irregular except that a former O'Neill associate had been indicted for alleged bank fraud. The second story was, in O'Neill's words, "outrageously false," and, in McIlwain's own words "a piece of real sloppiness." McIlwain insisted, however, he thought the "thrust" of the story was correct. A crucial date was reported inaccurately. If correct, O'Neill might have violated federal conflict of interest laws; incorrect, it said little of substance. Both stories ran on the front page and were given an extra dose of authenticity with a copyright line that signaled a *Herald* exclusive.

The first story was written by Paul Mindus, a political and investigative reporter, and Wayne Woodlief, called to Boston from Washington to become (briefly) political editor. Five other reporters had worked on the project, which focused principally on Maurice Shear, a Malden, Massachusetts, businessman, who was indicted in 1977 (and later convicted) for alleged misuse of state and federal vocational education funds. The story, published on Saturday, October 29, was headlined, "Speaker O'Neill Had a Partnership in '70 With Voke Ed Figure." It was a complicated and, in some ways, odd story, appearing to say that O'Neill did something wrong by agreeing to invest in the Bristol Nursing Home in Attleboro, Massachusetts, with eight other men in 1970. One of the eight was O'Neill aide Jim Rowan. Another was Shear. There was only passing mention of John Shea.

In the same story, O'Neill was quoted as saying he did not know Shear was involved in the nursing home project at the time, and that he had withdrawn from that business—and most others—shortly after being elected to a House leadership position in 1971. He noted that the Bristol home agreement had been a "conditional" partnership that was dissolved before the home was licensed in 1972. Later, O'Neill explained that the reason he became involved with the Bristol Nursing Home at all was that his friend Shea, who had invested earlier, was about to lose all his own money if he couldn't get additional funds to bring the project up to state standards for licensing.

On Sunday, October 30, the *Herald* ran a second story, "O'Neill had interest in firm receiving $1.3 M HUD backing." It was written by William J. Lewis, former political editor who was later eased off the *Herald* payroll and into work as a freelance columnist. Lewis wrote that O'Neill had been on the board of directors of Glenside Hospital when it received a mortgage guarantee from the Department of Housing and Urban Development (HUD) to buy a sixty-unit apartment house in the Jamaica Plain section of Boston. Under federal conflict-of-interest law, a congressman may not be a partner in a business at any time during the life of a federal contract. In the graceless language of federal law, Title 18, Section 431, states: "Whoever, being a member of or delegate to Congress . . . directly or indirectly, himself, or by any other person in trust for him, or for his use or benefit, or on his account, undertakes, executes, holds or enjoys in whole or in part any contract or agreement made or entered into in behalf of the United States . . . shall be fined not more than $3,000."

But the story was not true, O'Neill said. Not content with the usual denial statement issued by his office, O'Neill and his lawyers wrote a long rebuttal of the Lewis story and demanded that the *Herald* print it, which they did. They also demanded that the original clip, filed in the library, contain a notation that the story was incorrect, which it does. O'Neill declared that Glenside had bought the apartments with a bank loan but then sold them to another corporation before the HUD aid came through for the new owners. In a long letter, which the *Herald* printed in full, O'Neill detailed ten factual errors in the story and presented his view of the truth. "The magnitude of the errors is so great and is such a departure from normal and customary journalistic standards," O'Neill wrote, "that I am led to conclude that the *Herald American* recklessly and willfully set out to misrepresent the truth in order to maliciously impugn me."

Key dates went like this. With a bank loan from Garden City Trust Co., Glenside, Inc., purchased the apartment house on April 15, 1971. O'Neill, a stockholder since 1958, also was on the board of directors. Glenside then asked HUD to guarantee an additional loan to rehabilitate the project. Before HUD acted, however, Glenside sold the apartments to Pond View Apartments Associates and, on June 5, 1972, notified HUD of the new ownership. Final papers for the sale were signed July 18. HUD agreed to provide the loan guarantee July 21.

In its own defense, the *Herald* said HUD made a formal commitment for the guarantee, in writing, on March 31, 1972, three and a half months before the apartments were sold by the O'Neill group. Such a "commitment," they said, is the last critical step in the approval process.

The *Boston Globe* picked up the story November 10, referring to the original *Herald* version and to O'Neill's reply and concluding, "The sequence of events and the information contained in the HUD files in its Boston office appear to indicate there was no violation of the federal conflict-of-interest law." HUD officials were quoted as saying O'Neill's association with the firm had nothing to do with ultimate approval of the loan guarantee.

But O'Neill's press troubles weren't over. On April 9, 1978, the *New York Times* printed a wrap-up story on the O'Neill case by Wendall Rawls, Jr., that went back over the *Herald* stories, and posed the question of whether "the gregarious white-haired Speaker has used his political office for financial advantage and whether he has been less than candid about his transactions."

Again, O'Neill himself was responsible for some of the reporter's suspicions. Five times, he had refused the *Times*'s requests for interviews for the April 9 wrap-up. In earlier comments (on other *Times* stories about the allegations) O'Neill had been careless, scrambling figures and dates, leaving

Gary Hymel to issue correcting statements and leaving some reporters with the notion that he was trying to hide something. O'Neill couldn't be bothered to take the time to doublecheck his files and comment carefully. Instead, he would get angry at the mere suggestion of impropriety contained in a question. "Oh Leo," he would lament to his old friend, Diehl, "they're gonna cut me to ribbons."

No one cut him to ribbons, however, not even the *Times*, which had spent months on the O'Neill investigation and haggled weeks over the wording of the story and even the question of whether to run it at all. (John Finney, an editor in the *Times* Washington bureau, had cautioned, "If you're going to run the story, be sure you've got something on him." Afterwards, he would say only that he stood by the story as it appeared.)

Rawls reported that he sifted through hundreds of pages of court records, real estate documents, state and federal government papers. and past statements from O'Neill himself. He came up with a seven-point recital of "questionable" acts—in addition to references to O'Neill's relationship with Tongsun Park. Among other items reported by Rawls were these:

— In 1970, with Rowan's influence O'Neill obtained unsecured loans from two banks. The implication was that O'Neill had somehow circumvented state banking laws. Nonsense, said O'Neill later. "I was a member of Congress, no pauper in the street. I could get unsecured loans easily."

— HUD speeded up action on the loan agreement for Glenside only after O'Neill added his signature to the firm's application. It was a bank loan he had put his signature to, O'Neill said, not a HUD loan guarantee.

— On December 4, 1976, in the *Times* interview with Richard D. Lyons, O'Neill had undervalued his holdings in the Life of America Insurance Co. It was $7,500, not $4,000. The earlier statement, O'Neill said, was "off the cuff." Later checking corrected the figure. He also had said (in that December interview) that the Bristol Nursing Home had gone bankrupt when it hadn't.

— In the 1976 statement of his assets, he failed to mention his partnership in a high-risk securities investment venture named Broadway Capital Fund whose other partners included Maurice Shear and three others convicted of banking or real estate fraud. "There were thirty people in the Broadway Fund," O'Neill said. "Now they say these are my partners. Anybody who knows anything about a stock club knows that I didn't know these people."

The *Times* story provoked an angry response from the Speaker. In an unusual thirty-five-minute press conference on April 11, 1978, O'Neill refuted the *Times* allegations one by one.

There's never been a more honorable man to be seated in this chair. Nor a poorer one. I've never done an illegal act. I've never done an unethical act. I've been true to my country. I've been true to my God. I've been true to my government, whether state or federal or local. . . . Just because I'm a member of Congress does not deny me the rights [against libel or slander] of an American citizen. Wild Bill "They-know-I'm-crazy" Barnstead—that's what he calls himself, accused me of all these things. There's no truth to them. This is a ridiculous story. There has never been a more humble man or a poorer man to ever sit in this office than me. I'm the poorest man to be Speaker in the history of the nation.

Still, the *Boston Herald* wasn't finished with O'Neill. In October 1978, a special investigative "Probe" team headed by Dick Levitan (who was to run afoul of the law himself, in a tussle for a parking space at Boston's Logan Airport when he sprayed chemical Mace at the other driver) produced another story dealing with the Bristol Nursing Home. This time the reporters and editors were confident they had found a sure sign of conflict of interest. As the team gathered facts earlier in the year, one reporter excitedly wondered: "Are we eligible for the Pulitzer Prize this year?" The word circulated on the news office grapevine: the *Herald* is out to get O'Neill—and a Pulitzer. *Herald* executives deny that.

The October 1978 story reported that O'Neill had been a part owner of the Bristol Nursing Home in 1971 when it had received a Small Business Administration guarantee on a $150,000 second mortgage. SBA lawyers had looked into the case in the summer of 1978 when the issue was raised, apparently by Barnstead, and referred the whole thing to the Justice Department. Nothing more was done because more than five years—the limit of the conflict-of-interest law's backward reach—had elapsed since the incident.

Subsequent *Herald* stories reported that the House ethics committee and the U.S. Attorney in Boston also had reviewed the O'Neill case and done nothing, also because the five-year statute of limitations had expired.

Left hanging was the clear implication that O'Neill had violated the law and, if caught in time, could have faced criminal charges. O'Neill denied any wrongdoing.

Did I have any difficulty signing on [the SBA agreement]? None whatsoever. The law very specifically excludes congressmen. We went to three different lawyers. Do I have a problem? No problem. Did I do anything to break the law? No way did I do anything to break the law.

Nonetheless, when the *Herald* story broke, O'Neill hired a Washington law firm to research that law. They found that when the SBA was established in 1953 to succeed the Reconstruction Finance Corporation, it had not included a conflict-of-interest section. The old RFC had been specifically excluded from the statute in the 1930s, and in the absence of any other directive, the SBA had adopted the same policy. All agencies that fall under the conflict law (enacted in 1808) must carry a warning on federal contracts that Members of Congress cannot be included. SBA contracts carried no such warning. In 1975, SBA lawyers looked into the matter and decided that perhaps congressmen should be included after all but there still was no change on SBA agreements; SBA officials argued that a loan guarantee is not a contract. The legal conclusion was that the language is ambiguous and O'Neill violated no law. Furthermore, as his lawyers pointed out, the SBA agreement actually was signed with the bank that made the loan, rather than with the Bristol Nursing Home. SBA's role was to guarantee the loan between the bank and the private corporation, although both signed the original application to SBA.

It's a very technical thing. But no matter how you look at it, I didn't break the law. Believe me, you'll never know what it cost me to have this thing checked out—because of what the *Herald* did. . . . Let me tell you something. Has my life changed right now? You bet my life has changed. . . . They look at Tip O'Neill as an Irish politician and they say all Irish politicians are crooks so Tip O'Neill must be a crook. I know it. I live with it. It is the toughest thing I have to live with, the toughest thing I have to live with.

13

A "DO NOTHING"
CONGRESS?

B
Y THE TIME the Ninety-sixth Congress convened in January 1979, O'Neill had settled comfortably into the Speaker's office and had refined his leadership style the way one might expect—with a mix of toughness and humor. He was the boss, but he was still a pal to his fellow congressmen. "Tip relaxes and jokes with them and kids the pants off them," said Majority Leader Wright, "and he gets along better as a result." He was as accessible as ever, always ready to listen to gripes and problems from any member of Congress, Republican or Democrat. "I wouldn't hesitate to go to him with any problem," said a Western Republican. "He has tremendous empathy. He really understands this place and this job."

Many congressmen had feared—or expected—that O'Neill would rule with a heavy hand. Time and again, he had been quoted as advocating that the House have a "strong Speaker." He had talked of his days in the Massachusetts legislature where the Speaker ruled with total power and where party loyalty demanded that everyone fall into line when the Speaker gave the order. But times change. The trick for O'Neill in the late 1970s was to learn how to be firm without being arbitrary, how to cater to the younger independent-minded congressmen without alienating the old-timers. O'Neill has succeeded by just being Tip O'Neill. "Tip has an extraordinary sense of what can, and cannot, be accomplished around here," Representative Benjamin S. Rosenthal (D–New York) told the *New York Times* after his own consumer protection bill had been shelved by O'Neill for lack of votes. "He also has the interests of the members at heart. He'll never try to push a person into trying to do something if it's against his personal interests."

That view is widely held by House members. They feel that O'Neill understands their problems, both at home and in Washington. At the same time, however, O'Neill expects a certain amount of loyalty from those he helps. "He feels very strongly," Bolling said in an interview, "that people ought to do right, ought to be good Democrats, and he conveys that clearly. . . . And he's highly intelligent. Don't be fooled by that [old pol]

199

manner. I don't think he's an intellectual. But he makes great use of his intellect. When he's got something thought out, when he looks ahead, he does well. When he forgets to do that, he gets in trouble. . . . He is a worthy Speaker, a good man, and he is good for this institution."

Naturally, not all O'Neill's Democratic colleagues are admirers. One ultra-liberal Northerner has faulted him for failing to push legislation to carry out such Democratic party platform promises as national health insurance and the horizontal divestiture of oil companies. But he also concedes that O'Neill does not press for action if he thinks it a losing cause. In this congressman's view, O'Neill "should make noises and educate the people. He never goes on national television. He is undistinguished and unknown, a nonintellectual."

It is true that O'Neill seldom appears on national television. He has an inexplicable distrust of television, complaining, as Gary Hymel once explained, of TV editing that boils down the most complex statements to a single sentence. When other members of Congress race up to the Capitol's third-floor television gallery to offer comments on the subject of the day, O'Neill ambles into his office and goes back to work.

O'Neill was also skeptical of the television system set up for covering House debates, even though it was designed to meet his demand that House technicians, not the commercial networks, should operate the cameras, and he was the one who personally steered the necessary rules changes past the competing proposals of Representatives Jack Brooks (D-Texas, and John Anderson (R-Illinois). Still, O'Neill felt there were opportunities for abuse, or congressional grandstanding, and he grumbled about the ever-present cameras. They remained, however, and O'Neill has adjusted. On the day televised coverage first went public, O'Neill showed up in a newly pressed suit, blue shirt, and fresh haircut. There was no major legislation scheduled for the day, and O'Neill jokingly told reporters he had wanted to take off and play golf, "but Paul Duke [of the Public Broadcasting Corporation] said, 'You have to be here and wear a blue shirt.'"

The O'Neill leadership style was seen most clearly in the House Democratic Steering and Policy Committee. Under O'Neill's guidance, the group finally has lived up to its name, steering a course for the House by making committee assignments, and setting goals by taking policy positions. It should be noted, however, that the committee has steered only in the directions O'Neill wanted, taking policy positions only as proposed by O'Neill. He does not need to threaten and shout. He just presides in his own special way. Take, for example, the opening S-and-P sessions of January, 1979:

The members sat at two long tables arranged at right angles to O'Neill's roughly forming a U-shape. The atmosphere was informal—coats off, sleeves rolled up, coffee and sweet rolls on a table just outside the door. The group, twenty-four in all, arrived in ones and twos, chatting casually. They were unusually prompt: there was important business ahead. Except for Bill Gray of Pennsylvania, they all knew each other from previous years. Gray was a freshman whose reputation as a bright young politician had preceded him. He had defeated the incumbent for election to the House of Representatives, and was the chosen delegate of his fellow freshmen congressmen to this committee. Respectful of his position, the older members made him welcome.

The members gathered in what had once been the dining room of the old Congressional Hotel. The entire building had been taken over several years earlier by Congress in its constant search for more office space. The group's task: to decide which Democrats should serve on which committee in the new Ninety-sixth Congress. These decisions could affect national policy and personal careers.

Tip O'Neill arrived right on time and immediately shed his coat, revealing a broad expanse of white shirt with short sleeves. In a show of restraint that would break down later in the day, he skipped the donuts and went straight to the head of the table. He was clearly in charge. This was his committee. The staff was his staff (headed by the wise and faithful Ari Weiss). Half the members had been named by him personally. The rest had been elected in regional caucuses with the general understanding that O'Neill loyalists went to the head of the line.

Until 1975, Democratic committee assignments had been handled by a separate "committee on committees"—namely, the Democrats on the Ways and Means Committee. The Speaker had had little control except through whatever influence he could exert on the initial assignments to the committee. O'Neill had had his first experience with the new Steering and Policy Committee system in 1977. Things are different now. By 1979, the committee was functioning smoothly with O'Neill in undisputed command.

Even the choice of the meeting room had some significance that day in 1979. Two years before, the same committee had convened in the House Appropriations Committee room in the Capitol. It was crowded and uncomfortable. Members seemed to be moving around and talking all the time. Reporters stood right outside the door demanding to know what was going on. Now, two years later, in the larger room and away from the Capitol, the meeting became more structured in a uniquely unstructured O'Neill way. "He ran the meeting," said Representative Charles G. Rose (D–North Carolina), "more like a shepherd herds his flock, not like you lasso a steer to be branded. I have never felt, nor have I seen, the Steering and Policy Committee as the Thomas P. O'Neill Drum and Bugle Corps Marching Society. Yet it's very loyal to the House and to Tip O'Neill, and he lets the process rather gently work." "It helps," said another Democrat, "that Tip is so big. He just looks like what you'd think the Speaker of the House should look like, and he immediately dominates any group he's with."

Thus, when Bolling, a very senior member of the House, and third-termer Henry A. Waxman (D-California) tangled verbally over Waxman's effort to leap over some older House members to become chairman of a health subcommittee, O'Neill just let them talk it out. No one was arbitrarily gaveled into silence. "Tip just rolled the cigar in his mouth," Rose said, "and gave everybody a kind of hazy stare as if to say, all right, go at it." When it seemed they had talked enough, O'Neill simply said, "I think it's time we moved along." And they did.

At another point, when Representative Eligio de la Garza (D-Texas) angrily charged that the three New Yorkers on the committee had reneged on a deal to support his nominee for a key committee assignment, O'Neill broke in—as he often did—with a story. It went (doubtless better in the telling than in the retelling) something like this:

There was a time when Earl Long was running for governor of Louisiana. He was campaigning in a rural community in the northern part of the state where the people wanted a new road built. The local sheriff was Long's campaign manager and he told the candidate about the problem. So, when Long got up to speak, he promised straightaway that if elected, there would be a new road. The district voted for him, one thousand to four. Sometime afterwards, when a road still hadn't appeared, the sheriff went down to Baton Rouge to ask the new governor when they would get a road. Long just looked at him and said, "Hell, I can't build a road way out there." The sheriff was dumbfounded. "What shall I tell the people who voted a thousand to four for you?" he asked. "Well," said Long, "you just tell them ol' Earl lied."

The steering committee tension broke up in laughter and the group went back to work. "Tip has a great capacity to kid other guys out of their anger," Wright said later. "I've seen him do it dozens of times."

Steering committee negotiations were often sensitive. Each of the twenty-four members had been contacted by dozens of their fellow

congressmen and by each other, seeking choice committee assignments for
worthy allies. Hard decisions had to be made. At this meeting, twenty-four
requests had been received for seven vacancies on the budget committee,
seventeen requests for seven vacancies on Appropriations, eighteen requests for three vacancies on Government Operations, and so on. Everyone
wanted to be where they expected the action to be in the new Ninety-sixth
Congress. Such things ebb and flow. The Judiciary Committee, glamor spot
in 1974 when the impeachment of Richard Nixon was under study, went
begging in 1979. By 1979, concern over rising federal spending made the
Budget and Appropriations committees attractive, and those who wanted to
pay off on campaign promises to cut back the size of the federal government
wanted to be on the general oversight committee, Government Operations.

It paid to have well-placed friends. Massachusetts freshmen did well.
James M. Shannon, the youngest member of the Ninety-sixth Congress,
managed to beat out five other freshmen and five senior members for a
coveted seat on the Ways and Means Committee. O'Neill had passed the
word quietly that he had only a few preferences this year. One was to put
Shannon on Ways and Means. Shannon, he said with a smile, was a bright
young fellow who had, among other talents, written his senior thesis on
Thomas P. O'Neill, Jr. That started a good-humored round of wisecracks
from other committee members. Their nominee should be awarded a
particular committee slot, they would say, because: "At a young age, he
showed great wisdom by writing his sixth-grade term paper on Thomas P.
O'Neill" or "When he was in high school, he did a prize-winning essay on
Thomas P. O'Neill." It is not recorded how each of these other wise men and
women fared; Shannon won easily.

The banter illustrated the O'Neill style of governing. Easy going.
Friendly. "Tip can always disagree without being disagreeable," said Jim
Burke, who served with O'Neill in the Massachusetts state legislature and in
Congress for a total of forty-two years. "That's why he's a great Speaker."
Behind O'Neill's low-key approach, however, members of his staff make
certain that the steering committee's work is done the way the Speaker
wants. All committee assignment requests are considered in the light of the
applicant's past record. On a blackboard at the front of the room, "loyalty"
scores—namely, the percentage of votes cast with the Democratic
leadership—are posted as each name is read off. Although other factors are
considered, the vote scores are important. Once again, in O'Neill's book,
loyalty counts.

"If he has a choice among several people for a given committee slot," Jim
Wright said, "obviously he will take that person whom he regards as most

friendly, most reliable, the most likely to be amenable to his persuasion. Who wouldn't do that? I'd do it. But he doesn't consciously punish anyone. I've never heard him say, 'I'll get that bastard.' . . ."

O'Neill can get very mad. Wright found him "seething with anger" over the news stories in the *Boston Herald*. "It just infuriated him [that the stories would be printed]. Those things really burn him up." But O'Neill's anger usually is short-lived. He blows up and then, minutes later, it is all over.

And he can be impatient, especially with the often needless fussing that goes on among congressmen trying to protect their own areas of responsibility—"turf," it's called. On one occasion, Representative John D. Dingell (D-Michigan) was trying to ward off a Republican effort to force a House vote on a motion demanding that the Carter administration supply Congress with detailed information on the supply of oil in the United States. Dingell said his subcommittee already had gathered together all available data and a summary report was at the printer. The Republicans refused to back off until they could see the report. Dingell insisted on a vote dismissing the GOP request. Snide comments were exchanged on both sides until, finally, O'Neill, who was presiding over the House session, had had enough.

In the language of exaggerated civility that rules congressional debates, O'Neill said: "Would the gentleman from Michigan kindly withdraw the resolution until such time as the summary is printed and the gentleman from Indiana and the gentleman from Maryland have had an opportunity to read the document?"

"I am reluctant to do so," said Dingell, "but if the Speaker is sending me a suggestion that that be done—"

O'Neill interrupted to repeat his request. The House had important legislation to consider. "We would like to go forward," he said. But Dingell kept talking.

"Mr. Speaker," he said, "I am, of course. happy to respond to the wishes of the chair. I gather I cannot let the staff of the minority leader speak for the minority leader. I do not think I can, therefore, very well let the Speaker speak for the minority leader, and if the minority leader has no objection to that and will so indicate, I will—"

O'Neill interrupted again. Without further ado, he banged the gavel and announced: "The gentleman withdraws the resolution."

Dingell, sputtering, stalked up to the rostrum. But the matter was closed. The House moved on to other business.

Later, in his office, O'Neill fingered an ever-present cigar, a Daniel Webster, probably, though he preferred the fine Cuban cigars traveling members of Congress brought him from time to time. He was in shirtsleeves. The first thing he usually did when he entered the office was shed his suitcoat. He liked to be comfortable. But he also was aware that he often was described as "rumpled." That didn't seem dignified. So he would hang up his coat.

He sat at a huge oak desk once used in the White House by President Grover Cleveland and discovered in the basement of the Smithsonian by O'Neill's personal secretary, Eleanor Kelley. Capitol Hill craftsmen had refinished the dusty and abandoned relic into something like its former glory. Large and sturdy, it seemed the perfect desk for Tip O'Neill.

He leaned forward and fixed his visitors with a heavy lidded gaze. No jokes. He was serious, a man determined to accomplish something others said was impossible—to run the House efficiently and to represent the country accurately. A small clock on a table at the far side of the room chimed prettily.

Let me say this. The Congress of the United States is just the greatest grass-roots organization in history. They read the people. When Proposition 13 [the balanced budget amendment] came along, people would ask me what does it mean to Congress? It meant nothing to Congress. Congress was on that track. They had read the American people, that the American people wanted a cutback. So, what did they do? From the original proposal of the president for a $60 billion budget deficit, we came down to about $29 billion. So, Congress reads the people. That's exactly what's happening around here.

They do read the American people. Sometimes, you can almost see it happen, see an idea taking hold. Like when House sentiment swung around on the Vietnam War and on the impeachment of Richard Nixon. And when House members "read" that the American people wanted Congress to do something about the continuing shortages of gas and oil.

The House is much more volatile in this way than the Senate. House members must stand for election every two years from relatively small geographic areas, areas more homogeneous than an entire state (except the five smallest states which have only one House member) represented by two senators. House members often start running for reelection immediately after winning the first time. As a result, they spend more time in their home districts and feel closer to the people they represent than many senators. When the people become impatient or angry, they voice their opinions to the first federal official they see—and, often, that is their delegate to the House.

In 1978, the American people were telling their congressmen that there was too much government: too many laws, too many regulations, too much money spent on the bureaucracy and, somehow, because of all this, too much inflation. They wanted less.

Tip O'Neill was determined to give them less. "We're going to get into oversight," he said in an interview. "That's going to be one of the hallmarks of this Congress: sunset legislation [to phase out unnecessary agencies], and oversight to make sure the existing programs are working. And whatever programs are obsolete, we ought to get rid of them."

O'Neill recognized problems with "oversight." It usually meant hard, unglamorous work. It's more politically exciting to announce new programs to save the nation from something or the other. Oversight involves painstaking examination of existing federal agencies reluctant to surrender information that would make them look bad. But the word went out: this will be an "oversight Congress." It would fit in very nicely with President Carter's goal of trimming back the size of the federal government.

Neither worked out very well.

Carter discovered he had higher priorities for his administration: Panama and SALT treaties, energy conservation, hospital-cost controls. By the end of his term, any effort to significantly reduce the federal government had fallen by the wayside. Other things were more important and demanded his full attention.

For O'Neill, congressional oversight backfired. Although many committees and subcommittees duly set up oversight operations, the results were uneven and hard to measure. The most frustrating result was that people started criticizing the lawmakers as a "do-nothing Congress" because they weren't passing as many bills as usual. "Congress," said NBC News Correspondent Tom Pettit on a "Nightly News" show in July, "has been awash in a sea of indecision. . . . The leadership feels persuaded to follow the public—from a position at least one step behind." O'Neill found the criticism puzzling.

We started this year [1979] off with all the editorials in America saying: it's time to retrench. A mariner when he's on a storm-tossed sea should look at his compass and steer his ship to a safe port. They said we've had too many programs, we ought to have sunset legislation, oversight; the cause of inflation is the government.

We've done everything they wanted. We've cut back. There are no new innovative programs. Now, I've read three or four editorials in the last few weeks about a "do-nothing Congress." They say we've passed only twelve pieces of legislation. Hey, that's what we set out to do, to reassess ourselves as to where we are.

So, no matter what you do, you're going to be criticized. . . .

People say how does it feel to be Speaker of the House when it has such a low image? And I say Congress has been the whipping boy since the days of Thomas Paine.

A funny story. I'm talking to the chairman of the board of Hyannis Community College and I says when I retire I'd love to come down and teach a couple of days a week on the Cape, just to keep my mind activated and I says, y'know, I wouldn't want much, a pittance, just to keep myself activated and maybe write a few memoirs. I could tell the class a lot of things they'll never read in the history books. Christ, I could tell you stories about Nixon and the closing days I've never put down on tapes or anything like that. Geez, the next day I get a letter from them saying the board of the community college has accepted me. And I had to write back to them and say I had no intention of quitting Congress. Wait a while.

14

TRAVELS WITH
CARTER

THE silver-gray Lincoln Continental slipped through the city's nearly deserted streets carrying the driver and, seated beside him, his one passenger—a big, rumpled figure of a man. Twice during the short trip, the passenger reached for the portable telephone and told the anxious caller that he was on his way and to stall until he got there. He was angry. It was a rotten way to end a beautiful evening.

Thomas P. O'Neill, Jr., Speaker of the United States House of Representatives, had left the Capitol at six that evening, June 13, 1979, assured that there would be no problems with this bill so eagerly sought by the president. He did not often leave the House when controversial legislation was on the floor, but this was a very special occasion, a family gathering to celebrate his wife's birthday and the thirty-eighth anniversary of their marriage. Even O'Neill, with his notorious inability to keep secrets, had managed to hide from his wife the fact that all five children, together with their own families and a few close friends, would be there. A gathering of the clan.

The O'Neills are proud of that clan. The children—tall and sturdy, and black-haired as their parents once were—have done well. Rosemary, thirty-six, is a political officer in the foreign service. Tommy, thirty-four, is lieutenant governor of Massachusetts and an ambitious politician in his own right. Susan, thirty-two, a former junior high school teacher who also worked as a lobbyist for the National Association of Government Employees, is married now and living in Providence, Rhode Island. Her lawyer husband, Bruce Daniel, is carrying on the political tradition as a member of the Rhode Island state legislature. Christopher, or "Kip," twenty-nine, is a lawyer in Washington; and Michael, twenty-seven, is an investment broker in Boston.

For the anniversary celebration, they all gathered at the suburban Maryland home of Kip and his wife, Stephanie, for an evening of charcoal-broiled steaks and good-humored political talk.

As he had every year since their marriage, Tip O'Neill sang to Millie: "I'll be with you in apple blossom time. . . ." It is their favorite song, a family tradition. His voice is strong and spirited, even if slightly off-key. It was a warm and pleasant evening, just the O'Neills and good friends, comfortably away from the pressures of trying to keep the House of Representatives running on schedule. Then, around 10 P.M., the phone calls began.

First it was Danny Rostenkowski, O'Neill's deputy whip, with the news that opponents of the president's bill to create a cabinet-level department of education were seeking to mortally wound the bill by moving to strike the enacting clause. That was like lopping off its head, he said.

O'Neill told Danny not to worry; they wouldn't try that after debating the bill for more than fifteen hours. "The troops are restless," Rostenkowski warned. Like O'Neill, the Chicago congressman is a political pro, sensitive to the moods of the House. But O'Neill thought he had left the situation firmly in control. "I can't believe it," he said and stubbornly returned to his dinner party.

Ten minutes later, Majority Leader Jim Wright called with the same story. Wright hadn't been O'Neill's first choice for majority leader in 1977, but the two men had grown close during their months of working together. A mutual respect had developed and O'Neill valued Wright's assessment of the political outlook for the education bill. Privately, both men doubted the wisdom of creating the new agency. But publicly, out of loyalty to the president, they were committed to doing everything they could to see the bill enacted. It was one of Carter's top legislative priorities.

Finally, when Ari Weiss, O'Neill's young legislative strategist, phoned to say the bill-killing motion, one allowing only ten minutes of debate, was imminent, O'Neill said, "I gotta be there." He told Weiss to ask Wright to hold off the vote until he had a chance to speak on the floor.

He grabbed his suit jacket and straightened his tie. Roger Brooks, his driver for several years and, before that, McCormack's driver, met O'Neill with the car and they drove off together through the June night.

O'Neill might not have been so unhappy if he thought the education department was a good idea. But this bill, as he had told Vice President Mondale earlier that day, was a "lemon . . . that belongs on the garbage heap." Besides, organized labor and the U. S. Catholic Conference were opposed to it—good enough reasons by themselves to abandon the project.

But Carter had promised the National Education Association, largely as a condition for its support in 1976, that he would push for a separate Department of Education, and push he did.

As O'Neill drove to the Capitol, Representative David Obey, (D-

Wisconsin), author of the motion to torpedo the education bill, objected to
Wright's request for a delay. Although Obey, a shrewd legislative strategist,
had doubts about whether he had the votes to kill the bill, he thought that in
the madness of the late hour, his colleagues might be angry enough to vote
no in order to be able to go home for the night. He hated being asked to
surrender his tactical advantage.

But when a man like O'Neill, who has done so many favors for others
over the years, asks for one in return, few turn him down. Obey said OK to
the delay. Some others, however, disagreed, and a number of them,
according to Obey, came up to him and said, "Bullshit, let's vote now." It
was finally agreed they would wait no longer than 11:30 P.M.

Gary Hymel, one of O'Neill's top aides, hovered near the Obey
negotiating group, and when the 11:30 deadline was set, he raced again for
the telephone, telling O'Neill to hurry. By then, O'Neill was already
approaching the Capitol. OK. OK.

As he moved up the steps and into the House chamber, O'Neill's thick
straight hair fell across his forehead. Except for brief, formal occasions, his
hair is always out of place. He looked his age, sixty-six. He was tired, his
jowly face fell in deep folds. He was annoyed; he did not like to keep the
House in session late into the evening. He lumbered over to a seat near the
committee table and listened.

Obey, speaking in the awkward language of Congress, then said, "I move
that the committee do now rise and report the bill back to the House with
the recommendation that the enacting clause be stricken."

The debate was brief and O'Neill, exercising one of the prerogatives of
leadership, had the last word. He stayed on familiar ground, not arguing the
merits of creating a new government agency, but talking—as he often does
in House debates—of party loyalty. "To thine own self be true," he said,
recalling a line from Hamlet that James Michael Curley often used. "Be true
to this body [the House] for which we have such a high regard. . . . Do not
let this bill go down this way. Vote your mind, your conscience, when you
have heard the entire argument."

It was just about midnight when the vote was taken. Obey lost 146 to
266.

The House then adjourned for the night. The education bill remained on
the calendar for another month while both sides tried to line up votes. It
finally passed the House on July 11 and, after lengthy negotiations with the
Senate, was sent to the White House October 17.

O'Neill had delivered. Carter had won.

Jimmy Carter and Tip O'Neill met for the first time on January 10, 1975. O'Neill, then House Democratic leader, was in his office down one flight of steps from the House floor. Through the window behind his desk one could look down the mall toward the White House, a splendid view. The Ninety-fourth Congress, bent on shaking up some old congressional traditions, was to convene in a few days, and O'Neill was deeply involved in balancing the competing claims of the old and the new. But his door was always open. And Jimmy Carter was paying a courtesy call.

Carter, the lean, soft-spoken Southerner, and O'Neill, the oversized garrulous Northerner, offered sharp contrasts—physically, emotionally, and temperamentally. One was intense and moralistic, a late-blooming politician and a born-again Baptist, educated as an engineer. The other was hearty and uncritical, a devout Catholic and a born politician, educated in politics. They probably would never have sought out one another as friends. But they held one thing in common: Both men were lifelong Democrats, and that fact brought them together.

Under Georgia law, Jimmy Carter couldn't run for a second term. That day, he had a mission that only he and a close circle of friends fully understood, and he wanted to discuss it with the leaders of his party. Tip O'Neill listened in amazement, later recalling:

He comes in and he says, "Tip, you know in your heart that Ted Kennedy is not a candidate and that Hubert Humphrey won't be a candidate and Scoop [Senator Henry M.] Jackson is going to be out of it after three or four primaries." And then he says, "I'm telling you right now I'm going to be nominated on the first ballot without opposition and I'm going to be elected President of the United States."

I laughed.

But, by God, he did everything he said he was going to do. Now, he went out and made promises to change the ethics of politics in America, to reorganize the departments, to stimulate the economy, and to come up with a national energy policy. I have every confidence he can do these things.

What O'Neill did not know in 1975 was that Carter had started his 1976 presidential campaign shortly after George McGovern was wiped out by Nixon in 1972. Carter had earlier made an amateurish pass at the vice-presidential nomination during the 1972 Democratic convention but had never even gotten into McGovern's presence. Carter was then in his second year as governor and little known outside Georgia. And he had not been a McGovern supporter.

Back in Atlanta, Carter immediately started planning for 1976. In long memos hailed as politically brilliant, Carter aides—notably Hamilton

Jordan—laid out the strategy that would carry Carter steadily forward. He more or less launched his campaign in January 1973, with a speech at Washington's National Press Club outlining his vision for America—not just Georgia. He wanted to be known as a *national* figure. Jules Witcover, in his book, *Marathon, the Pursuit of the Presidency*, reported that former Representative Andrew J. Young (D-Georgia) (later Carter's ambassador to the United Nations), sitting at the head table, had slipped a note to a Carter aide saying: "I'll be damned if he isn't running for president." Carter knew that already even if no one else did.

In January 1975, Tip O'Neill didn't believe him. Few in Washington did. But that didn't bother Carter. He was running as an outsider, running against Washington and the bureaucracy and the old pols like O'Neill whom he liked to blame for the sorry condition of the country.

The 1974 elections had appeared to confirm the wisdom of the Carter strategy. The nation was ready for something different. In November, voters shook off the trauma of Watergate and sent new younger men and women to Congress. In the House, there were more freshmen (seventy-five Democrats and seventeen Republicans) than at any time since Truman's triumph over the "Do Nothing" Eightieth (Republican) Congress in 1948. For the first time since World War II, the average age of House members had dropped below 50—to 49.8.

Americans were weary of corruption and disappointed in big government. The presidency had been tarnished. Although Ford's short term in the White House had helped restore confidence, the view of Washington from Iowa caucuses and New Hampshire coffee klatches still was one of a quarrelsome and divided government—a Democratic Congress endlessly fussing with a Republican president.

Carter offered a new face. He was squeaky clean. His credentials were a nice mix of all-American boy (out of the U.S. Naval Academy) and hard-headed businessman-farmer (out of Plains, Georgia). He was polite, hard-working, and smart—an "achiever" to some, a "climber" to others. He campaigned nonstop for more than three years, and he won. Narrowly.

At the same time, House Democrats ran much stronger than Carter. Three-fourths finished well ahead of him, maintaining in the new Congress a lopsided two-to-one ratio of Democrats over Republicans. In the joy of victory, Democratic leaders were elated. With a Democrat in the White House and Democrats controlling both House and Senate, they looked forward to four years of great accomplishment. Carter had promised action, and they were ready—on ethics, national health insurance, welfare reform, energy policy, tax revisions. Carter talked of a "honeymoon" that would last his full four-year term.

The euphoria was short-lived.

From the beginning of the Carter campaign, congressional Democrats had been skeptical of the avowed "outsider," sometimes even offended by him. The Carter camp's anti-Washington attitude seemed arrogant, disdainful. Carter, himself, misread and underestimated Congress.

"Congress is inherently incapable of unified leadership," he told *Congressional Quarterly* in a long pre-election interview. "That leadership has got to come from the White House. And in the absence of that leadership, the country drifts. That's what it's been doing lately."

At the same time, Carter tried to sound reassuring. He promised to consult Congress and work closely with its leaders in developing legislative programs. "I think just a few personal moves on my part—treating Congress members as though they were presidents themselves, returning their telephone calls, letting my staff members respect them thoroughly—might alleviate the present disharmony and total separation of the White House and Congress."

But Carter didn't stop there. He kept reiterating one position that inevitably rankled congressional leaders. If he couldn't get his way on legislation, he said he would do what he had done in Georgia as governor, he would go over the legislators' heads. "I would never hesitate," he said, "to go directly to the American people with my side of the debate, and through this mechanism, hope to influence the Congress to accept my position." O'Neill advised him not to do that. He pointed out Congress was not the Georgia legislature.

Carter called himself a Democrat and he ran as the candidate of the Democratic party. But he was different.

Nevertheless, for O'Neill, the election returns erased all doubts about Carter. Ever the party loyalist, O'Neill cheered the Carter victory. A Democrat was a Democrat. They would be a happy team.

Hey, Carter will come in and he'll say, "Look, I've been critical of Washington, but now I'm going to work with you to restore faith in government." And, working together, we can set guidelines to get things done and to clean up the bureaucracy. . . . It's our obligation to put forward his program in Congress. I'm loyal to the party. That's paramount.

O'Neill's loyalty was sorely tested in the next few years. He held firm—Carter was his president. Publicly and privately, O'Neill stuck by

Carter. "He's a beautiful guy," he said. Other Democrats grumbled. Some fought Carter as much as they had fought Ford. "We won the election," one Democrat groused six months after Carter took office, "but you'd never know it."

Carter-Congress troubles started even before the Inaugural. The president's congressional liaison, Frank Moore, wouldn't return telephone calls. Moore, forty-one-year-old public relations man from Dahlonega, Georgia, had been picked as Carter's chief contact with Congress. When Carter had been governor of Georgia, Moore had served in a similar capacity, as liaison to the state legislature. He had worked as coordinator in the southern states for Carter during the presidential campaign. From Carter's standpoint, Moore was ideal for the congressional job. There was no question of how his priorities lined up, he was a loyal Carter man. And he was a Georgian. But he got off to a bad start with Tip O'Neill and his friends.

Moore affected Congress like chalk squawking across a blackboard. He knew nothing of the ways of Congress and had no one on his staff—at first—who did. Worse yet, he refused to acknowledge how much he didn't know. He acted more like the teacher than the student—a teacher too busy to fiddle with student problems. What Moore—and others in the Carter inner circle—failed to realize was that these members of Congress were anxious to cooperate with the new president. They had been looking forward eagerly to working with a Democrat in the White House.

Over the months, as Moore settled into the job and learned his way around Capitol Hill, relations improved slightly. O'Neill never was fully convinced, however, of Moore's ability. "I don't think O'Neill thinks that operation is competent or professional," a fellow Democrat said late in 1979. "Moore isn't around here very much."

Moore recognized that he had a problem, and early in 1977 he started looking around for an aide with Hill experience. He found William H. Cable, who had worked closely with House leaders on both the House Administration Committee and the Education and Labor Committee. House leaders liked him and trusted him. "He's the guy we feel at home with," Brademas, who had worked with Cable on the House Administration Committee, said. "He understands the place and we respect his abilities."

Moore's decision to add Cable to his liaison staff helped, but a certain wariness remained. As O'Neill said of the White House operation in an April 1977 interview with the *New York Times*:

They came up here and they didn't understand us Irish politicians or Jewish politicians from the urban areas. The average Southerner is a sweet talker and a charmer and charismatic, a smooth type that can skin you alive with sweetness and kindness. Politics are different in the North. There's a terseness and a toughness and an infighting. The Northern House member gets into the fray as soon as possible. The Southerner steps back.

Although O'Neill eventually made peace of a sort with Moore, he never could get along with Carter's top staff man, Hamilton Jordan, nor with his press secretary, Jody Powell. And, apparently, the feelings of mistrust were reciprocated. O'Neill considered them smart-alecks: they considered him the very model of the kind of old politics they had fought so hard to beat.

The O'Neill-Jordan disintegration actually had begun before the Inaugural. O'Neill, as the Speaker of the House, was scheduled to sit in a special box at the Kennedy Center for Carter's Inaugural Gala. a pre-swearing-in party. In addition, he sent in a check for $300 for ten seats so that he could take some members of his family and close friends. When the tickets arrived, he was surprised to find his friends had been assigned seats in the last two rows of the orchestra. He protested to Jordan: "When a guy is Speaker of the House and he gets tickets like this," he recalled to a reporter later. "he figures there's a reason behind it." Jordan cooly said if O'Neill didn't like the seats, the money could be returned. With that, O'Neill exploded: "I'll ream your ass out, you sonofabitch!" The seats were not changed and O'Neill started referring to Jordan (pronounced "Jerdan") as "Hannibal Jerkin." Powell he ignored. "You guys," O'Neill said early on, "have got a lot to learn if you want to play in the big leagues."

They clashed regularly. For O'Neill, an especially sore point was patronage, the oil that keeps political machinery moving. Republicans had held the White House for eight years when Carter came to town. The Hill Democrats were waiting eagerly with their friends and followers to fill the hundreds of patronage and policy jobs expected to open up.

The Carter people moved slowly. They found the give and take of Washington politics slightly demeaning. "We don't play the heavy patronage game," Jordan said at one point. Such wheeling and dealing seemed to contradict Carter's commitment to rational government. Carter set up a special committee to screen jobs and applicants, seeking—they kept saying—the best persons for each position, regardless of political ties.

The outcome of this policy was not comforting to O'Neill. Before Carter's first month as president was over, he had tromped on O'Neill toes twice. The first two White House appointments to Massachusetts men went to Republicans. Evan Dobelle, the former Republican mayor of Pittsfield, Massachusetts, was named chief of protocol, and Elliot L. Richardson, former Nixon cabinet officer and Ford's ambassador to Great Britain, was named ambassador to the Law of the Sea Conference. O'Neill had not been consulted in advance. "As a Democrat," he said bluntly, "I'm upset." But he didn't blame Carter: he blamed the staff. As an O'Neill aide commented at the time, "Tip says that he just loves Jimmy Carter, but he says we're going to have to keep an eye on all those other Georgians."

The angriest exchange concerned O'Neill's old friend Bob Griffin, and Carter was directly involved in that one: there was no blaming "all those other Georgians." Both O'Neill and Carter were shaken by the confrontation. O'Neill was personally affronted that Carter had upheld the abrupt firing (from GSA) of Griffin, an O'Neill crony. Carter was upset at the emotional pitch of the O'Neill reaction. After a stormy breakfast meeting at the White House, O'Neill returned to the Capitol "almost in tears," according to one friend. Two days later, in another White House meeting, this time with Jim Wright and John Brademas, the president said the encounter had been his "worst day" since taking office.

There is a photograph on the wall of Tip O'Neill's outer office where receptionist Pam Colvin and O'Neill's personal secretary, Eleanor Kelley, sit. The photo, autographed by Jimmy Carter and Vice-President Mondale, was taken from a distance. The two men appear as tiny figures. They are talking earnestly—and in the dark. Artistically. the photo is very attractive; politically, it symbolizes to some visitors a recurring congressional view that Jimmy Carter is—at least when it comes to dealing with Congress—in the dark.

For O'Neill, the first weeks of the Carter administration were among the most difficult, politically, of his life. He had traveled thousands of miles and raised thousands of dollars to get Democrats elected to Congress. He had played the congressional game diligently, rising to his goal, the Speakership. He had welcomed Carter—not his first choice for president because he had endorsed Mo Udall in the 1976 Massachusetts primary, but the winner and that's what counts. He had looked forward to working with a Democratic president on Democratic programs, people programs. Work and wages. And, right from the start, he found himself colliding with that Democratic president and a new breed of Democratic programs. O'Neill was perplexed.

Part of the problem, as John Brademas explained later, was that Carter failed to understand two important things about the House of Representatives in 1977. First, with O'Neill in the lead, Congress had been striving in recent years to reassert powers lost to previous presidents. From the opening day of this new, Ninety-fifth Congress, O'Neill repeatedly had emphasized its independence; Congress must be an equal partner with the president, Republican or Democrat, and would not just sit back and take orders from the White House. Pennsylvania Avenue, O'Neill said, was a two-way street.

Second, a Congress of 535 men and women, elected on individual merit, divided into two large bodies and subdivided into committees and subcommittees, operates differently than one man sitting in the Oval Office. Of necessity, Congress approaches problems in a piecemeal manner. Various aspects of one major issue may be handled in half a dozen different committees. No one person is in charge of all of it.

"Carter tended to think comprehensively and rationally," Brademas said. "Not that we think irrationally. But Carter tended to say, 'Okay, what's the problem? Let's analyze it, look at the pros and cons, what's best for the country?' Then he'd say, 'We're going to have a comprehensive this and a comprehensive that.' We don't operate that way and we cannot operate that way. We're piecemeal incrementalists."

O'Neill tried to bridge the gap between the comprehensive approach and the piecemeal approach on the first big issue of the Carter administration—energy—by creating the ad hoc committee as an umbrella group to take the various pieces of the Carter program from a number of committees and paste it up in a single package. He wanted to control the subject logistically, even though major changes might be made in content at the committee level.

A reminder: Tip O'Neill today—as in his old Rules Committee days—still is not concerned with the initial development of legislative policy nor with the fine tuning of legislative draftsmanship. He becomes personally involved with legislation only when the time comes to figure a way to get a bill past opposition roadblocks and through the House. It is not necessarily a tidy process. It often involves last-minute changes in strategy and a continuing pattern of threats and cajolery. And that's where O'Neill's genius comes in. He is flexible and he is diligent. He pulls his weight within the Democratic whip organization, personally contacting the most reluctant congressmen, dickering for votes. At the same time, he is willing to change his mind, will pull bills off the calendar at the last minute, listen to advice. More than once, O'Neill has flopped into a chair in the parliamentarian's office and turned to a close circle of aides and said, "OK, you guys. What the hell do we do now?"

At the same time, however, O'Neill may be going out of style. He is an old-fashioned Democrat who knows what he wants only in the broadest of terms: jobs for everyone, decent wages, freedom from inflation, plenty of oil. He relies on others to figure out how to achieve these goals. And he trusts them completely. Thus, if a Democratic president said tomorrow that the nation's woes could be cured with a 30 percent tax cut, O'Neill would be out there fighting for passage of a 30 percent tax cut. He would not attempt to study the tax code or memorize flow charts. Similarly, when a Democratic president working with Democratic advisers comes up with a legislative program, O'Neill seldom questions it. His job, as he sees it, is to get the bills passed. But to succeed, he might have to call on some of his old political skills and offer rewards here and there to reluctant colleagues.

Which brings us to a third aspect of Congress that Carter failed to understand: the manner in which seemingly unrelated issues become intertwined. Some might call it vote trading: I'll vote for your bill if you'll vote for mine. Or parochialism: no way will an oil-state congressman vote for continued oil-price controls or a farm-state congressman give way on target prices. A federal construction project in a congressman's hometown becomes more important than any comprehensive national policy Carter might send to Capitol Hill.

If there was a honeymoon, it didn't last long. By mid-spring, Congress and Carter were deadlocked over two issues that may have appeared unrelated but that were linked in an intricate pattern of presidential and congressional politics, of campaign promises and local demands. The topics were oil and water.

Water came first.

Carter, picking up where ex-President Ford had left off, sent his version of the 1978 budget (for the fiscal year beginning October 1) to Congress on February 22. It was $19.4 billion higher than Ford had suggested and it tilted federal spending back toward domestic aid programs trimmed by the Republicans.

The change in emphasis pleased congressional Democrats but they were instantly displeased by one of the Carter budget cuts aimed at offsetting some of the increased spending. He suggested eliminating nineteen federal water resource projects, mostly dams, that eventually would cost more than $5 billion. Carter said the cutback was just a first step. His administration was reviewing all of the existing 320 federal water projects in an effort to fulfill a campaign promise to reduce wasteful programs.

Congressmen were irate. These water projects were scattered throughout the country. Whether good or bad, they were political gold, the most coveted of "pork barrels." They provided jobs, created recreation areas, supplied irrigation water, attracted tourists. A congressman could spend his whole political career pumping federal dollars into his district through the careful development of a big water project. O'Neill knew that; Carter didn't, or he chose to ignore it.

Many congressmen also complained to O'Neill about the manner in which Carter handled the decision to cut back water projects. Despite his pre-election talk of consulting with Congress, and treating its members as equals, there was no advance discussion. Letters of notification went out the Friday before the Monday that the proposal was sent to Capitol Hill. Some learned of the president's decision from newspaper and television reports.

Congressmen stormed into O'Neill's office and stopped him in the hall to complain. O'Neill tried to intervene, tried to explain to Carter that these projects, known derisively as "pork barrel," were politically vital to the re-election prospects of Carter's own party in Congress. But Carter was hard-headed. He stuck by his resolve to eliminate water projects that his advisers told him were unneeded—no matter how individual members of Congress might holler. It was a seesaw battle. The hit list was expanded to thirty-two, then cut to eighteen with five other projects sharply revised. Then the Senate pared the list back to thirteen and the House battled to a compromise at ten. "I note," Carter said as he finally signed the bill into law, "that this bill contains funding for ten projects for which I recommended deletion of funds. I remain very concerned about these projects."

The battle continued into 1978 when Congress tried to restore money for six of the projects on the original Carter hit list. Again Carter fought back, threatening to use his ultimate weapon, the veto.

O'Neill was caught in the middle. He did not want to see a bitter split between Carter and congressional Democrats. But his heart was with Congress and the water projects. Publicly and privately, he urged Carter not to veto the bill. He talked of party unity: Democratic presidents don't veto the pork barrel projects of Democratic congressmen, he said. He talked legislative strategy: compromise is the heart of the system. And, finally, he talked pure politics: "If you tackle this Congress, you're not tackling the Georgia legislature. You're tackling able, talented, dedicated, educated, independent, thinking people who, since the Ninety-third Congress [1972], have come to Washington just like you did. They, too, ran against the establishment. And if you start telling these people they're wrong, they'll go back to their areas and they'll think nothing of attacking you."

Carter vetoed the bill.

And, with a little help from House Republicans, Carter won. The veto stuck. On a 223-to-190 vote, House Democratic leaders failed to pull together the two-thirds required to override a presidential veto. Sixty-two Republicans voted with the Democratic president. Carter hailed the vote as "gratifying." O'Neill grumbled. "If you want to be known as a great president," he said, "you'll need the backing of your party."

Next: oil. Just two months after Carter laid down the gauntlet on water projects, he challenged Congress in another controversial area, energy policy. Carter energy advisers had put together a comprehensive bill aimed principally at trying to nudge Americans into wiser—and less—use of oil and gas. The legislation included a complicated mix of carrots and sticks, rebates and taxes, aimed at driving up the price of oil to world market levels. There were taxes on crude oil and gas guzzling cars. There were rebates for home insulation and other conservation measures.

Carter unveiled his energy plan in a media blitz that included a folksy televised talk from the White House, a major speech to a joint session of Congress, and a nationally televised press conference. "With the exception of preventing war," he said, "This is the greatest challenge our country will face in our lifetime. The energy crisis has not overwhelmed us, but it will if we do not act quickly. . . ."

Carter knew his program would not be popular. He said, however, that it was right and necessary. There is no evidence that he considered Congress's angry reaction to the water projects when proposing a new energy policy. They were two different subjects, both sent to Congress with a purist attitude: You may not like this, but it's good for you. But by the time the energy measure arrived, the honeymoon glow was fading. Congress was ready to haggle with Carter over every detail.

O'Neill did all he could. He (and House Parliamentarian William H. Brown) divided the massive energy bill into sections according to House committee jurisdictions. Under authority extended to the Speaker several years earlier, O'Neill then set deadlines of July 13. 1977, for each committee to act. The separate pieces of the package then would be reassembled by O'Neill's new temporary supercommittee on energy.

Many doubted the House could meet O'Neill's schedule, but it did. Along the way, however, the Carter plan was cut to pieces. At each step O'Neill struggled to hold the Carter bill together, but the president kept coming up with new legislative requests, veto threats, patronage problems. At home and among his close friends, O'Neill was discouraged. He wondered what had gone wrong.

"He wanted to help," O'Neill's son Tom said of his father. "Everything in him said to be loyal. And then to have this guy come in and just be pitted against him, well, he didn't understand."

O'Neill kept trying. "We're part of the same team," he said, "and I'm a team player."

All was not grim. There were minor triumphs. Take breakfast, for example. When Democratic congressional leaders first started going to the White House for regular 8:00 A.M. Tuesday breakfast meetings, the frugal Mr. Carter served coffee and pastry. O'Neill spoke up. "This is a helluva breakfast," he told the president. "Why don't you feed us when you bring us over here?"

From that day on, they started to give us sausages and bacon. They have scrambled eggs and poached eggs. They have toast, a danish roll, and grits. I don't eat grits.

And coffee. After we'd been going there about a month, I said, "Y'know, I can't stand coffee black and I can't stand it with milk. I've always used either cream or Coffee Rich." And they've served it with cream from then on. Y'know, if you're in the family, you're supposed to talk up about things like that.

Talk up he did. O'Neill talked up bluntly. Did Carter pay any attention? "He only says, 'Uh-huh, I understand. I appreciate that.'" O'Neill told reporters in mid-1977. "My mother used to say a good listener is better than a good story-teller. He hasn't commented. I know he's listening."

To O'Neill, the White House breakfast meetings were gatherings of "family" and, therefore, the logical place to air family problems. The White House breakfast table was a natural extension of O'Neill's Cambridge dinner table where the O'Neill family, children, and friends, had talked politics for years. O'Neill the insider simply was talking politics with Carter the outsider—and the advice flowed, solicited and unsolicited.

Asked by reporters early in 1977 whether he relayed Democratic gripes to the president, O'Neill said: "Do we tell him? Right to the teeth, no question about it. But I don't call that confrontation. I call that sitting around the family table discussing things that are happening, what's wrong and what's right."

Brademas remembered one breakfast when Carter administration spokesmen had been discussing the next year's budget. To keep Carter on course toward his campaign pledge of a balanced budget, they said deep cuts would have to be made in social programs.

According to Brademas, "Tip said, 'I'm hearing things I've never heard from people who call themselves Democrats, and I didn't come here to work against poor people and handicapped people and jobless people, the underprivileged.' . . . He was clearly hot under the collar. Tip is not one to hide his views easily."

On another occasion, O'Neill risked international embarrassment by publicly rejecting a request to have the president of Mexico address a joint session of Congress. Such ceremonies had become almost automatic whenever a foreign head of state came to Washington. O'Neill said they were a waste of time. Few congressmen attended them anyhow. It was always a hassle to find people to fill the seats in the House chamber. More often than not, there would be rows of bored staff members and shiny-faced teenage pages sitting in for absent congressmen.

Carter went along with the O'Neill position without protest: the House was the Speaker's turf.

The Carter-O'Neill relationship continued on a kind of dual track. On one level, they were personal friends. Each said he liked the other. They were able to talk candidly. They seemed to enjoy one another's company—though one gets the feeling that O'Neill did most of the talking. Carter once said he especially enjoyed sitting with O'Neill on the Truman balcony one evening after dinner, listening to the Speaker tell old political stories. A souvenir photo from one such dinner was autographed by Carter: "Thanks for another political lesson."

On the other level, they were political allies, drawn together by the accident of position rather than by natural political affinity. They probably never really understood one another's definition of politics nor of the role and goals of the Democratic Party.

One source of intermittent tension grew out of those differences. Carter, the world leader, and O'Neill, the meat-and-potatoes Democrat, were not communicating.

It came to a head in 1979. Carter, the president in search of world peace, had spent months in intense—and dramatically successful—negotiations for an Egypt–Israeli peace treaty and for a nuclear weapons agreement (the Strategic Arms Limitation Talks) with the Soviet Union. He had led the United States into formal recognition of Red China and into new trade agreements around the world.

O'Neill, the street-wise pol looking after his own folks. applauded the president's international triumphs but said Carter should spend more time on domestic affairs. Inflation was eating into everyone's pocketbooks. Gas was scarce. Winter fuel shortages threatened. At one of those Tuesday breakfasts in late spring, O'Neill exploded.

I says, "Lookit, Mr. President, we've been coming to these breakfasts and all we ever talk about is foreign policy. Foreign policy doesn't elect anybody." Every president follows the same route. Nixon loved to talk about foreign policy, and all of the sudden, Jerry Ford, who didn't know where the hell Rhodesia was, became an expert on the subject. I'm a domestic operator. They came in to me again this afternoon, the State Department. They said the president [Carter] is all upset about Rhodesia. He'd like to call a leadership meeting on Rhodesia. I says, "Lookit, we went through that for three months, talking about Angola and Rhodesia, everywhere else under the sun." I says, "The people on Montgomery Street where I was born are interested in energy and inflation."

National opinion polls backed up O'Neill. Despite bursts of enthusiasm when Carter scored an international success, the American people generally gave him low marks for his handling of the U.S. economy.

O'Neill was confident, however, that if Carter would just follow his advice to work with Congress and concentrate on domestic issues, all these Democrats, working together, could solve any problem that might come along. Even before the presidential campaign and before his own election as Speaker, O'Neill refused to be discouraged by reports that Carter was stubborn and reluctant to compromise. "You just give me the chance at the Speakership," he said, "and we'll make this guy, whoever he is, a great president."

Three years later, with Democratic congressmen grumbling about Carter, O'Neill stood firm.

Hey, it's no secret. I get along beautifully with the president. I have the highest regard for him. He's a beautiful guy. He's able. He's talented. I've never met a guy who's more brilliant than he is.

It is almost as if O'Neill, by the force of his own personality, insists on holding the Democrats together. He is openly dismayed when any Democrat publicly criticizes Carter as president. It is all right to oppose some Carter legislative proposals, but not to attack him publicly. "No way is he going to sell out the philosophies and ideals which we stand for," O'Neill said time and again.

O'Neill refused to join the early move to draft his friend Ted Kennedy to run against Carter for the 1980 Democratic presidential nomination, and he was distinctly uncomfortable when Kennedy became an active candidate. O'Neill had been saying he expected Carter to run and to win. With Kennedy in the race, O'Neill fell silent and slipped into the convenient neutrality of his 1980 role as chairman of the Democratic National Convention.

O'Neill also refused to listen to talk that Carter, frustrated with a legislature that mangled his programs, would run against Congress in 1980. Washington political pundits said Carter advisers were toying with the idea of running—a la Harry Truman—against a "do nothing" Congress. They figured Congress was vulnerable. Polls showed it had slipped in public esteem.

"That doesn't bother me," O'Neill said. "It's just their strategy." He noted that Congress had been a handy whipping boy throughout American history and was not likely to change. But, when any presidential campaign gets down to basics, he said—Republican against Democrat—the Democrats pull together. It was natural to quarrel—and make up.

And, just in case all of this intraparty quarreling confused anyone, O'Neill issued a rare press release as Carter left to sign the SALT treaty in Vienna.

"No matter which party controls the Congress or the White House, there will always be differences between these two independent branches of government. Our democratic system rests on the framework of compromise and accommodation between an elected president and an elected Congress.

"No one—here or abroad—should misinterpret these inevitable differences as a sign of weakness or a lack of national unity. We share with President Carter the same goals for the future of the country we all love. When we in the Congress disagree with the president on specific issues, we do so with respect for the president's dedication to the best interest of our nation."

Hey, I think everything is going absolutely fantastic.

But it wasn't. During O'Neill's terms as Speaker, Congress has been almost constantly under attack—from the White House, in the press, and among the public at large. Approval ratings, measured by national opinion pollsters, have slipped steadily. By the fall of 1979, an Associated Press–NBC News poll showed that only one of every eight Americans, or 13 percent, gave Congress a good or excellent rating. It was a new low. In the face of rampaging inflation, chronic fuel shortages, and rising interest rates, Congress appears helpless.

O'Neill offers no easy answers. To charges that he presides over a "do nothing" Congress, he says it depends on how you define "nothing." True, it has not been a bill-writing Congress: it wasn't intended to be. When the Ninety-sixth Congress convened, O'Neill announced it would be an "oversight" Congress determined to take a close look at the sprawling federal bureaucracy, reviewing existing government programs and trying to make them more efficient. O'Neill's position echoed a widely held view that there already were too many laws on the books.

Even effective oversight is elusive, however, in a Congress that has become fractious, virtually unmanageable. No one knows that better than O'Neill. He blames the stridency of special interests and the resulting parochialism of his colleagues, and he delivers stern lectures at regular intervals. His colleagues listen and do not heed. It does little good for O'Neill to state a Democratic party position and expect others to follow. Newer, younger members of the House have new definitions of their responsibilities. As John Kenneth Galbraith noted in a 1979 assessment: "They [congressmen] answer to their constituents and to their special interests. Those arrayed demands do not necessarily respond to the national good."

In referring to Congress, one must remember there are two bodies, House and Senate. It takes both to make a law. So when Congress fails to act, it is not necessarily the fault of the House. Under O'Neill's prodding, in fact, the House legislative record is better than the Senate's—a sore point with House leaders suffering attacks broadly aimed at Congress as a whole. All too often, the House has moved fairly swiftly—on energy legislation, for example—only to have the Senate haggle for months.

Comity between House and Senate is not helped by the fact that House members harbor little jealousies toward senators, particularly in the field of public relations. A senator can attract national attention easily; House members are virtually ignored. Yet individual House members are more likely than senators to become intimately involved in drafting legislation, and they are sensitive to charges of inaction or bumbling that they feel should be laid at the senate's door. O'Neill gets even in a small way: He addresses Senate Majority Leader Byrd with the diminutive, "Bobby." Byrd doesn't like that.

In many ways, O'Neill yearns for the old days when big city machine bosses in New York and Chicago and Philadelphia could issue a call and have dozens of Democratic congressmen fall into line. He likes and admires the new, more independent members of the House. They are better educated than the old-timers, more thoughtful and harder working. But he would like these newcomers to see things his way a little more often.

In the final analysis, however, and obviously to O'Neill's surprise, his job has been made increasingly difficult by the Democratic president he greeted so enthusiastically. Carter has been unable to shed an inborn distrust of Northerners in general and the legislative branch in particular. To Carter— although he has never said so publicly—O'Neill typifies the corrupt old ward-heeling, deal-making politician. Carter refuses to join. He refuses to do the little things that make congressmen happy, such as inviting them to informal gatherings at the White House and consulting them on policy matters. He refuses, in short, to be their friend. O'Neill cannot understand that at all. Democrats are Democrats. A Democratic president should try to get along with a Democratic Congress. O'Neill keeps saying admiring things about Carter, only to be greeted by silence. As one top House staff man said: "They [O'Neill and other Democratic House leaders] go down to the White House to embrace the president and before they know it, they're hugging each other—and Carter has vanished."

"Tip is very loyal," Majority Leader Wright said in an interview. "I've seen situations where the Speaker would gently try to advise the president against a course of action, and the president would go ahead and follow that course of action, and Tip would march right back here and carry the ball across the line for him. He's very loyal. . . ."

By the end of 1979, some of O'Neill's frustrations with Carter began to show publicly. First, by praising former Health, Education and Welfare Secretary Joseph A. Califano, O'Neill indirectly criticized Carter for the mid-summer cabinet shuffle that left Califano on the outside looking in. Then, O'Neill began grumbling more openly about political mismanagement at the White House. Little things irked him—for example, the question of who should choose the small army of workers to conduct the 1980 national census. O'Neill said the congressmen should handle it. Carter put the White House in charge. After a series of angry exchanges, a compromise was worked out: Congress would "nominate"; Carter would do the hiring. In most of these confrontations, O'Neill blamed Carter aides, not the president himself. But, in the end, it was the president who assumed responsibility.

Part of Carter's problem with Congress is his own low standing in popularity polls. There is little incentive for a recalcitrant congressman to follow a falling star. Each has his own reelection to worry about. In O'Neill's office, phrases like "contain the damage" crept into the 1979 political jargon. Each Carter bill, the routine requests along with the pacesetters, became a major project and there were cliff-hanging votes over the Department of Education, the Panama Canal turnover, the federal budget itself, the national debt ceiling, energy bills, windfall profits, the Tellico dam, welfare reform, hospital cost controls.

O'Neill pushed his fellow House Democrats as much as he could, but they became tougher as a new election year neared. Time after time, faced with almost certain defeat, O'Neill agreed to major compromises to win over a few more votes. As a result bills like tax reform and energy conservation, described as "tough" when they left the White House, became "weak" after Congress finished with them. After one bad week, when four Carter-backed bills were defeated in the House, O'Neill regrouped for a second (and, as it turned out, successful) try. One day as he rumbled from one closed-door meeting to another in a desperate attempt to forge agreements, he paused briefly, wearily, and said, "You're looking at a guy who has nothing but troubles."

Things improved for Carter in the winter of 1979–1980. His position in the national opinion polls shot up during the Iranian crisis. Americans rallied to show the world a nation united behind its president's efforts to free American hostages from their captivity in Teheran and to stand up to Soviet aggression in Afghanistan. "We're just not hearing so many complaints about Jimmy Carter around here these last few weeks," one Democrat has said. "They [the Democrats] are much happier now about having him at the top of the ticket." But the situation is volatile. Carter popularity could fall again as fast as it rose.

O'Neill added a totally unexpected dimension to his role as Speaker when, in April 1979, over the objections of the State Department, heled a congressional delegation to Northern Ireland and sat down with rival political leaders there to see if he could persuade them to settle their differences. Never before had a Speaker of the House acted as a broker in such delicate foreign negotiations. But O'Neill could not see how any situation, especially one so totally unreasonable, would not yield to compromise. It was a role he seemed to have been made for, especially in this place, among his Irish cousins.

O'Neill had been working with a potent Irish-American "gang of four"—the others were Senators Kennedy and Daniel P. Moynihan, D-N.Y., and New York Governor Hugh Carey, a former House member— that attempted to end the political impass in Ireland by, among other things, putting pressure on the British to bring about a settlement. It was a difficult and, for then anyhow, a losing cause. O'Neill even persuaded President Carter to bring up the subject with British Prime Minister Margaret Thatcher during a June meeting in Tokyo.

Hey, the last election, the non-Paisley people—the rational Protestants and the rational Catholics—got about 72 percent of the vote, and it seems to me they ought to be able to put a government together. It's just a shame. Here we have 2,000 people killed and 20,000 wounded in a period of nine years, right in the center of the original culture of the Western world, and nobody does anything about it.

But the fighting continued.

Tip O'Neill is the last of a vanishing breed of political leader. He typifies the old politics of street corner rallies and baskets of fruit for the poor, of personal loyalties that override issues and of a straightforward world in which a few old friends and all Democrats stick together. The next Speaker of the House will be quite different, younger, less rigidly partisan, more intellectual, a man of the 1980s at home with the complexities of an era increasingly mechanized and computerized. But they will look back fondly on Tip O'Neill as a man who could run the House in a time of fundamental change and who has believed fervently that the job of a leader is, quite simply and to the best of his ability, to lead.

I'm supposed to be the typical Irish ward city politician, a kind of a leader, a fella who can put out a fire when a (political) party gets problems; even the way-out liberals ask how the hell does he do it. Is O'Neill a myth or a fact? Just amazing.

I'm a politician and I'm proud of it. I've been with every type businessman in the world. There's no profession more honorable than politics. We're barraged. We're criticized. But, percentagewise, there are more people in public life who are honest than there are in any other profession in the world. The politician is criticized because that's the way of American life: kick the hell out of Congress. So I'm part of that American life that's kicked hell out of.

Hey, that doesn't bother me a bit.

CHAPTER NOTES
AND SOURCES

CHAPTER 1

The story of O'Neill's effort to salvage the Department of Education bill was pieced together from interviews with O'Neill, his son Christopher (Kip), his aide Gary Hymel, and Congressman David Obey, and from the *Congressional Record*.

Martin Tolchin's article in the July 24, 1977, *New York Times Magazine*, "An Old Poll Takes on the New President," was helpful in describing O'Neill's legislative philosophy. The James Joyce characters appear in his *Ivy Day in the Committee Room*.

Information on the history of the Speaker's office came from "The House Shall Chuse Their Speaker," by Neil MacNeil, *American Heritage*, February 1977; and from *Sam Rayburn, A Biography* (New York: Hawthorn Books, 1975). Also useful was *The American Heritage History of the Congress of the United States* by Alvin M. Josephy, Jr. (New York, 1975).

CHAPTER 2

The story of Walter Johnson's pitching performance was based on an O'Neill interview, the Boston newspapers of July 2, 1920, and a book, *Great No-Hit Games of the Major Leagues* by Frank Graham, Jr. (New York: Random House, 1968).

Books that were helpful in understanding the Boston Irish were William V. Shannon's *The American Irish* (New York: Macmillan, 1963), Andrew M. Greeley's *The Most Distressful Nation, the Taming of the American Irish* (Chicago: Times Books, 1972); Edward Wakin's *Enter the Irish Americans* (New York: Thomas Crowell Publishers, 1976; and Carl Witthe's *The Irish in America* (Baton Rouge: Teachers College Press, 1956).

O'Neill's sister, Mary Mulcahy, provided much of the material about his boyhood and his relationship with his mother and stepmother. Bruce Mazlish of Cambridge and Joseph Herzberg of Washington, both specialists in political psychology, helped relate some of these boyhood experiences to his political aspirations. Some of the information on Cambridge's ethnic and political history came from *Cambridge Reconsidered* by S.B. Sutton (Cambridge: MIT Press, 1976).

Profiles of O'Neill's father were supplied by O'Neill, Mary Mulcahy, Thomas O'Neill III, and John Carver, a longtime associate. The Irish tunes come from a music book, *In Dublin's Fair City* (Dublin: Walton's Ltd., 1968), and the Gaelic expressions from O'Neill, with help from the Irish Embassy.

Some sources for background on early Boston politics were *Boston in the Age of John F. Kennedy,* John Muir Whitehead (Norman, Okla: University of Oklahoma Press, 1965); *Boston,* Nancy Sirkin (New York: Viking, 1965); and *The Last Hurrah,* James O'Connor (Boston: Atlantic Monthly, 1956).

CHAPTER 3

Stories about growing up on Barry's Corner were related, in interviews, by O'Neill, Francis X. (Red) Fitzgerald, William (Skip) McCaffrey, Jed Barry, Thomas Mullen, and Joseph Healy. The story about fracturing his only line in a class play was reported in the *Washington Post,* March 23, 1979. The Horatio Alger material came from O'Neill and *From Rags to Riches, Horatio Alger and the American Dream,* by John Tebbel (New York: Macmillan, 1963). There are several volumes of Father Blunt's poetry, including the one cited here, *Poems by Rev. Hugh F. Blunt* (Concord, N.H.: Rumford Press, 1911). As for the story about the rigged pay phone, it is from Jimmy Breslin's *How the Good Guys Finally Won* (New York: Viking, 1975).

The quote from O'Neill's father upon his son's entry into politics came from a *Time* cover story, February 4, 1974. Highlights from the Boston College years were supplied by classmate Tim Ready and the school's 1936 yearbook.

CHAPTER 4

Useful background on the Boston Red Sox came from *The Red Sox, the Bean and the Cod,* Al Hirshberg, (Boston: Waverly House, 1947).

Details concerning early political campaigns were compiled from interviews with O'Neill, John Carver, Thomas Mullen, Joe Healy, Skip McCaffrey, Red Fitzgerald and Jim Furgeson. The Curley quote was from a speech O'Neill made in the House of Representatives at the time of Curley's death. Accounts of legislative antics were supplied by Judge Charles J. Artesani, Leo Diehl, and an interview by Bob Poole, then of the *Boston Herald,* with Congressman James Burke. Poole also conducted the cigar interview with O'Neill.

Ed Crane, former Cambridge mayor, and Diehl provided background on O'Neill's stint as a city clerk. The episode involving O'Neill and the Cambridge School Committee was related by Crane, Jed Barry, and Eliot Spalding, former editor of the *Cambridge Chronicle.* The view of O'Neill as politician-husband emerged from an interview with his wife, Mildred O'Neill.

O'Neill supplied the dialogue for the confrontation with Curley. The story is supported by accounts of the delegate fight in the *Boston Globe.* Details were also provided by Whitehead's *Boston in the Age of John F. Kennedy.*

Former Speaker John W. McCormack smoked two cigars during an interview for this book in May 1978.

CHAPTER 5

The story of the Republican "plot" to buy the speakership came from O'Neill. His inaugural speech was quoted in the *Boston Globe,* June 6, 1949. Stories about his reign as Speaker came from O'Neill himself, Healy, Mullen, Artesani, and others, and from various accounts in the press, including the *Worcester Telegram*, June 3, 1949, and *Time*, February 4, 1974. The testimonial dinners were reported in the *Boston Post* of May 11 and June 24, 1949. The incident involving the supposedly anti-Catholic bank president came from an interview published in *Yankee Magazine*, July 1978.

The story of the meeting with Kennedy in 1951 came from interviews with O'Neill and Healy. The news of his announcement for Congress was carried in the *Boston Post*, April 17, 1952. Numerous stories about the campaign appeared in the *Cambridge Chronicle* during that period.

Information about the Curley pension fiasco was drawn from interviews with O'Neill and Walter Sullivan, a former legislator, and from numerous stories in the *Boston Post* in August 1952. O'Neill and Diehl supplied details about the primary campaign.

CHAPTER 6

Information for this chapter came from personal interviews, principally with O'Neill himself and with his closest friend/aide, Leo Diehl, and from newspaper files of the *Boston Globe*, the *Washington Post* and the *New York Times*. The newspaper files were not as helpful as one might think because news of O'Neill seldom reached the national press during these years. We found the most complete collection of O'Neill press clippings in his own scrapbooks maintained in his Washington office by his secretary, Dolores Snow.

All but one of the long O'Neill quotations scattered throughout the book are drawn from tape-recorded interviews with O'Neill in his Washington and Boston offices. The single exception is the first quotation in this chapter (dealing with Eddie Boland's tidiness), which is credited to Richard L. Lyons of the *Washington Post*.

In addition to O'Neill and Diehl, we interviewed Mildred O'Neill, Thomas P. O'Neill, III, former House Speaker John W. McCormack, former White House aide Lawrence F. O'Brien, Jr. (now commissioner of the National Basketball Association), Representatives Edward P. Boland (D-Mass.), Richard Bolling (D-Mo.), and Frank Thompson (D-N.J.), Kenneth T. Lyons of the National Association of Government Employees, Joseph Healy, and Dr. Victoria Schuck, president of Mt. Vernon College.

In this chapter, as in all those dealing with O'Neill's years in Congress, the *Congressional Quarterly*, both the annual almanacs and the four big volumes of the Congress and the Nation series, 1945–64, 1965–68, 1969–72, and 1973–76 were relied upon heavily.

For details of the 1961 Rules Committee fight, facts were collected from several other sources, including Neil MacNeil's *Forge of Democracy* (New York: David McKay, 1963) and the two Bolling books, *House Out of Order* (New York: E. P. Dutton, 1965) and *Power in the House* (New York: E. P. Dutton, 1968).

CHAPTER 7

Early in 1965, the Elder half of this writing team began covering Congress, mostly the House of Representatives, for the *Washington Star*. Much of the information that eventually found its way into this book, therefore, comes from her notes and experience.

Details of O'Neill's reversal of his position on the Vietnam War were not known at the time, however. The story was pieced together for this chapter from O'Neill's own recollections and from interviews with many then on the scene, including O'Neill's daughter, Rosemary, a State Department political and economic officer now stationed in Rabat, Morocco; Pat McCarthy, who, after an unsuccessful try for Congress himself, went to Washington as administrative assistant to Representative Joe Moakley (D-Mass.) and then joined the Small Business Administration; John D. Walker, now director of the English Speaking Union; Thomas F. McCoy, now a Washington political consultant; Richard P. Conlon, staff director of the House Democratic Study Group; Common Cause President David Cohen, and former Representative John J. Flynt (D-Ga.).

Reports differ as to exactly what Martin Sweig may have said when contacting federal agencies in Speaker McCormack's name. But there was no dispute over the fact that he did present himself as "the Speaker." The initial story, by reporter William Lambert, appeared in *Life* magazine of October 23, 1969. On January 18, 1970, Haynes Johnson wrote in the *Washington Post:* "When Martin Sweig was riding high on the Hill, he would pick up the phone in his congressional office and announce, 'This is the Speaker calling. . . .' Those who received such calls remembered that Sweig's voice even took on the timbre and pitch of his boss's."

CHAPTER 8

Among those interviewed for the story of O'Neill's selection as House Democratic Whip were O'Neill, staff aides Gary Hymel and Linda Melconian, and Representatives Lindy Boggs (D-La.), John J. McFall (D-Calif.) (now retired), Boland, and Bolling.

The most valuable source of all was Robert L. Peabody's *Leadership in Congress* (Boston: Little, Brown and Company, 1976) in which Peabody, a professor at Johns Hopkins University and close student of Congress, presented case studies of a number of congressional leadership battles. Additional insight came from *New York Times* reporter Warren Weaver in *Both Your Houses: the Truth About Congress* (New York: Prager, 1972).

Details of the Senate Foreign Relations Committee inquiry into the activities of O'Neill's friend Martin Camacho are contained in part eight of the printed hearings entitled "Activities of Nondiplomatic Representatives of Foreign Principals in the United States," executive session, released on August 1, 1963.

Also useful here, as in other chapters, was a long O'Neill interview in the July 1978 issue of *Yankee Magazine,* and the unpublished senior thesis written by Representative James M. Shannon (D-Mass.), for a degree in political science from Johns Hopkins University.

As we've noted on a number of occasions, O'Neill was philosophically attractive to national Democrats because of his voting record as a consistent urban liberal. Ratings compiled by *Congressional Quarterly* from the most liberal (Americans for Democratic Action and the AFL-CIO's Committee on Political Education) to the most conservative (Americans for Constitutional Action) break down like this:

YEAR	ADA	COPE	ACA
1959–60	100	100	11
1961–62	100	100	5
1963–64	88	100	5
1965–66	88	92	0
1967–68	83	100	5
1969–70	76	100	6
1971–72	69*	80	5
1973–74	65*	92	8
1975–76	60*	75	8

*In 1972, the ADA changed its method of scoring to count absences as negatives, thus lowering all scores.

As Speaker, beginning in 1977, O'Neill only voted on the rare occasions necessary to break a tie.

CHAPTER 9

Former President Gerald R. Ford, in his book, *A Time to Heal* (New York: Harper & Row and Reader's Digest, Inc., 1979) tells of Agnew's efforts to have his case heard in the House Judiciary Committee. Additional information came from a telephone interview with Ford, newspaper clippings, Elder's reporting at the time, and later interviews with O'Neill, Representative Robert F. Drinan (D-Mass.), and pollster William R. Hamilton.

Jimmy Breslin's O'Neill quote was first published in Breslin's entertaining story on O'Neill and the impeachment process, *How the Good Guys Finally Won* (New York: Ballantine Books, 1975). Specific data on the Judiciary Committee's handling of the Nixon impeachment charges can be found in *High Crimes and Misdemeanors* (New York: W.W. Norton, 1978) by former United Press International reporter Howard Fields.

Former Speaker Carl Albert quarrels with the assessment that he was a weak speaker, but that is clearly the image he projected publicly. In his 1979 interview with Alan Ehrenhalt, Albert seemed to resent the media attention given O'Neill and complained that when O'Neill was majority leader, he spent too much time in Massachusetts and wasn't around when needed.

There's much more to the story of O'Neill and Nixon than reported here. At least, O'Neill says there is, but he also says he won't talk publicly about that period until the principals are dead or he is out of politics. Nightly during the impeachment months, O'Neill dictated thoughts and impressions that were typed up by his private secretary, Eleanor Kelley. But he declined to make these available.

Nixon's resignation was not the end of the impeachment story in the House. On August 20, the House voted 412 to 3 in favor of a resolution presented by O'Neill that formally accepted—as an official document—the House Judiciary Committee report recommending three Articles of Impeachment against the president of the United States. O'Neill was anxious that this final action be taken so that the committee's work would not be left hanging. It was an act that, in effect, nailed Nixon's list of impeachable offenses to the White House gate.

CHAPTER 10

Again, as in earlier chapters, news clippings, follow-up interviews (as acknowl-edged in the text) and on-the-scene reporting form the basis of this chapter.

P.S. Mills went into private law practice in Washington, often working as a volunteer for Alcoholics Anonymous. Hays went back to Ohio and ran successfully for the state legislature. Fanne Foxe and Elizabeth Ray both went onto the night club song-and-dance circuit.

CHAPTER 11

The full text of O'Neill's inaugural speech as Speaker can be found in the *Congressional Record* of January 4, 1977; his remarks (as well as those of John Rhodes) when elected to a second term can be found in the *Congressional Record* of January 15, 1979.

O'Neill started off the ethics code battle by releasing publicly a list of his own personal assets (*Washington Post*, April 28, 1978. Page C 13), which added up to a net worth of $181,192, consisting largely of homes in Cambridge, Harwichport, and suburban Maryland.

The saga of the pay battle, from the Peterson Commission report of December 2, 1976, through final congressional action, can be found in the 1977 *Congressional Quarterly Almanac*, beginning on page 751.

Co-author Paul Clancy was a staff assistant on the Obey Commission and provided special insight into Obey's personality and the commission's fate. The commission's report was printed as a public document, House Report #95-73, dated February 14, 1977.

CHAPTER 12

As a congressional reporter, Elder attended a lot of Tip O'Neill press conferences. These anecdotes are from her notes.

The history of Boston newspapers came from Louis M. Lyons's *Newspaper Story: 100 Years of the Boston Globe* (Cambridge: Belknap Press of the Harvard University Press, 1971) and a *Boston Magazine* article (April 1979) by Charles Dawe, entitled, "The Incredible Shrinking Newspaper."

The story of the *Boston Herald American*'s apparent campaign against O'Neill was assembled from the *Herald*'s own newspaper library clippings and from interviews with key people (some of whom asked not to be identified), including McIlwain, Barnstead, Richard D. Lyons, Chris Black, William Safire, and Jim Rowan.

Most of the McGarry story came from *Congressional Quarterly Weekly Report*'s regular coverage of the Senate confirmation process.

Specifics on the Tongsun Park parties, the Jack Kelly affair, and other ethics questions concerning O'Neill can be found in an official statement (absolving O'Neill of any wrongdoing) released by the House Committee on Standards of Official Conduct on July 13, 1978, and entitled, "Contacts of Congressman (later Speaker) Thomas P. O'Neill, Jr., with Tongsun Park."

Postscripts:

Park, indicted September 6, 1977, by a federal grand jury in Washington on thirty-six counts of bribery and other charges, fled to Korea. After lengthy and complex negotiations between the Korean government and U.S. State and Justice Department officials—and including Park's agreement to return briefly to the U.S. to testify in several trials of others involved in the case—the Justice Department dropped all charges on August 16, 1979.

Don Forst, who succeeded McIlwain as editor of the *Boston Herald American,* quietly launched a new policy. No formal orders were issued but the results were plain: there would be no new tough O'Neill investigations. "Basically," said one reporter, "the dogs are off." Instead of uncovering possible scandals, the *Herald,* in the summer of 1979, began writing of such friendly O'Neill events as the reunion with his old pals from Barry's Corner and an interview called "First Break"—one of a series on how "influential Bostonians got their first break." (Characteristically, O'Neill said: "No one gave me my first break. I did it myself. . . . I ran for public office." *Boston Herald American,* July 2, 1979).

CHAPTER 13

The remarks of people such as Jim Wright, or Richard Bolling, and others quoted, come from tape-recorded interviews for this book.

In taking a closer look at the Steering and Policy Committee, we talked with Representatives Charles G. Rose (D-N.C.), William D. Ford (D-Mich.), and Wright's former administrative assistant Craig Raupe, among others.

CHAPTER 14

Congressional Quarterly reporter Don Smith's interview with candidate Carter appeared in the September 4, 1976, *Weekly Report.*

Elder, left the *Star* in 1975, a time covered by this chapter, to try freelance writing, and was back covering the House for the *CQ* newsletter, *Congressional Insight.* In May of 1979, Elder joined the Washington bureau of Media General, which publishes daily newspapers in Richmond, Tampa, and Winston-Salem—still keeping an eye on Tip O'Neill.

Among those interviewed for this chapter were Majority Leader Jim Wright and Democratic Whip John Brademas.

Failing to obtain a personal interview with President Carter, Elder relied instead on conversations with White House aides and reporters, and on a particularly helpful article by *New York Times* reporter Martin Tolchin, "An Old Pol Takes on a New President," in that paper's Sunday magazine of July 24, 1977.

INDEX

ABOUT THE AUTHORS

PAUL CLANCY, a native of New York City and graduate of Columbia University, has been in the news business fifteen years. He went to Washington as a correspondent for the *Charlotte* (North Carolina) *Observor* and now works for the *Washington Star*. He is the author of *Just a Country Laywer*, a biography of former Senator Sam J. Ervin, Jr. Clancy and his wife, Barbara, live in Reston, Virginia, with their two daughters.

SHIRLEY ELDER is a westerner, born in California and raised in Seattle, Washington. She is a graduate of Stanford University and has worked on all three Washington newspapers (one, the *Washington Daily News* has since folded). She covered the House of Representatives from 1965 to 1975 and is now in the Washington bureau of Media General newspapers. She is the co-author, with Norman J. Ornstein, of *Interest Groups, Lobbying and Policymaking*. Ms. Elder and her husband, Richard L. Lyons of the *Washington Post*, live in Fairfax County, Virginia.